W9-ARB-757

Breaking the Code

The New Science of Beginning Reading and Writing

J. Richard Gentry

LIBRARY
FRANKLIN PIERCE COLLEGE
RINDGE, NH 03461

HEINEMANN
Portsmouth, NH

Heinemann
A division of Reed Elsevier Inc.
361 Hanover Street
Portsmouth, NH 03801–3912
www.heinemann.com

Offices and agents throughout the world

© 2006 by J. Richard Gentry

All rights reserved. No part of this book may be reproduced in any form or by any electronic or mechanical means, including information storage and retrieval systems, without permission in writing from the publisher, except by a reviewer, who may quote brief passages in a review.

The author and publisher wish to thank those who have generously given permission to reprint borrowed material:

Figure 1.1 from "Minds, Brains, and Learning: Understanding the Psychological and Educational Relevance of Neuroscientific Research" by J. P. Byrnes. From *Psychological Review,* 1989, 96. Reprinted by permission of the American Psychological Association.

Figure 4.1 adapted from "An Analysis of Developmental Spelling in GNYS at WRK" by J. Richard Gentry. From *The Reading Teacher* (36 [2], November 1982). Copyright © 1982 by the International Reading Association. Reprinted by permission.

Figures 6.2, 6.3, 6.4, 6.5, and 6.10 from *Nursery Rhyme Time: Reading and Learning Sounds, Letters, and Words* by J. Richard Gentry and Richard S. Craddock. Copyright © 2005 by Universal Publishing. Reprinted by permission.

Figures 7.15 and 7.17 from *The Science of Spelling* by J. Richard Gentry. Copyright © 2004 by J. Richard Gentry. Published by Heinemann, a division of Reed Elsevier, Inc. Portsmouth, NH.

Figures 8.1 and 8.4 from *Kid Writing: A Systematic Approach to Phonics, Journals, and Writing Workshop* by E. G. Feldgus and I. Cardonick. Copyright © 1999. Published by The Wright Group. Reprinted by permission of The McGraw-Hill Companies.

Acknowledgments for borrowed material continue on p. vi.

Library of Congress Cataloging-in-Publication Data
Gentry, J. Richard.
  Breaking the code : the new science of beginning reading and writing /
J. Richard Gentry.
    p.   cm.
  Includes bibliographical references and index.
  ISBN 0-325-00922-8 (alk. paper)
  1. Reading (Primary).   2. English language—Composition and exercises.
  3. Reading, Psychology of.   I. Title.
LB1525.G46 2006
372.4—dc22   2005028902

Editor: Lois Bridges
Production management: Denise Botelho
Production coordination: Vicki Kasabian
Cover design: Night and Day Design
Typesetter: Technologies 'N Typography, Inc.
Manufacturing: Louise Richardson

Printed in the United States of America on acid-free paper
10 09 08 07 06 EB 1 2 3 4 5

To Bonnie Wright Gentry,

my beloved mother and my first grade teacher

Contents

Figure 8.2 from *The Nuts and Bolts of Teaching Writing* by Lucy Calkins. Copyright © 2005 by Lucy Calkins. Published by Heinemann, a division of Reed Elsevier, Inc. Portsmouth, NH. Reprinted by permission.

Figures 9.3 and 9.4 from *Spel . . . Is a Four-Letter Word* by J. Richard Gentry. Copyright © 1989 by J. Richard Gentry. Published by Heinemann, a division of Reed Elsevier, Inc. Portsmouth, NH.

Figure 10.5 from *Comprehension and Critical Thinking Level 3*. Published by Teacher Created Materials. Reprinted by permission.

Acknowledgments

Having worked on previous projects with most of the outstanding Heinemann team that worked with me on this book, I was no stranger to the high level of professionalism and dedication they bring to publishing books of the highest quality for teachers. I would especially like to thank Karen Clausen, Amy Rowe, Doria Turner, Louise Richardson, Vicki Kasabian, Eric Chalek, and Denise Botelho for their fine work on this project. Words cannot express my gratitude to Lois Bridges, my editor. Lois was an incomparable shepherdess when I was a lost sheep.

The researchers, educators, and scholars whom I owe gratitude for helping to shape the thinking reflected in this book began with a group of professors and graduate students at The University of Virginia who studied with Edmund H. Henderson three decades ago and extend to present-day giants in the field including Regie Routman, Marilyn Adams, Ken and Yetta Goodman, Dorothy Strickland, Richard Allington, Marie Clay, Irene Fountas, Gay Su Pinnell, Don Graves, David Pearson, Pat Cunningham, Richard Hodges, Connie Hebert, Ronald Cramer, Tim Shanahan, Darrell Morris, Linnea Ehri, Connie Juel, Margaret Moustafa, Catherine Snow, Keith Stanovich, Tim Rasinski, and many others. I feel blessed to have chosen a career in education and to have friendship and acquaintanceship with many leaders in the field. I have great admiration and respect for the academic community in education and I am grateful for the scholarship that informs our practice.

I am fortunate to have a number of friends who are remarkable teachers and administrators whom I come back to over and over for counsel, and advice. Thank you to Richard Craddock, Bill McIntyre, Karl Studt, Jean Gillet, Judy Farley, Penny Jamaison, Gert Johnson, Lilia Nanez, Dalia Benavides, Patty Baxter, Kristin Davis, Carolyn Miegs, Jean Mann, Cecilia Aitkens, Larry Harriger, Kristin Sousa, and Beverly Kingery for your support.

I would like to thank Isabell Cardonick and Eileen Feldgus for their generous contribution to sections of this book and for lengthy discussions about early literacy. A special thank you also goes to Shelly Bromwich, Dot Solenski, and Nancy Creech for special contributions and insightful comments.

I have deep respect for the Sandra Wilde's scholarship and for her understanding of the nuances of beginning literacy. Sandra reviewed my manuscript and was generous in encouragement and most helpful in offering many specific recommendations that went into this book. I am deeply appreciative for her help.

Thank you to all the parents and children who shared their experiences and their work and made direct contributions to this project. I am inspired by all of you, and by the letters and emails that come back to me with expressions of your genuine interest in providing better educational opportunities for all children. Many parents and teachers mentioned in these pages are my heroes. A special thank you to Ginger Berki, George Lakatos, and Daniella Jabbour.

Rosemarie Jensen, both a loving parent and a brilliant teacher with an academic command of the educational literature, read large sections of my manuscript, and was a friend and contributor throughout the process. All writers should be so lucky as to have a friend like Ro.

Writing is not easy for me, and while I enjoy it, the process is slow and painstaking. I would not be successful without the incalculable contributions and support of Bill Boswell in my work and in my life.

Introduction

In 1982 Marie Clay gave us *Observing Young Readers,* a brilliant synthesis of the previous twenty years of reading research in developmental psychology along with her own powerful research from careful observation in natural classroom settings. This work along with her other volumes helped pave the way for progress in the next twenty-five years in reading education, underpinning powerful movements such as Reading Recovery, guided reading (Fountas and Pinnell 1996, 2001), comprehensive balanced reading (Routman 2000), and designing research-based programs (Allington 2001). In *Observing Young Readers,* Clay predicted the potential of early writing to complement the early reading program while pointing out that very little had been written about early writing up to that time. She ended *Observing Young Readers* by imploring educators to "go far beyond" her brief review of the developmental aspects of early writing, inviting educators to find the writing/reading connection. Marie Clay was right, as were her eminent reading educator predecessors such as Donald Durrel, whom she quoted "We have known for years the child's first urge is to write and not to read, we haven't taken advantage of this fact" (in Graves 1978 quoted in Clay 1982).

This book is my own thirty-year synthesis of what I have learned about the importance of early writing for teaching reading. It stands on the shoulders of many with whom I have worked and others who came before me. It adds to fine ongoing work—good research-based teaching such as Reading Recovery and excellent comprehensive balanced reading—and it responds to the invitation Marie Clay issued over twenty years ago calling for new tools for capitalizing on the reciprocity of early writing and reading. My intent is to help add the missing component that Marie Clay invited educators to search for in 1982, when she had wisdom and foresight to recognize the powerful connection between early writing and learning to read.

There is now a new understanding of the reading process, a new blueprint, and new tools for reading teachers based on the reciprocity of writing and reading and how these systems work together. This book will provide the blueprint for beginning reading and new tools for teaching it. Most importantly, it will show exactly when and what type of instructional intervention is needed in the beginning phases of breaking the code. The new tools and blueprint for teaching beginning readers make it easier to implement the research-based practices in beginning reading instruction that find support in the most current under-standings of the reading process.

I believe one problem in reading education is that even though we have many garden-variety reading teachers working successfully with children who already know how to read, too many of our teachers are not prepared to deal with the exigencies of beginning reading instruction. This book addresses the important differences in beginning and skilled reading and provides special tools for teaching beginners or children who struggle with breaking the code.

I have met many beginning-reading teachers who are frustrated as I would be if I were required to do something like plumbing or dentistry for my living. I don't fully understand how plumbing and dentistry work, and I don't know how to use the tools to get the job done.

Let's think a moment about plumbing. Like reading problems, every plumb-ing problem is different. I can detect the leak easily enough, but I'm not very good at analyzing the problem and coming up with a solution. Just as the mas-ter plumber must understand how the system works, carry along a tool kit with the right tools, and know which tools work best to get the job done, the teacher of beginning reading must have a kit of fine precision tools and be able to pull out the right tool at the right time.

Let me give you an example of a child who was left behind because her teachers had neither a good tool kit nor an understanding of how to use the proper tools at the right time. I began working with a second grade struggling reader whose parents were paying for an expensive tutor at a private summer reading clinic, hoping to give their daughter the boost she needed to read well enough to succeed the following year in third grade. They weren't getting good results. This nine-year-old had not become an accomplished reader who loves books, and the parents and child were distraught. It was the summer before third grade and she was still reading at beginning first-grade level. When I first met her she lacked self-esteem and confidence and she felt defeated because she couldn't read as well as her classmates. I did an assessment and easily discov-ered her problem—she hadn't broken the complex English alphabetic code or made the move from beginning to skilled reading. If she saw the word *feet*, she called it *foot*. She was very bright and engaging and the main reason she was struggling with reading and fluency was that she had not discovered how Eng-lish orthography works. She didn't recognize common spelling patterns and sight words—an aspect of code breaking. She was still trying to read words by cueing on beginning and ending letters to sound words out and had no concept of how English letters may be chunked into spelling patterns. If she saw the un-known word, *interesting,* she tried to decode it by attaching a sound to a few prominent letters with no understanding of how to chunk these letters into *in-ter-est-ing.*

Furthermore, she hadn't experienced the volume of reading with appropri-ate easy books to develop the necessary fluency to become a proficient reader. For over a year she had been "instructed" as if she were a skilled reader in materials that were far too difficult for someone who read at her level. The expectations at school were that she be a reader, but with little understanding of how English spelling patterns map to words, she was unable to recognize a large repertoire of words automatically, a prerequisite for skilled and fluent reading. The kind of work she needed was no longer being taught in second grade and the next year could be even worse.

The mother showed me the work that was underway at the summer reading clinic and it was unsettling: the tutor was drilling the child on using context clues. Working on context clues is a great technique for readers who may not be using syntactic cues as a backup for the information one needs to process during reading, but this child's problem was that she saw *feet, bat,* and *mail* both in and out of context and said *"foot," "but,"* and *"meal,"* respectively. She didn't automatically process that –eet, -at, and –ail are common chunks of letters in the English spelling system that make it easy to decode *meet, beet,* and *feet; bat, hat,* and *cat; nail, mail,* and *sail;* or *meet*inghouse, comb*ativ*eness, and unass*ail*able. The good news is that as a child breaks the alphabetic code, consolidates an understanding of how the code works with the other processes for reading, and has enough reading practice with easy material so that many words and patterns are recognized automatically, the child will combine this decoding ability with her perfectly good phonological, syntactic, and meaning-processing circuitry to read English easily. At the time, however, this child simply hadn't broken the code and her tutor didn't realize it. I could tell what she needed not only by observing her reading but also by looking at her writing. It was right there in front of me. The work to be done that summer should not have focused on context clues—she was already overdependent on them. It should have focused on automatic recognition of common spelling patterns and analogizing—something achieving second graders do easily with the patterns in *meet, bat,* and *mail.* The work should have focused on rereading easy and engaging material until these patterns could be read fluently. To read skillfully and fluently (and to write with confidence), this child had to learn to recognize spelling patterns and many one-syllable words automatically (and to produce an abundance of these patterns when she wrote). Along with recognizing the patterns, she had to practice them over and over in fairly easy text until specialized parts of her brain could take over the job of analyzing and recognizing the spelling and word patterns automatically. Then she could get in the flow of reading and the words on the page would sing in her mind like a symphony, harmonizing with the prosody, phonology, and syntax of spoken language into one meaningful voice. She would have become a skilled reader.

After extensive interviews with the child and her parents, I learned that this child's former teachers apparently had too few tools for working with emerging readers and no blueprint for a real understanding of what should be happening as a child advances from nonreading, to beginning reading, to skilled reading. Skilled reading is achieved once the child's brain activates the same critical regions of the brain that you are activating at this very moment. (A *beginning reader's* brain activation would look different from yours at this moment with fMRI [functional magnetic resonance imaging] because different specialized areas are activated. A *skilled reader* who is reading second-grade-level material would produce a brain scan that probably looks a lot like yours as you are reading this page.)

Regrettably, this particular child had floundered for three years in school—no reading instruction to speak of in kindergarten and two years of misplacement in one-size-fits-all scripted reading programs, lockstep in implementation but out of sync with what *she* needed, through no fault of her own. By the time I first met the child, the summer tutor was awkwardly trying to fix the problem using the wrong tools. She was using a hammer to unscrew the gooseneck from the pipe. Context clues may have had some effect on this reader's processing, just as one might very well bang on the pipe with the hammer a couple of times before attempting to unscrew it, but the real work of unscrewing the pipe should be done with a pipe wrench. The reading tutor just didn't know which tool to use to do the job.

The new tools in this book have been selected based on new understandings of what is needed for children to be successful in learning to read (and write), including brain imagery studies, which are allowing researchers to see what's going on *inside the brain* at the same time teachers observe what goes on *outside the brain* with beginning and struggling readers. More importantly, the tools go far beyond what many teachers currently do to take advantage of writing and reading reciprocity, which Marie Clay predicted we needed over twenty-five years ago. This book is designed to provide a tool kit to help teachers work with confidence and precision. It will show you exactly what tool to use at the right time, what you are trying to accomplish with the tool, and why it's important for the beginning reader. The selection of the tools and the guidelines for using them is predicated by the most up-to-date theories of how learning to read works. We now know what signals to look for when a beginning reader is falling behind, and we know what kind of instructional intervention can help them.

Part of the exciting message of this book is that with the right tools at the right time, most brains can learn to read English, which is harder to read than other alphabetic languages. Even more encouraging is that, with early intervention, brains that initially struggle simply may have a glitch in the reading circuitry in a specialized area of the brain for automatic word reading, and with the tools highlighted in this book, the glitch can be fixed.

In the chapters that follow, I use plain language to show you what the latest theory and research tell us is needed to teach reading successfully. We will follow a plan of assessment-driven instruction, guiding children through four phases of beginning reading by selecting the best tools in each phase for moving them to the next higher level. To assure your success with assessment-driven instruction, I provide a blueprint to enable you to connect teaching writing and spelling with teaching reading in ways that aren't predicated by convention.

Beginning writing and reading share commonalities that haven't been high-lighted in teacher training or the teaching-reading literature. Many well-trained, veteran reading teachers who read this book will see the spelling/writing/reading connection explicated clearly for the very first time. You'll learn why high-lighting the spelling component not only makes sense for emerging readers but also revolutionizes assessment-based instruction. We will highlight early writing and reading reciprocity and show how kindergarten writing is a means for ensuring reading success. Emerging readers who are guided through phases of writing using invented spelling can use their writing knowledge for learning to read because both systems share the same underlying knowledge base. Early writers use knowledge about sounds, letters, syllables, words, word parts like onsets and rimes, and phonics patterns, so early writing *advances* reading. But we haven't taken full advantage of it. Too often early reading and writing are not connected; they are treated separately. Teachers are doing things with phonemic awareness, not understanding when certain phonemic awareness work is needed or how it fits in the whole process of becoming a reader. Phonemic awareness has become an isolated objective, not a part of the natural development of early reading, spelling, and writing. Regrettably, writing and spelling are not even taught in some kindergarten classrooms. Very specific techniques used concomitantly for teaching beginning reading and writing at particular phases in early development greatly assist the child's move toward the goal of skilled reading. Many teachers still do not realize that beginning reading and writing are almost the same thing, identical processes unfolding in four identical phases in what for some children is a two-year journey in kindergarten and first grade on the road to skilled reading—a two-year journey to breaking the code.

While beginning reading and writing phases are identical, assessing writing phases has a value-added component: writing phases are easier to detect. It is often easier to nudge children forward in literacy development teaching into their writing than focusing only on guided reading instruction or separate phonemic awareness instruction. Working with beginning writing is like fixing the drainpipe under the sink and all of a sudden the dishwasher works because, like the sink and the dishwasher, reading and writing are hooked up to the same system. And while things unrelated to drain pipes can go wrong with the dishwasher, it makes sense to check out the basic systems first.

A huge advantage of tracking the writing phases instead of relying solely on reading levels is that writing is right there on the paper, marvelously explicit and easier to see than the reading phases. That's important because assessment-driven instruction based on the reciprocity of beginning writing and reading not only makes the work of the reading teacher a lot easier, it allows you to add a few precision power tools to your toolbox to replace some of the crude instruments you may have used in the past.

The research base in this book provides new understanding of what it takes for a child to become a reader by focusing on differences between *beginning* reading and *skilled* reading. You'll find a contemporary model for reading and a synthesis of phase theory of sight-word reading and stages of developmental spelling remarkably corroborated by brain scan research to support a newfound emphasis on the spelling/writing/reading connection during this important time in development. You'll see how all three sciences point to the same fact: the child becomes a skilled reader after a protracted process of breaking the letter code.

A major goal of this book is to expand our understanding of what it means to "break the code" by clearly mapping out the important role of the spelling/writing/reading connection for beginning reading. Deciphering the English spelling system and understanding how the printed symbols of the alphabet—namely, letters or chunks of letter combinations and patterns—combine to represent comprehendible, meaningful, pronounceable words and subword parts, are at the fulcrum of beginning reading (and writing). *Once this chunking breakthrough is accomplished, the brain can activate circuitry for recognizing words automatically and read with much more proficiency, precision, and independence.* (We will see that early independent reading, which is much more dependent on repetition and memorization of easy material, may be an entirely different process and activate different brain circuitry than later skilled independent reading.) It may surprise you that it normally takes some children two years to break the code. (And too many never really break it!)

Chapter 1 surveys a model of reading many psychologists believe to be the best current psychological perspective on how reading works. Whether you think it's the best model or not, it's one worth thinking about because it does provide new perspectives on beginning reading. After surveying the model I provide my own five propositions to help rethink the requirements of teaching beginning reading, which may lead one to retool by taking advantage of writing and reading reciprocity.

Chapter 2 leads us inside the brain to reveal stunning new findings from brain scan research and the neurobiology of reading. You'll find evidence of two separate pathways for reading that define beginning versus skilled reading. You'll better understand the critical role spelling plays in the beginning reading and beginning writing process, and why studies show that writing is "the context in which word analysis most often took place, typically as using phonological analysis in the service of 'figuring out' the spelling of words" (reported in Snow, Burns, and Griffin 1998, 187). We'll also see why spelling instruction may play a role in overcoming some reading disabilities.

Chapter 3 presents a new perspective from which to retool assessment-driven instruction, adding assessment of a child's advancement in "figuring out" words or breaking the code from no letter use, to pre-alphabetic, partial alphabetic, full alphabetic and consolidated alphabetic levels of beginning reading and writing to support and foster the child's reading efforts. Looking from outside the brain, we'll see differences in early phases versus eventual skilled and automatic reading. At each phase we will be learning specific strategies to establish and stabilize the level of word analysis the child is capable of and then move them to the next level. We'll see how observations by phase theorists for word learning and developmental spelling research outside the brain corroborate what neuroscientists see happening inside the brain. In Chapter 3, we focus on research in the development of phase theory for sight-word learning and begin to lay the foundation for both an instructional and an intervention blueprint.

In Chapter 4, the blueprint becomes more tangible by showing the child's advancement through clearly apparent phases of writing and spelling development. You will learn that the writing phases and the reading phases are directly connected, and so provide a clear research base for reading and writing reciprocity. Taken together, findings in these two chapters lead to a clearer understanding of what happens in the brain to allow for skilled and automatic reading and spotlight early intervention as a key to successful reading instruction.

Chapter 5 begins by showing how children are prepared for success with literacy before entering kindergarten. You will learn why it's important to capitalize on the child's first urge to write. You'll find a discussion of the reading wars and an attempt to stretch our understanding and perhaps bring two warring camps closer together in ideology by highlighting reading and writing reciprocity. We begin to look at how and why to intervene during the early phases of beginning literacy.

Chapter 6 is a blueprint for intervention—essentially the when, why, and how to intervene with beginning readers and writers who are straying off course. Capitalizing on reading and writing reciprocity and the compelling writing connection to reading, the easy intervention procedures needed during the "tadpole" phases of beginning literacy are clearly presented. Beginning with a mission statement and a set of values that all teachers of beginning and struggling reading will be eager to embrace, the Intervention Blueprint will help delineate each of the phases of development and show when and how to intervene with the right kind of instruction at the right time. You'll learn to use a new set of tools to build what is needed and to fix what goes wrong. And in so doing, you'll discover a powerful new paradigm for ensuring that all beginners and struggling readers break the code and read automatically.

Chapters 6 and 7 are the centerpiece of this book. If you are short on time, you may go directly to Chapters 6 and 7 for detailed information on when and how to intervene and instruct beginners, as well as dozens of specific strategies for supporting developing readers and writers. You'll see the tools in action moving the child level by level toward breaking the code. You'll glean nuances that will sharpen your observation and instructional skills, enabling you to guide beginners and those who struggle toward successful code breaking. You'll see how instruction can be crafted to be individualized, age-appropriate, and engaging at all levels and you'll learn how to be a responder to a child's specific needs for breaking the code.

Chapter 8 shows how to set up a kindergarten writing program that is as important for learning to read as reading instruction itself. You'll hear the voices of the best kindergarten teachers in the nation as they invite you into their classrooms to visit powerful learning environments for literacy learning and to see how to teach reading through writing. They'll share their favorite literacy techniques and strategies. The chapter includes schedules that show times for teaching writing explicitly and also times for creating play-based instruction to increase not only oral language but written language as well.

In Chapter 9 you will journey deep into the dark side of reading disability. In a case study of a struggling reader and explications of the cases of three children with probable neurologically based reading and spelling disabilities, you will see how missteps in reading instruction, a lack of early intervention, and bad advice can be devastating, not only to children but to the adults who surround them.

Finally, Chapter 10 is an amazing story of one recovered reader; and in a Postscript you'll learn how the work you do leaves a legacy.

I hope to take you on a remarkable journey deep into the world of teaching beginning readers and writers—we may go farther than you can imagine. If you are a reading teacher, our journey may change your teaching.

A Model of Skilled Reading Before We Look Inside the Brain of a Reader

A neuroscientist comparing the fMRI brain scan of a first-grade level *beginning* reader to the brain scan of a second-grade level *skilled* reader might see images as different as a tadpole and a frog. In my view, that distinction is one of the great contributions of recent brain scan research. There is no question that beginning reading and skilled reading, like the tadpole and the frog, are the same animal; but when viewed through the lens of a neuroscientist, the immature version looks different. The second-grade skilled reader is like the frog; she has crossed the threshold to maturity and from inside the brain the activation of her reading circuitry probably looks very much like yours. She is able to do grown-up reading.

Brain imagery is providing a new prism for viewing reading and shedding new light on the process. Of special interest to me is a new way of viewing beginning reading; as a two-year metamorphosis between nonreading and skilled or "grown-up" reading, with changes not only observable inside the brain, but also easily recognized outside the brain by classroom teachers. The outside-the-brain changes in beginning readers are as easy to detect by the knowledgeable kindergarten and first grade teacher as are the growth of legs, loss of tails, development of lungs, and ingestion of insects (not plants) in the four phases of tadpole development.

Perhaps the world of the beginning, not yet mature, reader needs supports as different as do the worlds of the tadpole and the frog. Mature and immature readers thrive in and around the classroom just as frogs and tadpoles thrive in and around the pond, but the tadpole eats differently, breathes differently, and survives only in the water. A tadpole's experience is very different from a day in the life of a frog. Perhaps the beginning reader should have different experiences too, in kindergarten and first grade, to sustain and nourish the changes that must take place between nonreading and skilled reading.

I believe brain scan research, phase theory for word learning, and research for developmental spelling are converging to support such a view. In Chapter 2, we will have a look inside the brain through the lens of a neuroscientist and later, in Chapters 3 and 4, outside the brain through the lens of reading and spelling researchers to gain some new perspectives on what's happening in the life of the beginning reader. But first, let's survey an important model of reading.

Looking at Reading Through the Lens of Contemporary Psychology

The brain processes information by searching for patterns and processing them within component parts of attention as the mind focuses selectively on a tiny fraction of the stream of information it takes in. The beginning reader may need to rely on some types of information that may not be needed by the skilled reader, just as the tadpole has to rely on a different environment than the frog. If so, it follows that teaching practices for mature versus immature readers may need to be geared to these differences and provide different kinds of support. To better understand the types of information readers must focus on, let's begin with a psychological perspective on reading derived from recent constructivist theories and illustrated in a current model of what many contemporary psychologists believe to be the four important operational components of the reading process: (1) a meaning component inextricably connected with (2) a spelling component, (3) a sound component, and (4) a context of spoken language component. These are the reading-related processes. During reading, attention must be focused on all the processes—meaning, sound, context, and spelling—as the reader is actively engaged in drawing on past experiences in each of these areas and chunking patterns or building new conceptual schemes to construct new sense and new meaning. James Byrnes (2001) in a wonderful chapter on reading in his book, *Minds, Brains, and Learning,* credits the 1989 Seidenberg and McClelland model of reading, made famous and extended by the work of Marilyn Adams (1990), as what many psychologists believe to offer the best psychological perspective on how reading actually works. It's useful for us to review it briefly here because it has had an impact on brain scan research and may have huge implications for our teaching.

The Seidenberg and McClelland model of reading, presented in Figure 1.1, shows what kinds of information the brain is likely to be focusing on during the reading process. The model doesn't attempt to physically show how the brain reads by matching processes with brain activation; rather, it identifies the likely focus of attention and the operations necessary to explain what kind of information the brain of a skilled reader must pay attention to and how this information must be acted upon to make reading possible.

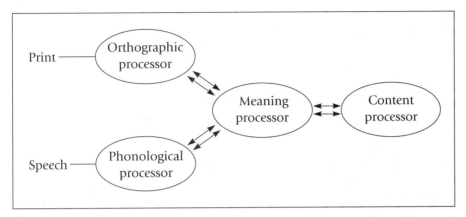

FIGURE 1.1   The Four Processors of the Reading System (After Seidenberg and McClelland [1989])

The Seidenberg and McClelland model has four components for mature reading, called *interactive processors*, each processing important kinds of information thought to be necessary for skilled reading—a meaning processor interactively connected to an orthographic (spelling) processor accounting for the role of spelling, a phonological processor explaining the role of sounds in language for reading, and a context processor accounting for important pragmatic, grammatical, and syntactic features of language. Each of the processors detects patterns of regularity or conceptual schemes within the realm of information it reacts to in its area of specialization. All four components work together to drive the reading process. Information flows back and forth between these processors, with especially important connections between each of the components with the meaning processor. One component affects the work of the other allowing for a good bit of redundancy, which in turn provides important backup systems to keep the reading process running smoothly. Arrows in the model between processors indicate how one processor can interact with another to affect the outcome. For example, meaning and syntax might provide information to enable the reader to determine whether the word *lead* when it appears in text is automatically recognized as a noun meaning a heavy malleable metallic chemical element, or a verb meaning to show the way to, or direct the course of, by guiding. This interaction of processors would account for whether the reader would settle on a pronunciation of *lead* that rhymes with *bed* or one that rhymes with *seed*. I find the model very evocative for helping me think about what's happening when I work with children and their reading.

This model has influenced some of the brain researchers too. For example, some processors are believed, in the words of Byrnes, "to contain a large quantity of interconnected 'units' that are thought to bear a close correspondence to neural assemblies" (2001, 116). Just as we have seeing and hearing circuits, readers likely have systems of interacting modes for orthographic, phonological, syntactic, and semantic aspects of language. Some of these are piggybacked instinctive circuitry already in place for spoken language. Some must be activated specifically for the acquired ability of reading. Later, when we look at the brain scan research, we'll see how some of the neuroscientists who think they have identified the underlying neural mechanisms for reading in the brain believe the neural assemblies actually do their work. The work presented in this book doesn't depend on the Seidenberg and McClelland model, but the model corroborates this work and is certainly compatible with it.

The Seidenberg and McClelland model helps us understand some of the core mechanisms of reading and provides some broad sense of how skilled reading might work. Importantly, it helps us better understand key contributions from the brain imagery and perhaps see research findings in a new light that has extraordinary importance for our teaching. Among the findings that will be highlighted in the chapters to follow are these propositions:

1. Spelling knowledge is much more important for reading than has been acknowledged.

2. Beginning readers differ from skilled readers. We may need a separate model (or blueprint) for beginning reading.

3. Reading teachers must guide beginning readers to make the chunking breakthrough. Chunking spelling patterns and automatic word recognition are necessary to skilled reading. Without ability to recognize words automatically, the reader cannot advance to a skilled, mature level.

4. The brain learns to do things automatically by firing neurons over and over. Certain kinds of repetition are hugely beneficial for readers because repetition leads to automaticity.

5. At various stages in development, some component operations of the reading process are more important than others. The processes needed for beginning reading may become automatic in skilled readers. Our teaching will improve if we focus on the right operational components at the right time.

Before looking at the brain scan research, let's flesh out each of these propositions in a bit more detail.

1. *Spelling Knowledge Is Much More Important for Reading Than Has Been Acknowledged.* Notice the prominence of spelling in the model. All the other processors are aspects of spoken language. To some extent, they develop naturally and are already in place when children begin to read. The orthographic processor is the only part of the model that must be acquired uniquely for reading. Spelling, how the child thinks letters or combinations of letters represent meaningful words, may be much more important than it has been regarded in the past. The brain of a very literate person has some mechanism for storing and re-trieving the exact *spelling* of a word. At the same time a reader sees a known word in print or a writer thinks of a known word to write down on paper, as-semblages of neurons in the brain of a highly literate person fire in sync, not only with the word's meaning and pronunciation, but with its correct spelling. (This happens in the region designated as Area C in Figure 2.1 on page 15.) The brain of a literate person has an enormous capacity to sort through the thou-sands of letter combinations on a page of print and find the regular patterns within it by chunking. *Spelling, in fact, is a chunking skill. The reader/writer/speller must learn to chunk strings of letters into discernable patterns.* Look at the following string of letters:

maercecidnaseikoocklim

Twenty-two bits of information are provided in this letter string. Study the se-quence for about ten seconds and then look away and try to recall the sequence.

The limitations of working memory make this a difficult task. It's virtually impossible to remember the letters unless one notices chunks of spelling pat-terns such as maerce-cid-nase-i-koock-lim, a chunking process, which makes it possible for one to remember them. Now for the next ten seconds, look at the same twenty-two bits of information again. This time they are presented in re-verse order.

milkcookiesandicecream

Do you now have an easier time remembering this sequence? Did your brain detect the spelling patterns first? Did you add sound, context, and mean-ing in processing the twenty-two letters in the string in the second example?

Spelling plays such a prominent role in the Seidenberg and McCelland model and, as we shall see, in the brain scan research that one might wonder why it plays such a minor role in most of our literacy programs. In most ele-mentary schools spelling is a "supplementary" subject, an afterthought, yet it is a key component of this highly acclaimed model of skilled reading with impli-cations for reading speed and fluency, and the only component uniquely spe-cific to reading.

Developmental spelling plays a huge role in beginning reading, and track-ing its development may be one of the most powerful ways to assess how well beginners are developing as readers (Snow et al. 1998; Gentry 2004). Tracking developmental spelling is at the core of good assessment-driven instruction for beginning reading. Chapters 3 and 4 illustrate how the beginning phases of reading and writing unfold in the same phases as developmental spelling, which are as easy to see in invented spelling as the four phases of the tadpole's metamorphosis into a frog.

2. Beginning Reading and Skilled Reading Are Not the Same. Seidenberg and McClelland propose a model of skilled reading, and much of the research and understanding of reading that has come out of this model has focused on differences between *poor* and *skilled* reading. We also need to look at differences between *beginning* and *skilled* readers. If beginning reading and skilled reading are different, it invites one to create a separate model (or blueprint) for beginning reading. Would a model for beginning reading account for phases like the ones we see in tadpole development? Would it predict a need for a focus on moving children to rapid and automatic recognition of spelling patterns in words and subword units, since automatic recognition of spelling patterns appears to be the sine qua non of skilled reading? Would it help teachers of beginning reading to recognize the need for each child to make the chunking breakthrough for decoding? What is the role of repetition for fluency in beginning reading?

3. *A Necessity of Skilled Reading Is Automatic Word Recognition.* Think of a three-syllable word beginning with an *r* that means a boat race. Can you spell it? If the word has popped in your mind, a unique constellation of neurons have fired triggering its meaning, its sound, and its spelling. (Four out of five of you can see the word's spelling in your mind, but one in five cannot see it. If you are in the group of one-in-five struggling spellers, you may be puzzling over *ragatta, regatta, regata, regotta,* or *rigatta.*) Your automatic word processor is at work. You are calling on the word module in your brain for *regatta.* If you know this word, your automatic processor enables you to read *regatta* instantly. (Some of you who are in the struggling-spellers group may use different circuitry to activate words.)

If the defining feature of skilled reading is automatic word recognition—and I believe it is—a major focus of beginning reading may be to get the child to a point that word recognition *is* automatic. After automatic recognition is accomplished, it's much easier for attention to be focused on higher levels of processing like sentence integration and, ultimately, comprehension and meaningful connections. A primary concern for beginning reading, therefore, may be how to teach automatic word recognition and automatic recognition of common spelling patterns—that is, to get beginning readers to make the chunking breakthrough. In my opinion, much progress has been made in the classroom with techniques such as using word walls in first grade, a technique that connects with brain research because good word wall work is multimodal, invoking multiple assemblages of visual circuitry, auditory circuitry, kinesthetic circuitry, and tactile brain circuitry working together along with lots of repetition to get words into an automatic processor. There are additional techniques to accomplish the critical role of automatic word recognition with particular emphasis on learning how spelling works, analogizing, and rapid recognition of chunks of phonics patterns.

4. *The Brain Learns to Do Things Automatically by Firing Neurons Over and Over.* In this book I highlight the role of appropriate repetition in our teaching, especially at beginning levels. Recognizing the role of repetition is nothing new. Much has been written recently about the benefits of increasing the volume of reading because higher reading volume gives all four component operations—using context, using spelling, making meaning, and using phonology—a healthy workout, and the residual benefit is that reading skills such as sight-word recognition, vocabulary development, reading fluency, and conceptual development grow exponentially as a result of lots of independent reading practice (Allington 2001). This is readily apparent in studies such as the one by Cunningham and Stanovich (1998), which found that readers who scored at the 10th percentile on reading tests read about 8,000 words per year contrasted with 282,000 words per year by readers who scored at the 50th percentile *and 1.8 million words per year by readers who scored at the 90th percentile*. The difference in the numbers of firing synapses for word recognition by readers at these various levels is staggering.

Remarkably, Marie Clay addressed the importance of repetition for building strong readers as well as the benefits of making reading stronger by practicing it, and she addressed it very specifically over twenty years ago in *Observing Young Readers*. Her brilliant observations sound much like she is making direct reference to current knowledge of how the brain works even through she wrote the following passage long before the Seidenberg and McClelland model or the possibility of brain scan imagery:

> A kind of learning occurs in natural language tasks [*such as reading and writing*], which is rarely thought about. Proceeding by rough and ready theories but operating self-correction processes the child practices old learning [*recognizing known words, for example*], giving a minimum attention, while new learning is laboriously worked over until it has found a place in the system [*like moving from an area of slow and analytical word analysis to an area where the brain specializes in recognizing words automatically*]. Every time a child reads a sentence or writes a story each letter sequence and language form in that sentence is, by its use, moving from somewhere in the novel language dimension towards being used with minimum attention. [*This is an excellent description of how some neuroscientists theorize the brain learns to read [and write] words instantly.*] The hard-to-spell new word seems to be the one which requires processing [*in the brain*] but every other word in the sentence profits [*in the brain*] by being used, moving further towards fluency, "automatic responding" and flexibility of use. High frequency words move most rapidly to this state. So when we record a series of "correct" responses for the child reader [*the brain is actively reinforcing itself—reinforcing the neural pathways for each specific word module, for example—and building automaticity*] we are not really noticing this continuing process of learning and overlearning. [*Note that today's psychologists include terms such as "redundancy" or "a backup system," which mesh well with the concept of "overlearning."*] (Clay 1982, 4) [Emphasis and parenthetical material added]

5. *At Various Stages of Development, Some Component Operations of the Reading Process Are More Important Than Others.* While all four operations—context, spelling, meanings, and phonology—work in concert to help the reader construct meaning from print, at various stages in development, some of these component operations may be more important for reading, with others backing them up. Here's an example: the Seidenberg and McClelland model accounts for the importance of both context clues and spelling clues, but which is *more* important? And when? In recent years many beginning reading programs placed context and meaning front and center—with only tiny emphasis on spelling and phonics. According to Byrnes (2001), the Seidenberg and McClelland model of reading calls that into question when considering poor versus skilled readers. One might wonder whether the same holds true for beginning versus mature readers:

> But research has shown that the context-meaning effects [*i.e., context clues*] are weak relative to the orthography-meaning effects [*i.e., spelling clues*]. That is, readers are much better at predicting possible meanings of a word based on its perceived spelling than they are at predicting which word will follow a preceding context (Adams 1990). When context-meaning links conflict with orthography-meaning links, the latter win out. Thus, skilled reading consists, first and foremost, of learning the correspondences between written words and their meanings [*i.e., spellings*]. Context effects occur after words are perceived and various possible meanings are accessed. (122) [Emphasis and parenthetical material added]

So while context, spelling knowledge, meaning, and knowledge about the sound system of language are all important for reading, spelling knowledge may come first and be more critical to the reading process at certain phases of development with the other systems backing it up. After all, the beginning reader already has brain circuitry for connecting sound and context to meaning due to his or her innate ability to speak language. The four-year-old who speaks English already uses the forty-four sounds of English to speak, though she may not be able to consciously manipulate them, and she is able to fill in the blanks if you say, "Turn on the ———," or "Let's ——— to the mall." By contrast, most four-year-olds have no knowledge of how spelling works—even if they have memorized how to write their names. There is no systematic letter–sound processing. The child has simply memorized an arbitrary set of squiggly marks. A good teacher of beginning reading must teach how the squiggly marks represent sounds and words.

Here's an example of how spelling cues may be more important than context clues. Remember the struggling second grader whom I wrote about in the introduction who read *foot* and *feet* indiscriminately? I observed her relying too heavily on context clues time and again, reading *prince* as *king,* for example, in a story about Cinderella when clearly the spelling p-r-i-n-c-e should not fire off neurons for *king*. Her overreliance on context clues, which signaled the need for a word to be a male member of the royal family, trumped the more important spelling cues. This underreliance on spelling cues persisted; even after she first began to recognize patterns like *hop, stop,* and *pot,* she still might substitute *cop* for *police.* Her tutor chose to focus on context clues in spite of the fact that she overrelied on context and underrelied on spelling patterns as in reading *po-lice* (*police*) as *cop.* The tutor chose the wrong instruction to mediate the problem.

In the chapters that follow, we will fine-tune your ability to choose the right teaching technique at the right time. You'll learn how what children are doing or not doing with spelling is a clue to what techniques you may use to help them advance as readers. You'll learn which of four phases a beginning reader is in at a particular point in time and specific instructional techniques to lead them into the next phase. You'll learn what kind of repetition is beneficial for readers in a particular phase to stabilize and establish word learning until word recognition becomes automatic. You'll learn how to tell when the child is falling behind the expected level of development and how you can provide early intervention to fix the problem.

2

Looking Inside the Brain— Glimmerings of Insight from Brain Scan Research and the Neurobiology of Reading

Did you know that some neuroscientists believe that they have not only found the location in the brain for dyslexia but also the cause of it? Did you know that they think your teaching practices might "cure" dyslexia if you provide intervention with dyslexic children when they are young enough? Wouldn't it be ironic if part of the reading problem is the lack of appropriate spelling instruction? Brain scan research addresses each of these questions directly. In my view, brain scan research is not an exact science and it does not tell the whole story of how reading works. It might, however, provide some glimmerings of insight.

First of all it must be acknowledged that the brain is incomprehensibly complex—admittedly incomprehensible even to most neuroscientists. Your brain has about 100 billion neurons or nerve cells, for transmitting electrical impulses, which is comparable to the number of stars in the universe (Sousa 2002). Secondly, like a fingerprint, every brain is different. Nonetheless, underneath this dazzling complexity there are core patterns that may be detected by brain scans, which are a kind of map of the brain (Byrnes 2001). While every reader's brain is different, with one's own unique working vocabularies and word modules in the brain, and different experiential memories and worldviews to bring to the reading process, there is commonality in the way people experience reading. We all very likely have similar systems of interacting modes for processing orthographic, phonological, syntactic, and semantic aspects of language; but then again, perhaps skilled readers, beginning readers, and dyslexics who have learned to read have differences in their neurological circuitry.

Some neuroscientists believe that brain scan work is helping to unlock some of the mysteries of reading and to provide important guidance for teaching it.

It's interesting to take a brief look at the ascendancy and newness of brain scan research for reading. Beginning in the early 1980s, neuroscientists began using a technology called positron emission tomography (PET) to see the brain's activity by measuring the blood flow in specified cerebral regions, raising the observation of the brain up a notch, so that for the first time, a brain scan might not only show a perfect picture of the human brain's structure, but also aspects of the brain's function during cognitive processes such as reading. When an area was activated, the blood flow increased, and by injecting radioactive compounds into the bloodstream, the scientists could record regional distribution of radioactivity. For the first time, neuroscientists were able to see "reading areas" of the brain performing various reading-related processes. PET was more recently replaced by a technology called *functional* magnetic resonance imaging (fMRI), which goes beyond the MRI picture of the brain. You are probably familiar with magnetic resonance imaging (MRI), which is commonly used in medicine to produce computer-processed, high-contrast images of the body's anatomy. In contrast, fMRI shows which areas are *functioning* by monitoring the magnetic properties in blood and recording activation and increased blood flow in an area where neurons are firing. Unlike PET technology, no injections are required for fMRI technology (Shaywitz 2003).

A benchmark crosscultural study was published in 2001 entitled "Dyslexia: Cultural Diversity and Biological Unity" (Paulesu et al. 2001) in which the researchers used PET scans to determine if dyslexia was biological or cultural. Dyslexia is any neurologically based specific reading disability. This study identified subjects with developmental dyslexia as opposed to acquired alexia, the latter being a loss of reading ability resulting from a stroke, tumor, or traumatic injury to the brain. Did normal readers' brains function differently than developmental dyslexics who had learned to read? Were dyslexics who had learned to read activating different regions of the brain? The answer was "yes." Not only did the normal readers show greater activation in all brain regions associated with reading, but they produced different brain scan profiles than did the dyslexic subjects who could read. The area of difference seemed to be an area associated with spelling. Does the brain of a skilled reader have some mechanism for storing and retrieving the exact spelling of a word and could this possibly not be activating in the brain of a dyslexic? The study found commonality in brain scans among normal readers across languages and in dyslexic readers across languages even when the languages had vastly different spelling systems. One of the interesting facts to come out of the report was that English was much harder to read and to spell than a language like Italian because readers of Italian only have to know thirty-three spelling combinations for its sounds, while the English reader has to know 1,120 spelling combinations for the sounds of English (Kher 2001, 56), presenting a formidable challenge to the beginning reader or writer of English. The implication is that teaching and guiding children who are emerging as

English readers requires great focus on how English letters represent the sounds of our language. Thus, the English spelling system, because of its complexity, may be a big part of what needs to be learned so that beginning readers may gain ability to read words instantly and to read with fluency. My own reading of the Paulesu study kept bringing me back to the importance spelling has for reading. Like the Seidenberg and McClelland model, this early important brain scan study showed that spelling plays an enormous role in skilled reading. Why is it then, that we tend to gloss over spelling when teaching literacy in elementary school?

The Paulesu study made me wonder about the role spelling plays in automatic word recognition as well. To me, the study implies that there may in fact, be a region where the brain stores memories of exact spellings of words (like *regatta*) enabling expert spellers to "see spelling in their mind's eye" (Gentry 2004). Paulesu and colleagues reported inactivity in areas linking language to visual cues in the dyslexic brain, which may explain why dyslexics are notoriously poor spellers. In my view there are three kinds of spellers—people who learn to spell with relative ease, people who seem to be naturally poor spellers, and people who are uneducated spellers. The latter category is eliminated by decent instruction, leaving two categories—natural spellers who acquire the skill if they work at it, and about one-in-five naturally poor spellers who may never be expert spellers no matter how hard they try. I believe the main difference between a naturally poor speller and an expert speller is that the expert speller is activating an area of the brain that can "see" the word in his or her mind and the poor speller cannot "see" the word because the area linking language to visual cues in not activated. Instead, a compensatory system of reading is being used, employing other areas of the brain. Is there an area of the brain on the boundary between language and visual processing where skilled readers eventually activate correct spellings automatically—an area that links language to visual cues? The Paulesu study seems to point in this direction. I am an atrocious speller myself, and probably a dyslexic who has learned to read. Suppose I'm writing and all of a sudden I need the three-syllable verb that starts with *r-e* and means to call past events or experiences to mind. Sometimes the only clue I have in a situation like this it to spell it like it sounds. I cannot "see" the word in my mind; however, if I see *reminisce* in print, unquestionably I recognize it. My attempt at spelling it, however, is likely to be something like *remeness*, which is so far off it is not even recognized by a computer spell checker.

It's also interesting to report that my reading is slow and I am conscious of a great deal of subvocalization. I usually pronounce every word in my mind when I read. Many readers are capable of reading much faster than I can—because they don't subvocalize! Very likely, I am activating different than normal left-sided brain circuitry for reading and spelling; nevertheless, the reading part works for me. It just takes me more time. Even though my reading is slow, I am an excellent reader. No matter how hard I try, however, I have been unable to become an excellent speller. The Paulesu study suggests an important spelling/

reading connection between spelling and reading, and that the role of spelling in literacy is central. (Though, literally, the activation of perfect spelling is *posterior* according to brain scans!)

Probably the best known of the brain scan work that is influencing reading education is work by neuroscientist and professor of pediatrics, Sally Shaywitz, and her colleagues at the Yale Center for the Study of Learning and Attention, reported in her book *Overcoming Dyslexia* (2003). Shaywitz and her colleagues' fMRI studies have been focused on creating a reading map of the brain by charting the neural circuitry for reading. Initially, Shaywitz identified specific neural sites for sounding out words (77). Then her work focused on looking at differences in brain activation patterns for dyslexic versus normal skilled readers. This work, according to Shaywitz, has uncovered the basic brain mechanisms underlying reading, not only leading to knowledge of "exactly where and how dyslexia manifests itself in the brain" (4), but by contrasting dyslexic and normal readers' brain scans she believes the basic neural pathways of reading have been identified (10). She found dyslexia to be specifically localized within the phonologic component of the language system, the part of the brain "where the sounds of language are put together to form words and where words are broken down into their elemental sounds," and she calls this part of the brain the "word form area" (40). Her findings indicate that the upper levels of language processing, those for semantics, syntax and the basic neural sites for speaking and understanding language, are not affected by dyslexia. The problem is in the lowest level, the phonologic module where sound elements of language are mapped, or chunked, onto spelling (41). While reading does rely heavily on brain circuits already in place for spoken language, that brain circuitry functions normally in dyslexics. Dyslexics have no problem with higher-order processes needed for comprehension such as vocabulary, use of context, reasoning, and deriving meaning. In fact, according to Shaywitz, dyslexics often exhibit particular strengths in comprehension, problem solving, reasoning, critical thinking, vocabulary, and general knowledge (53). Indeed, dyslexics have not been shown to have visual defects, as is widely reported; they don't typically transpose letters or write backwards. Shaywitz says, in fact, "reversals are irrelevant to the diagnosis of dyslexia" (101).

The brain scan studies revealed that the problem resides in the basic circuitry for linking letters to sounds—Shaywitz alternately calls this region of the brain "the word form area," "the left posterior brain region," or "the occipito-temporal area." Since spelling is linking letters to sounds to form words, think of the area as "the automatic spelling circuitry," in other words, the area of the brain that allows expert spellers to "see words in their mind's eye." It's interesting to note this association of the spelling circuitry with dyslexia because severe spelling disability is a telltale sign of dyslexia.

The problem leading to dyslexia, according to Shaywitz, occurs at this lowest level of processing language, the decoding level, or spelling level, where printed words are translated into the phonetic code, that is, where text becomes the sounds of human language in the mind, and then is accepted and processed by the higher-level neural circuitry already in place for processing spoken language (51). In essence, dyslexia happens at the letter-chunking level. In fact, that's what English spelling is—it's chunking groups of letters to represent sounds. Part of the work of the brain is to sort through enormous amounts of information and find regular patterns within it. That's exactly what it does with spelling and reading, which turns out to be one of man's greatest intellectual accomplishments—figuring out how a language's spelling system chunks into representations of the sounds of spoken language. The brain discovers the chunking system for making alphabetic letters represent word parts and words. It's especially challenging for English because English has over one thousand combinations for its forty-four sounds.

The glitch associated with dyslexia happens in the reading process after the brain sees the words on the page, at the point when the brain tries to convert the letters into their sounds, by chunking. The problem occurs before the brain engages its innate abilities to process speech into meaning. The location of the glitch is in the phonologic component of the language system, more precisely, the automatic spelling area, the basic circuitry for chunking letters to sounds.

> The phonologic model tells us the exact steps that must be taken if a child is to go from the puzzlement of seeing letters as abstract squiggly shapes to the satisfaction of recognizing and identifying these letter groups as words. Overall, the child must come to know that the letters he sees on the page represent, or map onto, the sounds he hears when the same word is spoken. (44)

Shaywitz believes that the neuroscientists, with the technology of brain scan research, have been able to identify precisely where in the brain the child chunks the letters he sees on the page to the sounds he hears when the same word is spoken. It's the area that transcribes chunks of letters into sounds. This brain area, the word form area (occipito-temporal area), which I like to think of as the automatic spelling area, is where skilled readers recognize words automatically. (You can see it designated as Area C in Figure 2.1.) Dyslexics do not activate this area. The dyslexics who do learn to read activate different areas, including more in the front of the brain and often on the right side of the brain, which is unusual since the unimpaired skilled reader primarily uses a left-brain reading system. Shaywitz believes that dyslexics who do learn to read use a compensatory system of reading networks, that is, they activate different areas and exhibit different qualities for reading than do unimpaired skilled readers. They are slower at reading, since they can't use the word form area to recognize words automatically, and they use other areas of the brain to do the word form area's work. Dyslexics are also very poor spellers, perhaps because they don't activate Area C, the word form area, where the brain houses word modules with visual representations of words and their exact spellings. Instead of chunking *reminisce*

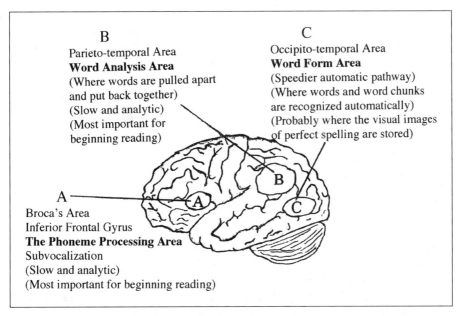

B
Parieto-temporal Area
Word Analysis Area
(Where words are pulled apart
and put back together)
(Slow and analytic)
(Most important for
beginning reading)

C
Occipito-temporal Area
Word Form Area
(Speedier automatic pathway)
(Where words and word chunks
are recognized automatically)
(Probably where the visual images
of perfect spelling are stored)

A
Broca's Area
Inferior Frontal Gyrus
The Phoneme Processing Area
Subvocalization
(Slow and analytic)
(Most important for beginning reading)

FIGURE 2.1   Left Hemishphere Brain Systems for Reading

Adapted from S. Shaywitz, *Overcoming Dyslexia.* Alfred Knopf, 2003. Reported in J. Richard Gentry, *The Science of Spelling: The Explicit Specifics That Make Great Readers and Writers (and Spellers!)* (Heinemann, 2004).

as *reminisce,* they may spell it as *remeness.* Because they can't "see" it in the mind, they must spell it like it sounds.

So who gets the blame for dyslexia? Shaywitz says it is a neurological glitch, perhaps even related to a set of genes (though identical twins don't necessarily share the condition), and that the glitch likely takes place during fetal life—during embryonic development when the brain is hard-wired for language (67). The glitch is confined to the wiring of the word form (spelling) area, Area C. One promising aspect of her work is that preliminary studies involving children who are just learning to read indicate that, with the proper instruction, the brain can fix itself—that is, it can bypass the glitch and activate Area C, the word form area, even in children who have the genetic predisposition to be dyslexic. Fixing itself requires early intervention, however, when the brain is plastic and malleable for rerouting neural systems (30), which apparently is best achieved around the ages of five and six. (Most learning disabilities in the United States are identified between the ages of eleven and seventeen, which is too late. [Gorman 2003])

Interestingly, both the Seidenberg and McClelland model and the Shaywitz brain scan studies have tended to focus mostly on skilled versus poor reading, or in the case of Shaywitz' work, skilled versus dyslexic readers. I think an aspect of the brain scan work equally promising for helping educators understand how best to teach reading manifests itself in glimmerings of insight related to beginning versus skilled reading. If we think about beginning reading as we focus on Shaywitz' report of how left-side reading works, we get some of these glimmerings of insight. Then we can begin to develop a separate model for beginning reading.

Look at Figure 2.1, a model of the left-side brain system for reading in the skilled, unimpaired reader. There are three areas activated for reading, which I have designated A, B, and C. In the skilled reader, most of the brain activation for reading takes place in the back of the brain incorporating areas B and C. Area C is the word form or spelling area, which as we have seen, has been identified as the area for automatic word recognition and perfect spelling. It's the area that is not activated in dyslexics and for most impaired readers it's the area of the dictionary in the brain, holding the word module for every word one has in one's vocabulary. Once activated when seeing a word on sight or thinking of a word to be written, this area produces the word's sound, its meaning, and, in expert spellers, its exact spelling. When one reads, this area reacts instantly to the whole printed word as a pattern by identifying the word automatically on sight (79). Since the brain works by drawing analogies and finding regular patterns, I suspect not only automatic recognition of words but automatic recognition of spelling patterns—the *sail* in unas*sail*able, for example—is extremely important for reading, especially for reading polysyllabic words. The brain is actively seeking out these chunks of spelling patterns.

Of course, beginners don't have very many words in Area C and it's only at the later phases of beginning reading that they are able to seek out chunks of spelling patterns and analogize. Shaywitz believes beginners must first analyze and read words correctly a number of times in order to form an exact neural model of that specific word to be permanently stored in Area C. Areas A and B, which are slow and analytic and most important for beginning reading, are responsible for that work. So the distinction between beginning reading and skilled reading made by the brain scan studies is that they are entirely different systems for reading, involving activation in different areas, or as Shaywitz calls it, two different pathways. To use my metaphor, tadpoles and frogs:

> Imaging studies have identified at least two neural pathways for reading: one for beginning reading, for slowly sounding out words, and another that is a speedier pathway for skilled reading. (78)

According to Shaywitz, the areas that are activated most for beginning reading are areas A and B. Area A, in the left inferior frontal gyrus in Broca's area, plays a role in slow word analysis. This part of the brain is activated for articulating spoken words, and during reading for subvocalizaton, that is, when a reader repeats words in her mind as she reads (81). Shaywitz believes this area plays an important role in beginning reading for processing sounds. For example, it's where rhyming and phoneme manipulation take place.

Area B, located on the left side in the middle of the brain a little above and behind the ear in the parieto-temporal region, is used by the beginning reader for word analysis. Shaywitz explains Area B this way: "Slow and analytic, its function seems to be in the early stages of learning to read, that is in initially analyzing a word, pulling it apart, and linking its letters to their sounds" (79). I presume skilled readers would activate this area if they encountered an unknown new word. But skilled readers mostly use Area C, which Shaywitz calls the "express pathway," which instantly and automatically activates a word form in the brain that not only identifies the word on sight, but its sound, its meaning, and its spelling. Shaywitz' work has revealed that the best readers show higher levels of activation of Area C, establishing "a strong link between reading skill and reliance on the word form area" (81). What can we do in our teaching of beginning readers to help get this word form area activated? To lay the foundation to better answer this question, let's move from the inside to look at what happens outside the brain as a beginning reader reads.

3

Outside-the-Brain Changes in Beginning Readers

Mature readers may use the spelling system differently than beginning readers do by activating a specialized area of the brain for recognizing words and spelling patterns automatically. The automatic circuitry isn't activated for beginning readers. As we have seen from brain scan research, this is one of the important differences in beginning and skilled reading. Looking from outside the brain, we also see differences in the beginning and skilled processes. We see beginning readers and writers morphing. Phase theorists for word learning and developmental spelling researchers have discovered the existence of four phases of early reading and writing development as children try to discover a pattern system for spelling that eventually leads to automatic word recognition. It is important for teachers of beginning reading to recognize these four phases, to understand how readers and writers approach decoding and encoding differently in each phase, and to plan instruction that moves children from lower earlier phases to higher later phases and eventually to skilled automatic processing. First we will observe concomitant changes in early reading and writing and take full advantage of writing and reading reciprocity. Then we will see how teachers in kindergarten and first grade and teachers who work with struggling readers help bridge the gap between nonreading and skilled reading by gearing instruction to the particular phase of development.

The four phases don't account for everything beginning readers and writers must learn in the beginning, but keep in mind that a lot of what we already do works very well in the teaching of reading. Teachers with Reading Recovery training, for example, are quite masterful at teaching reading by using tools for helping individuals who struggle with reading. And we have made remarkable improvement in our use of leveled text and guided reading in classroom instruction (Fountas and Pinnell 1996; 2001) and incorporating methods for increasing fluency (Allington 2001). The four phases will help us add a new, necessary component, however, which focuses on some of the more basic levels of processing. I believe these basic aspects of reading are the areas least understood by teachers and the areas of instruction where teachers might use new tools to increase the success rate with teaching beginning reading. These include work leading to the core mechanism of chunking spelling patterns.

The phases are really, in my view, spelling phases that the child applies to both reading and writing. These phases relate most specifically to the work of the orthographic processor in the Seidenberg and McClelland model (see Chapter 1). Spellings in English are patterns that must be detected by the brain for reading, but they are not one-letter-to-one-sound patterns; they are multiletter patterns or letter groups, and often, complex chunks of vowel and consonant combinations. *A lot of knowledge about spelling is necessary before a child can use the whole complex system the way mature readers use it.* During beginning reading phases, the child is attempting to discover the pattern or chunking system. There is no inborn and automatic recognition of the pattern system for spelling as is the case with the sound patterns or the contextual and meaning patterns of spoken language. Speaking comes naturally because the brain is innately wired to recognize and produce its complex patterns. A baby born in Italy almost immediately responds to patterns in the rhythm, pitch, and cadence in the mother's voice and after several months will recognize and babble the twenty-five sounds of the Italian language—the child now recognizes the sound pattern system for Italian. Likewise, after several months, a baby born into an English-speaking family begins firing neurons in his or her brain eliciting the forty-four sounds of English. The human brain's ability to find regular patterns in the native language is largely prewired. No one has to teach these sounds because the human brain recognizes the patterns of phonemes that make up the speech sounds of a particular language automatically. The same is *not* true of spelling patterns. We have to teach the child how to find the regular patterns within print. That's not to say, however, that the first thing to happen is necessarily the teaching of spelling in kindergarten.

Teaching reading can begin *very* early. I think it's important to pause at this juncture, and emphasize the possibilities for early beginnings. I believe teaching reading begins by teaching children to love books—even before they can speak. I watched my one-year-old godson on his first birthday, who was just speaking his first words, handle soft fabric books and board books. Books were already some of his favorite "toys." He attached meaning to the word *book* and responded to "Get the book, Aidan," by crawling to the box where the books were kept and pulling them out. At about the same time he learned to crawl up and down the stairs, and respond to commands such as "walk to Daddy" on the walker, and "sit next to Mattie" (the golden retriever), he already loved book experiences. At one year of age he was beginning to develop book-handling concepts; when his mother read to him he delighted in turning the pages and seemed to get the cue from the rhythm and cadence in her voice. I watched him sit with a book and turn the pages on his own. His early "spelling skills" included pulling ABC letter magnets off the refrigerator, throwing them on the floor, and squealing. He had so many toys that provided recordings of the ABC song that his dad swore he woke up one morning and heard Aidan humming the alphabet song—"da, da, da, da, da, da, da . . ." I mention this to underscore powerful possibilities for the true beginnings of reading. At one year of age, even as he spoke his first words, this child's mind was already curious and fascinated by the magic of reading and interested enough to join in with his parents, curious enough to begin unlocking its mysteries. Beginning reading can (and should) begin long before our more formal work in kindergarten. Early book experiences are absolutely fundamental for setting the best stage for reading.

The way the pattern system of spelling is discovered is equally marvelous. It's logical, and straightforward as it unfolds in phases. The first phase begins with no recognition of the pattern. In the next phase the child discovers that the pattern has something to do with matching letters to sounds, but he or she can only make a few matches. In the third phase the child gets the gist of the pattern system, can match many letters with sounds, and, quite logically, attempts to use a straightforward one-letter-for-one-sound system. Finally the child enters a phase heralded by the discovery that English spelling isn't necessarily one-to-one but often it's chunk-to-chunk, and with this new understanding there is enough regularity and pattern in the system that with a little practice finding the

An Early Beginning—Aidan Sharp and the Author

regular patterns, backed up by higher-level processes such as context and meaning, the brain can soon recognize the spelling patterns automatically.

Once the brain can recognize patterns like the ones in *in-ter-est-ing* and *Al-a-bam-a*, the assemblages of neurons fire in sync as the reader analyzes these particular pattern sequences correctly a number of times, eventually forming an exact neural model for the word, thereby recognizing the word automatically. Certain teaching strategies or "experiences" facilitate the move to pattern recognition starting with no recognition, to partial recognition such as recognition of the beginning letter and sound, to full recognition of a letter for every sound, and finally to consolidating groups of letters into chunks. These teaching strategies leading the child to certain "experiences" are important because patterns in the brain are shaped by experience as well as by genes.

The beginning phases anchored in the discovery of the spelling system are, admittedly, phases at the lowest level of processing, but that makes them even more important because they lay the foundation for skilled reading. Without recognition of the patterns, skilled and automatic reading cannot happen. The phases represent points on a continuum in the development of the alphabetic principle, and for many children, they are a two-year journey in breaking the complex code of the chunking system of English spelling. I believe much more can be done to match the type and timing of instruction with the particular phase in which children are functioning. Showing teachers how to do that is the major thrust in the chapters ahead. In my view, with appropriate instruction, we might reasonably expect most children to move through the beginning phases and acquire the basic mature, grown-up literacy skills by the time they are seven or eight years old. Shaywitz believes that this kind of work, what she would refer to as appropriate decoding instruction, may even go a long way in the elimination of dyslexia if intervention comes early in the child's development when the brain is still adaptable. The phases provide guideposts for early intervention.

Too often we have looked at aspects of beginning reading—learning letters, matching individual letters to sounds, phonemic awareness, learning phonics—as separate activities when, in fact, they are points on a continuum of the lengthy process of unlocking the alphabetic principle. In English this is not one-to-one but a chunking of letter groups to sounds. There's a great deal of research supporting the notion that phonemic awareness is a critical factor in learning to read (Adams 1990; Blachman 2000; Liberman, Shankweiler, Fischer, and Carter 1974; Mattingly 1972; Morris et al. 2003; National Institute of Child Health and Human Development 2000; Snow et al. 2000), but that's just the first part of the story. Ultimately the beginning reader/writer must learn the whole complex process—not just the phonemic awareness part, but ultimately, he must go through all four phases that lead to automatic chunking of spelling patterns. Only then are the lower-level processes that focus attention on spelling for decoding or encoding released to the automatic recesses of the mind (literally,

Area C in Figure 2.1, page 15) allowing the brain much more freedom to concentrate full attention to the higher levels of cognition such as comprehension, problem solving, reasoning, and critical thinking.

It's important to point out that the conception of phonemic awareness is important for reading only because it relates to the child's eventual need to pay attention to how spelling works. Other phonological awareness concepts such as recognition of rhyming words, syllables as units of sounds in a word that may be clapped out, recognition of onsets and rimes, word families, and the whole realm of knowledge surrounding recognition of phonics patterns, are all spelling concepts. There are certain times in early reading and writing development that particular instructional techniques mesh well with how the child thinks spelling works and what the child is doing with spelling at a particular point in early development when she reads or writes. In the beginning reading and writing classroom, however, too often we divide the child's world into a reading period and a writing period, and now the "phonemic awareness" period but if you ask the teacher about spelling she says, "Oh, we don't teach spelling in kindergarten." Good spelling instruction in kindergarten, among other things, moves children forward by degrees in their level of phonemic awareness as that level of awareness changes with each phase. Yet, too often, only one lockstep sequence of instruction is offered for all children regardless of a particular individual's level or phase of development, with too few teachers implementing multilevel instruction in the mixed ability classroom. Thus something called "phonemic awareness" becomes an isolated objective as opposed to a part of a developmental continuum.

Phase theorist Linnea Ehri points out the arbitrary division of reading and spelling in work that has received far too little attention from educators and teachers in the classroom, "Learning to Read and Learning to Spell Are One and the Same, Almost."

> The English language includes two terms, *reading* and *spelling*, that are used by researchers and teachers to divide the world. Researchers classify studies into those focused on reading, those focused on spelling, and those focused on relations between reading and spelling. Teachers plan lessons to teach reading during one period and different lessons to teach spelling during another period of the school day. All this presumes that there are two separate things that are being studied or taught. (1997, 238)

The problem Ehri identifies may not be so much that the teachers are focusing on different lessons at different times, but that the content of spelling instruction is often far off-base from what is needed at a particular phase of the developing reader or writer. Contemporary models of reading and brain scan studies both point in the direction that reading, writing, and spelling are connected processes in the brain. We need to bring the reality of what we do in the beginning reading classroom, or in our work with struggling readers, closer to the child's own reality—closer to what is happening in the child's mind as he or she develops reading, writing, and spelling skills reciprocally.

There are certain teaching strategies focused on helping the reader or writer understand how spelling works that are particularly well suited for particular phases of development. When is it best to point out rhymes, clap out syllables, do hand spelling with onsets and rimes, use finger spelling, or sort particular spelling patterns, for example? What are the particular spelling patterns that are important for certain phases of development? Many teachers miss these timely teachable opportunities and fail to make a connection with what is going on in the child's mind as he or she processes the spelling component when reading or writing. While I agree with Ehri's earlier point about the problems caused by the arbitrary division of spelling and reading, there is a caveat. It is not so much that spelling and reading are taught at different times, but that we do such a poor job of teaching spelling. Spelling is given low status by teachers because much of what we do with it seems to be busywork and a waste of time. For example, we don't need more one-size-fits-all spelling worksheets that are so common-place in the spelling components of many current reading programs (Gentry 2004). Rather, we need teachers who understand the spelling component of the reading process and who know how to *connect* the appropriate teaching of spelling in a particular phase with the teaching of reading and writing. Another problem is that *connecting* the teaching of spelling with reading and writing is often confused with *integrating* the teaching of spelling with reading and writing. An "integration" practice of pulling spelling words out of the reading material, for example, doesn't work, particularly if the words chosen for spelling are the wrong words. Most appropriate second-grade spelling words are words children learn to read in first grade—words such as *they, nail, funny,* and *hook.* Yet in many instances where reading and spelling are supposedly "integrated," the second-grade child who can't spell *they, nail, funny,* and *hook* is given reading vocabulary such as *America* and *country* to memorize. These are the wrong words. In my view, some of the worst examples of inappropriate spelling instruction have come out of attempts to integrate spelling with the teaching of reading and writing because children were treated as if they were prewired to pick up perfect spelling and appropriate spelling instruction receives short shrift (Gentry 2004). Ehri's comment about reading teachers dividing the world between reading and spelling is not supportive of the current surge of spelling components in reading programs, which, rather than pay attention to appropriate spelling instruction based on phase theory and research, provide packets of in-appropriate busywork, teach the wrong words and patterns at the wrong time, and waste the child's time with inappropriate activities often as absurd as sorting *swimming* and *chocolate* according to whether they have eight letters or nine letters. These materials provide little of what I would consider to be research-based instruction (see Gentry 2004).

The Development of Phase Theory for Sight-Word Learning

Linnea Ehri, a professor of educational psychology at the Graduate Center of the City University of New York, is the researcher primarily responsible for developing phase theory of sight-word learning, a theory that explains how the beginner reads words from memory. Ehri has provided a comprehensive description of the full range of word knowledge development for reading, which progresses in four phases between nonreading and skilled reading. There is considerable variation among individual children but it's not unusual for these four phases to take children as long as two years to accomplish: Ehri's pre-alphabetic, partial alphabetic, full alphabetic, and consolidated alphabetic phases greatly affect the way children read (and spell) words (1992, 1997, 1998).

Phase 1, Pre-alphabetic Reading. The first phase is called *pre-alphabetic.* In this early phase of reading, the teacher in the classroom or a parent often observes the child "reading" words using no systematic letter-sound processing whatsoever. In other words, these readers do not understand how the real system works. Pre-alphabetic readers match logos or visual memories of certain combinations of the squiggly symbols we call letters to particular spoken words. Often pre-alphabetic reading first occurs when the child notices print in his or her environment. The child may be observed to "read" the word on the stop sign or the name on a cereal box, but in reality, while the visual form of the word's spelling is cueing the reading, the child is not paying attention to letter-sound correspondences. He is paying attention to nonalphabetic information. The visual cue might be the design of the logo—an association between the *M* and the golden arches cueing the correct reading of the word "McDonald's," for example. Studies such as one by Harste, Burke, and Woodward (1982) showed that pre-alphabetic readers often made interesting miscues that show that they weren't attending to spellings. *Crest* was read as "toothpaste," or "brush teeth." Ehri called this phase pre-alphabetic because this type of reading occurred *before* a child understood the concept that letters represent sounds in spoken words.

Phase 2, Partial Alphabetic Reading. Ehri's work showed that beginning readers make a giant cognitive leap by moving from Phase 1 to Phase 2, from a pre-alphabetic to a *partial alphabetic* phase, a move signaling the dawn of the letter-sound concept. For the first time, Phase 2 readers can read words by matching a few letters—usually those at the beginning and ending of the word—with sounds. In order to do this the child must have some phonemic awareness and must know some letter-sound correspondences, thus making it possible to use one or two letters—often the first and last letter in a word—to cue a word when reading. Even though he or she is working with very limited letter-sound information, *for the first time the child is cueing on spelling.* No longer dependent on arbitrary visual cues like golden arches, the child is beginning to conceptualize a system for matching letters to sounds for cueing words by segmenting the spoken word into some of its sounds and matching it with a letter, beginning to see a pattern.

Readers at this stage generally don't pay attention to letters in the middle of a word, which are usually vowel letter-sound correspondences and often more complex than beginning and ending letter-sound matches. Medial letters (i.e., the letters in the middle of a word) may consist of patterns of chunks of letters and the child doesn't recognize these as patterns or know how the vowel spelling chunks work. What she can do is read a few words like *hop* by noticing the *h* and the *p*, but the Phase 2 system doesn't work very well if she must discriminate between *hop, hip, hit,* or *hot*. In studies where the Phase 2 reader is asked to read a nonword such as *kug*, it is very common for her to notice the *k* and *g* and give a real word such as *king* (Ehri 1997, 254). As Ehri says, Phase 2 readers "operate with rudimentary knowledge of some letter-sound relations" (204).

Another important finding is that readers at Phase 2, the partial alphabetic phase, probably don't have enough memory for detail in words to be able to read words by analogy unless they have the analogue or "word family" in view. If they know *cave* and see the new word *save*, they likely call it "cave" rather than make an analogy; they misread the new word because they are cueing from a partial spelling—in this case the *a*, the *v*, and the *e* which they remember for *cave* (Ehri and Robbins [1992] reported in Ehri [1997, 254]).

Darrell Morris suggests that it is very important for children to develop the ability to do the voice-to-print match at Phase 2, that is, to read a verse or short easy text from memory and point to the printed word at the same time she says it when reading out loud. This enables the child to grasp the concept of what a printed word is and, in effect, frame the word for analysis. So once the Phase 2 reader stabilizes the concept that a printed word matches a spoken word, he or she begins to realize words have middle parts, and that the middle part might give some cues too (Morris et al. 2003). Research has shown that the middle part is the hardest to read (Ehri 1998; Lewkowicz 1980; Morris et al. 2003).

Phase 3, Full Alphabetic. The next giant cognitive leap occurs when children start paying attention to all of the letters in the word; they have more letter-sound knowledge and start using more complete letter-sound correspondences when reading words. Ehri calls Phase 3 the *full alphabetic* phase, indicating that readers are paying attention to the full spelling, not just a few prominent letters at the beginning and end. Full alphabetic reading is heralded by the advent of full phonemic awareness when children have stabilized the concept of word, know that a word is made up of constituent sounds, and are able to provide all the phonemes in most words and manipulate them. It's also signaled when the reader begins to read more accurately than at the previous phase, since she is attending to each letter when reading a word.

Whereas [partial alphabetic] readers' limited memory for letters may cause them to misread *soon* or *spin* as *spoon*, full alphabetic readers' representations eliminate confusion because their representations are sufficiently complete to distinguish easily among similarly spelled words. (Ehri 1998, 21)

It appears to be easier to learn similarly spelled words at this stage. Ehri and Wilce (1987) found that Phase 3, full alphabetic readers learned a list of words such as *drip* and *dump*, or *bend* and *blond*, in only three trials. Phase 2, partial alphabetic readers could not learn as many similarly spelled words and when they did learn them it took them seven trials. Another great advantage at Phase 3 is that full alphabetic readers are able to read new words by analogy to known words, that is, to use known words to figure out unknown words. Unlike the Phase 2, partial alphabetic reader, if the Phase 3 reader knows *cave* and he sees the new word *save*, he is much more likely to read it correctly by analogizing. Still another advantage of Phase 3 reading is that Phase 3 readers tend to be successful at finger-point reading short memorized texts (Morris et al. 2003). But Phase 3 has limitations. English spelling is not a system of matching a letter to a sound; rather, it's a system of matching chunks of letters to sounds. In order to read a lot of words automatically, the beginning reader must make the chunking breakthrough.

Phase 4, Consolidated Alphabetic Reading. There is a difference in decoding and encoding that happens as the child moves from Phase 3 to Phase 4. In Phase 3, connections are formed in memory between individual graphemes and phonemes, but at Phase 4 the graphemes are *consolidated into chunks* of spelling patterns. Thus moving from Phase 3 to Phase 4 is a move from processing the word *interesting* virtually as individual letters (*i-n-t-er-e-s-t-i-ng*), to processing it in chunks (*in-ter-est-ing*).

The brain has finally found the patterns! That's what makes it much easier to read new words and store known words in memory at Phase 4. With some experience reinforcing the recognition of the patterns, the brain activates an area that can read many words automatically from memory and analogize hundreds of words (and syllables) operating with the same spelling pattern: *bat, hat, cat, mat, fat, sat, lat, pat, rat, splat,* and so on. It can apply these same patterns to syllables in polysyllabic words: *in-ter-est-ing, Cin-der-rel-la, tel-e-phone, el-e-phant.* Ehri calls this the consolidation phase because at this phase the letters that were formerly processed one at a time are now consolidated—they are processed in chunks. Many recognized one-syllable chunks pave the way for recognizing thousands of multisyllabic words with the same chunks, and once the child begins to recognize multisyllabic words other regular patterns in the spelling system reveal themselves—doubling consonant patterns, for example, in words such at *hopping, hoping, mopping,* and *moping* (Templeton and Bear 1992; Venezky 1970). Children generally learn to read these words first, and learning to spell them perfectly comes later because it's much easier to read words than to spell them (Bosman and Van Orden 1997; Ehri 1997).

It's a watershed event when the child begins to operate in chunks of letter patterns. With a little practice, the brain can begin to store words in memory and recognize them automatically. The whole reading process becomes much more efficient because the brain can pay even more attention to backup systems associated with spoken language, including use of context and other higher levels of processing to drive the system. Once the word recognition and spelling pattern recognition systems become automatic, the higher-level systems are in effect saying, "Turn the driving over to us!" Reading no longer has to be slow and analytical as it is in the beginning phases, but the reader can move toward fluency. New material can be read independently instead of being learned by echo reading, which depends upon repeating it from memory after the teacher has modeled it. I believe "Learning to Read and Learning to Spell Are One and the Same, Almost" and other works such as my book, *The Science of Spelling*, highlighting the reciprocity of writing and reading, provide bellwether understandings of how beginners learn to read, though little heed has been paid to it. Too often we are still lost sheep when it comes to helping beginning readers and writers make the important reading-spelling connection. Let's see how spelling unfolds in the exact same stages as phases of word learning, a discovery that largely *preceded* Ehri's discovery of these very same phases in reading.

4

Outside-the-Brain Changes in Spellers and Writers

Take a look at Figure 4.1, which shows the changes in spelling produced by Paul in early writing samples reported by his mother, Glenda Bissex, who was a literacy researcher and author of *GNYS at WRK: A Child Learns to Read and Write*, a seminal and now classic account of one child's early reading and writing (1980).

Level 1, Level 2, Level 3, and Level 4 are *exactly* the same phases as Ehri has reported for early word learning. Bissex's son Paul was precocious and advanced through the levels somewhat earlier and at a faster pace than many children, yet I remember reading this extraordinary book in 1980 and there were the developmental spelling levels staring me straight in the eye. I could see the critical aspects of each phase in Paul's development matching exactly the same developmental spelling levels researchers had been observing and writing about since the mid-1970s. Their genesis now seems to be the same as Ehri's phases of word learning for reading as reported in Chapter 3. While Bissex did not report the stages, I applied a *developmental spelling classification system* to the Bissex case study by using the spelling samples Bissex reported in *GNYS at WRK* to demonstrate the existence of the spelling stages "revealing developmental stages that researchers (Beers and Henderson 1977; Gentry 1977; Henderson and Beers 1980; Read 1975) have discovered in children's early spelling and writing" (1982, 192). The article entitled "An Analysis of Developmental Spelling in *GNYS at WRK*" first appeared in *The Reading Teacher* (1982) and was reprinted in materials such as *SET: Research Information for Teachers*. To me it seemed miraculous. We had discovered a metamorphosis outside the brain in developmental spelling and it had equally powerful applicability for the classroom or for rigorous research study. Here's a description of what the levels in the spelling metamorphosis looked like.

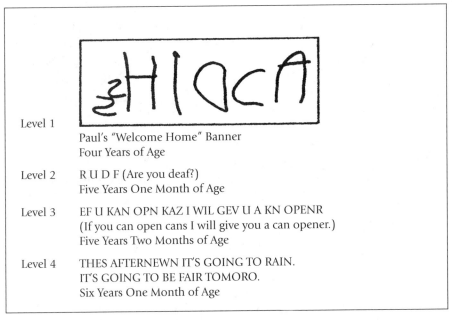

Level 1
Paul's "Welcome Home" Banner
Four Years of Age

Level 2   R U D F (Are you deaf?)
Five Years One Month of Age

Level 3   EF U KAN OPN KAZ I WIL GEV U A KN OPENR
(If you can open cans I will give you a can opener.)
Five Years Two Months of Age

Level 4   THES AFTERNEWN IT'S GOING TO RAIN.
IT'S GOING TO BE FAIR TOMORO.
Six Years One Month of Age

FIGURE 4.1   Four Levels of Paul's Writing Development

Level 1. Paul's writing (and other beginning writing) began at Level 1 in a phase of letter strings completely lacking letter-sound correspondence—very similar to the lack of letter-sound correspondence in a Level 1 logographic reading of "McDonald's" cued from the golden arches. At four years of age, Paul demonstrated fascination with writing and ability to write letters on paper well before he knew much at all of how alphabetic systems work. All alphabetic systems work the same way; they are operational systems of matching printed letters or letter combinations to particular sounds in a word. But just as beginning readers read words such as "stop" and "McDonald's" before they have any concept of how the letters of the alphabet do their work, beginning writers write letters on paper in a pre-alphabetic writing phase without awareness of what the letters represent. One might imagine that Paul was oblivious to the letter-sound alphabetic principle as he put down S-S-H-I-D-C-A on a 30 centimeter by 120 centimeter "welcome home" banner or when he typed strings of letters, which he described as notes to his friends (Bissex 1980, 4, reported in Gentry 1982). There was no alphabetic regularity in this four-year-old child's first attempts at writing—the pattern system was not yet apparent. There was not even regularity of a few matches of beginning sounds with letters; rather, a complete lack of letter-sound regularity was in evidence.

Much has been written about the *lack* of regularity in the English spelling system, but I now think researchers failed to recognize the regularity and were mistaken to think that it was too obscure to be discovered by children. In fact there is wonderful, full, and complete regularity in English spelling; it is a regular, systematic, pattern system of both frequent, and *very infrequent*, regularities. The 1,022 spelling-to-sound letter combinations are present in any text of written English. So instead of thinking that English spelling is irregular, we should think of it as complex. Ll spells /l/, the first sound in *llama*, on a very regular basis—it works that way every time one sees it in *llama*. The letter combination *-ough* always spells the same set of sounds whenever it appears in a particular word. For example, any time you read *dough, bough, hiccough, through, thorough, rough,* and *bought, -ough* always represents the same sounds. The system is complex, however, because *-ough* can spell seven different sounds—not to mention the fact that there are at least twenty-four different ways to spell /sh/ and *dreamt* is the only word in the English language that ends in *-mt!*

I'm sure Paul was gleefully oblivious to all this complexity as he ventured forth in this first "tadpole" phase of writing. Metaphorically, he was just beginning to grow his legs as a writer. While there may have been some reason for writing SSHIDCA with the production of the seven letters in that particular order on his welcome home sign, it was a nonalphabetic reason. Paul could write with letters by putting them down on paper using some nonalphabetic theory to choose his letters *before* he knew the alphabetic system. Ehri's Level 1 descriptive term for reading phases of word learning, "pre-alphabetic level," works perfectly well for describing Paul's (and other children's) first spelling attempts at writing. Level 1 writers are attempting to create written words using letters before they know the system is an alphabetic, letter and letter-chunk system for mapping letters to sounds. Just as children know the label on the cereal box says something, Paul hypothesized that his string of letters said something and he attached the welcome home greeting to this arbitrary set of letters. At the moment he was writing he may have had "welcome home" in mind, but sometimes Level 1 writers say "What did I write?" and attach the meaning after the writing.

One cannot read Level 1 writing because the writing is not alphabetic. When I worked with Ed Henderson and others in the 1970s and 1980s who were investigating the stages or levels of developmental spelling that we were seeing as beginners emerged as writers, I first called this level "deviant," meaning that it deviated from normal alphabetic spelling (1977). But the label implied that the child was deviating from what was normal which, of course, is absolutely inaccurate. Level 1 writing is as normal as babbling in spoken language, so eventually I settled on what I hoped was a better term, "precommunicative" (1982). Precommunicative indicates that Level 1 is a level *before* the writer can communicate (encode) in writing (i.e., a reader cannot read Level 1 writing because the writing is precommunicative). Notice the good agreement with Ehri's term "pre-alphabetic" for this phase, which in essence is the same concept, which she later applied to reading (decoding). In both instances Level

1 is a phase of nonalphabetic use of letters before the brain maps letters to sounds in order to encode or decode print.

Level 2. Paul's second phase of spelling development, first documented at five years one month of age, lasted only a few weeks, but this second writing level, as in Ehri's work in reading, marked the first use of letters to correspond to sounds. Not only did he produce RUDF (Are you deaf?) during this period, but quite a few other productions showing that he had learned a fairly large number of letter-sound correspondences: KR (car), BZR (buzzer), HAB (happy), OD (old), DP (dump), and even TLEFNMBER (telephone number) (Bissex 1980, reported in Gentry 1982). My first spelling classification system had used the term *prephonetic* to describe the second stage, meaning that it was *before* the child represented the full phonetic form. I described it this way in 1977: "Although prephonetic spellings do contain the rudiments of a phonetic system such as correct beginning and ending consonants, these spellings are usually greatly abbreviated and lack all the essential phonetic elements needed to represent the surface structure of a word" (Gentry 1977, 22). This original term, again, was misleading because obviously the Level 2 spellings are partly phonetic, not *prephonetic*. By 1981, I was using the term *semiphonetic* (1981) for Level 2 using the prefix *semi-* meaning "partly" or "not fully" as in *semiautomatic* or *semiconscious*. Again "semiphonetic" is in good agreement with Ehri's term for the second level of reading phases, "partial alphabetic" (Ehri 1997). I think it's interesting to show the closeness in the terminology that grew out of the studies of these early observations to describe the phases for spelling and reading because, to my knowledge, this work was largely independent: independent observers of spelling had seen the very same changes as later observations that were made in reading. In my view, Ehri's 1997 chapter, "Reading and Spelling Are One and the Same, Almost," is a hallmark publication citing the importance of reading and writing reciprocity because, for the first time, this study presented both the reading levels and the developmental spelling levels as simultaneously supporting reading/writing reciprocity.

   Paul remained at Level 2 for only a short stint and quickly moved to Level 3, full phonetic representation, largely, I think, because of the good teaching and intervention he was receiving from his mother during the first month after his fifth birthday (Bissex 1980). What she was doing intuitively is what all teachers should be doing consciously to take advantage of reading and writing reciprocity. She showed great interest and provided encouragement for his invented spelling, including explicit teaching such as supplying letter-sound correspondences and suggesting spacing between words, which helped stabilize Paul's concept of word. As we have seen in Morris' work, Level 2 is the exact appropriate time for children to stabilize the concept that the printed word is a match for the spoken word. The concept that the word is an entity helps children "frame" or think about the word as a unit, thereby allowing them to think of the beginning, middle, and ending of a word, or to think of consecutive word parts as sound elements (Henderson [1985] 1990; Morris 1981; Morris et al. 2003). By five years two months Paul had moved to Level 3 as documented in a message he typed that provides a letter for every sound in each word (except in the spelling of KN for *can*, which is Level 2): EF U KAN OPN KAZ I WIL GEV U A KN OPENR (If you can open cans I will give you a can opener.) (Bissex 1980, 11).

What happened with Paul in this short period is what should happen to all children as they begin to write and read. *They should be encouraged to test their hypotheses, praised for their attempts, heartened to create volume, and taught explicitly at their level of understanding with the right kind of instruction to move them to the next level.* Currently, this is not happening in many kindergarten classrooms. Too often we focus on isolated objectives. Rather than track each student's development through the phases of reading and writing and provide the type of instruction that fits the child's needs in a particular phase, teachers present isolated objectives, which may even be good instruction, but at the wrong time. Isolated objectives taught explicitly outside the child's level of understanding are a problem. Sometimes I wonder why we do so much elaborate and painstaking testing and talking about phonetic awareness, for example, when a child's level of developing phonetic awareness is so easily recognized by looking at their writing (if the child is in an environment where writing is encouraged and supported) just as Paul's phonemic awareness is so easily tracked from Levels 1, 2, and 3— from no awareness, to partial awareness, to full phonemic awareness at Level 3. Tracking this progress is the perfect measure of normal growth and any departure from this path is a clear signal that the child needs help, or early intervention. Tracking the phases of spelling and writing is a powerful and easy test for early interventions. In the chapters ahead you will learn not only to assess phonemic awareness by tracking writing development, but also to use exactly the right tools to move children through these critical levels of understanding.

Level 3. Paul was a prolific phonetic speller for about a year beginning at the end of five years one month and he wrote in a wide variety of forms such as signs, lists, notes, messages, letters, labels, captions, greeting cards, game boards, stories, directions, and statements (Bissex 1980, 15, reported in Gentry 1982). This is the kind of writing that should be routine and ongoing in every kindergarten classroom. Paul's Level 3 phonetic spelling is characterized by full phonemic awareness and his Level 3 strategy is to supply a letter for each sound in a word as in IFU LEV AT THRD STRET IWEL KOM TO YOR HAWS THE ED (If you live at third street I will come to your house. The End.) (Bissex 1980, 13, reported in Gentry 1982). Notice that this Level 3 strategy—a letter for each sound in each word—is in good agreement with the Level 3 reading strategy that Ehri describes as "full alphabetic" corroborating reading/writing reciprocity at Level 3. In the spelling classification system, Level 3 was described as "phonetic," a term that came out of the abundant literature that documented this particular stage (Beers 1974; Gentry 1977, 1978, 1981; Gentry and Henderson

1978; Henderson and Beers 1980; Read 1971, 1975, 1986; Zutell 1975, 1978). In essence, what we were all seeing at this level was that the child supplied a letter for each phoneme or sound in the word as the strategy for inventing the spelling.

While Bissex did not report levels of spelling development, her astute observations and comments show that she was aware of obvious changes in Paul's thinking about how the system works and changes in his productions, and she documented some of his first analogizing mental exercises and correctly predicted that mental analogizing would move Paul into a new phase of spelling development:

> While writing the song book, Paul observed, "you spell 'book' B-O-O-K. To write 'look' you just change one letter—take away the B and add an L." This mental spelling and word transforming continued after his writing spurt temporarily petered out: "If you took the L out of 'glass' and pushed it all together, you'd have 'gas,'" he mused while lying in bed. Such manipulation was the form that the next phase of his spelling development took. The following week (5:3) he mentally removed the L for "please" (for "peas" or "pee"), and after we had some conversation about Daedalus and Icarus, observed that "if you put an L in front of Icarus, you get 'licorice.'" And "if you take the T and R off of 'trike' and put a B in front, you have 'bike.'" (Bissex 1980, 15, reported in Gentry 1982)

Paul was discovering how the English spelling system works; he was learning to spell by analogy and would eventually move away from a letter for each sound to a chunking strategy for the regular patterns of English spelling.

Level 4. By about six years one month, Paul's Level 4 spellings reveal that he was using a chunking system to write in English, and although he was using chunks that spelled the sounds he needed, he had not yet learned the correct chunks or patterns for many words. That would come with experience and spelling instruction. His spelling, after six years one month, included a weather forecast: THES AFTERNEWN IT'S GOING TO RAIN. IT'S GOING TO BE FAIR TOMORO, and a news report FAKTARE'S (factories) CAN NO LONGER OFORD MAKING PLAY DOW (dough) (Bissex 1980, 46, reported in Gentry 1982). In the early research exploring the sequential development of spelling, this level was dubbed "transitional" (Beers 1974; Gentry 1977) because children were transitioning into correct or conventional spelling. We found Level 4 writers discovering and using the patterns—orthographic markers such as CVCe, for example, but with spellings such as MENE for *mean* and RANE for *rain* without the word-specific knowledge to determine correct use. With good spelling instruction and experience writing and reading, Level 4 writers activate the word form area of the brain, begin to produce many correct spellings automatically, and over time with study, they learn many more correct spellings, as Paul was beginning to demonstrate in Figure 4.1 with correctly spelled words such as *it's, going, to, rain, be, fair, can, no, longer, making,* and *play.* I now prefer Ehri's term "consolidated level" (1997) for Level 4 rather than the term "transitional," indicating that at this level children move from the Level 3 strategy of providing a letter for a sound to the Level 4 strategy of consolidating letters into chunks to spell both monosyllabic and polysyllabic words in parts by using chunks of letters to represent chunks of sound elements instead of one letter for each phoneme. Probably a better, more descriptive label for Level 4 than either "transitional" or "consolidated," would be "the chunking level." Paul's Level 3 message, produced with a-letter-for-a-sound strategy, IFU LEV AT THRD STRET IWEL KOM TO YOR HAWS THE ED, likely would have looked something like the following rendering in chunks of spelling patterns at the next level, Level 4: IF YUO LIV AT THERD STREAT I WIL CUM TOO YORE HUOSE THE IND. In the second rendering, a Level 4 chunking strategy replaces the Level 3 letter-for-a-sound strategy. Notice these changes: Instead of U for *you,* the Level 4 speller chunks the correct letters but gets O and U out of order. Instead of using R to spell /er/ in *third,* he or she uses the -ER chunk. Instead of a letter for each of the five sounds in *street,* he or she spells *street* in two chunks: STR- and -EAT. Instead of the W-E-L letter-for-a-sound strategy for *will,* he or she spells *will* as a CVC chunk so that WIL is analogous to *wit, wiz,* or *wig.* The Level 4 speller uses a CVCe chunk for *you're*—YORE—rather than a letter for a sound. In each instance there is a chunking explanation for the choice of letters used in the Level 4 spelling.

The Formulation of a Blueprint for Early Writing, Spelling, and Reading Development

Taken together, the spelling phases, writing phases, and reading phases provide a clear blueprint for what should be happening outside the brain as beginning writers and readers go through four phases of development. The blueprint is designed to chart a course of what to expect with early reading and writing development. While one should expect individual variation in the exact time and duration as children go through specific phases, the phases are consistent, easy to detect, and powerful in helping the teacher determine if a child is progressing normally. Both experience and exposure to print greatly affect individual development. These conditions accepted, the blueprint is an exact and detailed outline of what to expect, and it will help you plan for the type and timing of instruction that might best move the learner forward as well as help you determine when development seems to be off track, and whether special instructional intervention may be needed.

It should be noted that a number of conditions might exist making it possible for a child to be in one phase as a reader and in another phase as a writer at the same time. Sometimes we observe children transitioning from one phase into the next higher phase. Since reading a word is easier than spelling a word, a child may process chunks and patterns in reading a little before he or she consistently uses chunks of spelling patterns in writing. For example, as we saw in the Bissex case study, Paul discovered how to make spelling analogies such as *look* from *book, gas* from *glass, peas* from *please,* and *bike* from *trike* even while his primary writing strategy was the Level 3, one-letter-for-each-sound strategy. At the same time he was a Level 3 writer, his mother recorded some of his Level 4 musings ("you spell 'book' B-O-O-K. To write 'look' you just change one letter—take away the B and add an L") demonstrating that he began thinking about how word parts worked in chunks well before he consistently used the chunking strategy in his writing.

Sometimes, a considerable mismatch between reading phases and writing phases is a red flag to indicate that instruction is not well balanced. Children who receive little opportunity to write in school, for example, and too little appropriate writing instruction sometimes excel as readers but struggle as writers and spellers. I reported on one such incidence a number of years ago in my book, *Spel . . . Is a Four-Letter Word* (1987) in a case study of Dan, who came to the university reading clinic in January of his first-grade year reading above second-grade level but struggling, even refusing to write, demonstrating a huge discrepancy in writing levels and reading levels. His writing was Level 2 while his reading was Level 4. The etiology of his writing disability turned out to be simple: he never had experienced real writing in kindergarten and first grade. He did little writing in kindergarten that focused on socialization and self-concept, and during his stint in first grade it was customary in his school for writing lessons in the first half of the year to consist of copying the teacher's stories from the board with all words spelled correctly—which was not uncommon in the 1980s. At that time children were often discouraged from using invented spelling because it was presumed that inventing incorrect spellings would turn them into poor spellers. In fact, we now know that beginners greatly benefit from inventing spelling, which should be balanced with appropriate instruction leading to correct spelling. (Gentry 2000b; International Reading Association 1998; Snow, Burns, and Griffin, 1998).

One of the major benefits of following the Blueprint is that it helps the teacher determine when and what type of early intervention may be needed. Early intervention following the Blueprint enabled Dan to advance from his first week at Level 2 status in writing to Level 3 and then Level 4 in just sixteen weeks, as shown in Figure 4.2. During this period he wrote thirty stories, including titles such as "The Dukes of Hazzard," "Muggs," "Toothpaste," "Feelings," "James Bond," "$100.00," "Rocks," "Our Treehouse," and "My Dog." These are the kind of titles and self-selected topics that *all* kindergartners and first graders should be writing about. Dan invented 186 spellings during his sixteen-week spurt in writing at my Reading Center, allowing his neurons to fire over and over as his brain constructed new connections and a deeper understanding of how the English spelling system works. In just sixteen weeks his writing levels caught up with his reading (Gentry 1987). One point to be made here is that ignoring writing/reading reciprocity not only is a missed opportunity for fostering

Time	Sample	Writing/Spelling Level
First Week in February	If I had a magic pair of boots, I would I would make gold. 24 CRTS. (carats) I would play football. I would read CLFFORD (Clifford) books. I would BIY a CAMR. (camera) I would BLO up pluto. I would play BASKBALL. (basketball) I would go to New York and See the STATU of LBRTE (liberty) I would go out west. I'd go to the grand CANYN. (Canyon) And BIY a SLATITI. (stalactite) I would take a trip down the COLORDO (Colorado) RREVR (River) on a raft.	Level 2: Partial Alphabetic Writing (He leaves out some sounds when inventing most spellings.) Semiphonetic Spellings in the sample are indicated by showing the word spelled correctly in parentheses. BLO is Phonetic. STATU is Phonetic. BIY is Transitional.
First Week in March	My OL truck My truck is gray. My truck SHOTS water out. On the side it SES MOBOL. It ROLS and Jumps ramps. It's black, blue, Red, and white. I play WETH it.	Level 3: Full Alphabetic Writing (He invents with a letter for a sound and represents all sounds.) This sample has five Phonetic spellings. MOBOL is Transitional.
First Week in May	My Foot My feet are flesh. I WHAIR SIS 3. My feet take me EVREWHAIR My feet like to CLIME trees and BILLDINGS. I walk to school. My feet make me SWEM In water. My feet are TIYERD at the end of the day.	Level 4: Consolidated Alphabetic Writing (He invents in chunks of phonics patterns.) This sample has five Transitional spellings. SIS and SWEM are Phonetic.

FIGURE 4.2   Dan's Writing Development over Sixteen Weeks in First Grade

reading development, but it can also be the cause of literacy problems, as in Dan's case. (It's interesting to note that Dan grew up to become a medical doctor. I wonder what would have happened without early intervention for his struggle with writing.)

Monitoring phase development in both reading and writing, following the Intervention Blueprint in Chapter 6, allows the teacher to fine tune his or her planning for the appropriate type and timing of instruction by teaching into what children are doing both as a writer and as a reader (see Chapters 6 and 7 and the Appendix). The Blueprint allows the teacher to track and assess expected development. This powerful instrument for determining which children need early intervention enables the teacher to monitor each child's development and check the minimal expected time for movement through a particular phase. Both time and grade level indicators for *minimal expected competency* are provided, which is a gauge of the point at which failure to move through a phase or exhibit the expected behaviors of a phase should be construed as a signal that the child may not be progressing normally in literacy development. If a child is not functioning in the phase at the time of the grade level indicated, there is a need for intervention (Gentry 2004, 2000a, 2000b). These "minimal standards" are based on research syntheses including *Preventing Reading Difficulties in Young Children* (Snow, Burns, and Griffin 1998), *Learning to Read and Write: Developmentally Appropriate Practices for Young Children* (International Reading Association 1998) and my own synthesis of research (Gentry 2004a, 2000a, 2000b). With superior teaching, or under other optimal conditions such as early and ongoing exposure to literacy in the home, many children will exceed the benchmarks that are listed in the Intervention Blueprint for each phase as the "minimal competency expectancy level" (see page 47). In fact, many teachers in kindergarten and first grade classrooms where writing is being taught successfully will have whole classes where children achieve well above these minimal competency benchmarks, which is precisely my objective for *every* classroom.

In addition to determining whether there is a need for intervention, the Blueprint helps the teacher determine if a child's reading and writing development are in sync. If large discrepancies in reading phases and writing phases are noted, as in Dan's case as just described, the child may need intervention or a better balance of reading and writing instruction.

Here's a summary of what we have learned in Chapter 4: Just as tadpoles go through four visible phases in becoming a frog—losing their tails, growing legs, developing lungs, and finally eating insects—immature readers go through four phases leading to skilled, mature reading that are easily viewed in their writing. First they put letters on paper that do not correspond to sounds, next they use beginning and some ending sounds, and in the third phase they use a letter for each sound they hear in a word. Finally, they spell in chunks of letter patterns. This last phase, writing in chunks—*in-ter-est-ing; Al-a-bam-a; el-e-phant; tel-e-phone*—is the level where the brain begins to recognize and produce spelling patterns automatically. The four writing phases are the same phases that were later discovered by researchers in word reading. Phase 4 is necessary for the lower level processes of reading and writing to become automatic. Phase 4 is when the frog hops away from the pond!

Now you must make a choice. You may wish to tackle the complex Instructional Blueprint with all its nuances presented in its entirety in the Appendix. The Instructional Blueprint is academic and complex, which at this point some readers may find too dense for easy reading. (Once terminology presented in this book such as "Precommunicative Spelling," "scaffolded writing," "consolidated alphabetic writing," and "materialization" become second nature, you will find the academic treatment most useful in steering your instructional course. This treatment provides a complex and full research base for the more accessible Intervention Blueprint presented in Chapter 6. The Instructional Blueprint in the Appendix will guide you as you observe what an emerging writer or reader is doing with the code, and ultimately give you confidence to make appropriate and wise instructional decisions, no matter what theoretical stance, reading program, or instructional framework underpins your work. The Instructional Blueprint shows the phases all beginning writers and readers go through in breaking the code. It presents specifications and behaviors and helps you plan instruction for all literacy modes (writing, spelling, and reading) presented hierarchically from lower to higher levels of literacy sophistication, that is, from nonalphabetic, to pre-alphabetic, to partial alphabetic, to full alphabetic, and finally to consolidated alphabetic (or chunking) phases. This blueprint will show you what to expect at each level as a reader, writer, and speller operates in a given phase. While the Instructional Blueprint specifies phase behaviors at each level for writing, spelling, and reading separately, it also shows how these literacy modes are connected at each level. The treatment in the Appendix calls upon the reader to understand code breaking on an academic level through a synthesis of complex and technical academic information.

Many readers may prefer to go directly to Chapter 5 and then to Chapter 6, The Intervention Blueprint, and save the technical academic treatment presented in the Appendix for later analysis and synthesis. Chapter 6 will show you what to look for in a child's writing to signal appropriate early intervention during emergent literacy. Highlighting reading and writing reciprocity and providing the right kind of early instruction and early intervention is precisely what every kindergarten and first grade teacher must do to succeed with early literacy instruction to move pedagogy forward. The Intervention Blueprint makes it easy to see exactly when a developing writer needs early intervention to ensure that both writing and reading development are moving forward, and it will show what kind of instructional intervention the child needs so that no child is left behind.

Both blueprints will show precisely how children get to Phase 4—the final phase of breaking the code, which activates the brain circuitry for automatic processing of words and allows for automatic reading and automatic spelling, the nexus for eventual fluency for both reading and writing.

5

How and Why to Intervene During the "Tadpole" Phases of Beginning Literacy

The essence of profound insight is simplicity. In simple straightforward language, we will explore what to do to keep all beginning literacy learners on track for breaking the code. The phases outlined in the Intervention Blueprint are a natural part of a successful journey to lifelong literacy. *It is important to note here that code breaking is only one of the requirements for a successful beginning to reading and writing.* In addition to code breaking, the child must have background knowledge, motivation, and interest in literacy, and ultimately must develop academic vocabulary to decode and encode successfully. In fact, background knowledge, motivation, interest, and academic vocabulary are important at *every* level of reading, even into high school, college, and adulthood (Snow 2005). Additionally, the child must have access to age-appropriate books. Another important principle for beginning reading, replicated in study after study, is that preschoolers who have been read to often and who interact with books are much more likely to succeed with literacy once they arrive in school than do children who have not had book experiences before kindergarten (Moustafa 1997). Before looking at the Intervention Blueprint for decoding, it helps to consider some of these important precursors to literacy success.

How Do We Prepare Preschoolers to Be Successful with Reading and Writing?

Moving pedagogy forward in kindergarten and first grade by getting beginning reading instruction right from the start is simpler than most parents, educators, and policy makers think. It involves recognizing and acting upon some things that we already know. For example, we know that reading to children and bring-ing books into their lives from the first year of life onward is important (Wells 1985, 1986). When this happens at home, children often come to kindergarten with a repertoire of nursery rhymes, some knowledge of sounds and letters, and often with ability to write their names—all great precursors for success with writing and reading. Many preschoolers have read favorite books over and over to the extent that they come to kindergarten with nursery rhymes, reli-gious verses, songs and poems, and text from favorite stories already locked in the memory circuitry for language in their brains. Sometimes they already have ability to make the voice-to-print match and they know other impor-tant concepts about print. Parents often think that these children have taught themselves to read. But often without realizing it the parents have encouraged enough repetition of reading the same favorite books, along with pencil and pa-per activity, enthusiasm for literacy, modeling, and informal feedback about lit-eracy, to provide a focused "program" of reading instruction. Most kids who learn to read at home have had someone to teach them.

We know that when books have not been brought into the lives of pre-schoolers, teachers of literacy in preschool, kindergarten, and first grade must make up for this lack of preparation for success in school (Smith, Constantino, and Krashen 1997; Teal 1986). As Marie Clay once expressed it, "We have to do more, faster!" We know that we must give all children access to books beginning at a very early age (Gambrell 1996; Kozol 1991; Moustafa 1997). We know that we need to move forward with providing all children with preschool experi-ences, especially children from low-income homes who may be less likely to have bountiful experiences with books. We accomplish this by providing a fo-cused pre-kindergarten program to prepare kids for success with kindergarten literacy.

The Intervention Blueprint Highlights Reading and Writing Reciprocity

When we value the child's first urge to write and highlight reading and writing reciprocity, we move pedagogy forward by enabling educators to make peace on the battlefields of reading instruction. Writing and reading reciprocity can help us go far beyond devastating battles over parts and wholes, or phonics and meaning-based practices, and replace those tired soldiers and their tattered ban-ners that have promulgated us into internecine "reading wars" with something constructive.

Ultimately, moving pedagogy forward involves the simple recognition that we should open our minds to the fact that both phonics and meaning are essen-tial for beginning reading. Code-breaking practices, social practices, and mean-ing-based practices all go hand in hand. It's often been argued that reading is whole-to-parts (whole language) versus parts-to-whole (phonics and whole word approaches) and that each of these stances carries different assumptions (Moustafa 1997). Dorothy Strickland moved us forward when she pointed out that reading instruction is a whole-part-whole proposition—we expose children to whole meaningful text, we decontextualize and teach the parts, and the learner applies what he or she knows back into whole authentic context. Both the whole *and* the parts are important (Strickland 1998). In truth, we need a new paradigm for beginning reading instruction regarding wholes and parts. Unlike the chicken and the egg, *both* come first! The whole emphasizes meaning and the natural flow of language. But the parts are equally important for beginning reading. Words and word parts are used from the outset by every beginning reader and writer, as you will see in the Instructional Blueprint presented in the Appendix. At times, all beginning reading and writing teachers must decontextualize and teach the parts explicitly, right from the start. It is in observing children's writing and in connecting children's reading and writing that the teaching of parts and wholes at the same time becomes self-evident. When we leave writing out, we get a distorted view of what's happening. Children learn to read better when teaching focuses on overall story meaning (Goodman 1993) *and* on word parts and words (Adams 1990). Reading is conveying print into spoken language *and* making sense of it.

In a wonderful book entitled *Beyond Traditional Phonics,* Margaret Moustafa (1997) presents what I would consider one of the best syntheses of the whole language or whole-to-parts perspective. But within all the insightful information that is accurately presented regarding what is needed to teach literacy successfully, there are a few serious missteps, such as the following statement highlighted on page 12 of Moustafa's book. After citing studies by researchers, many of whom are great proponents of coding instruction, Moustafa concludes:

> Instruction in letter-phoneme correspondences doesn't make sense to children who have not yet learned to read.

This statement is patently inaccurate. I believe Moustafa, herself, would agree that children who invent spelling at Phase 1, at Phase 2, and at Phase 3 are all making sense and using letter-sound correspondences even though they are writing words they might not be able to read. Phase 1 Nicholas writes his name as N-I-C-K-Y, for example but he can't really read it. When asked what it says he shouts "Nicholas!" He's using logographic reading (i.e., *Nicky* is a logo for his name.) Even though he misreads his name, he gets some of the parts correct. This is a good example of when the parts may come before the whole. There are many instances when beginners, especially writers like Nicholas, get the parts before they get the whole, and they profit from Don Holdaway's model of shared reading. This process uses whole text as the teacher and his or her students share the reading of the text as the teacher reads *to* them and *with* them, ultimately allowing the reading to be done *by* them after they memorize the language of the text (Holdaway 1979). But at the very time that the beginning reader profits from memorizing Bill Martin's *Brown Bear, Brown Bear, What Do You See?* (1979) (beginners read from memorization, not like you read it), this same reader is *writing* "My MOTR BT GOZ FST! (My motor boat goes fast!). It certainly makes sense to give this child direct coding instruction to move him to the next higher phase of writing (and reading) development that enables him to write and read at a higher level by chunking. In this case, code instruction might help him move to the level of inventing spellings in chunks such as My MOTUR BOTE GOSE FASSED. Moustafa's notion of teaching whole-to-parts phonics instruction after a story has been read *to*, *with*, and *by* children is certainly effective. But we must also teach the parts, building on children's natural learning processes long before children are reading words and analogizing onsets and rhymes, an idea that Moustafa espouses. The part comes first in Phase 1 when the child, who is asked to shout out the rhyming words in "Jack fell DOWN and broke his CROWN," shouts out the rhyming word *crown*. His choice to shout *crown* is based on recognition of the word part that sounds like *down*. Perhaps he can't read *crown* and he may not know what Jack's crown is, but he can respond to the rhyming element, which is a word part. Matching the sounds in word parts instruction is perfectly suited for children long before they can read and make analogies. We teach parts before wholes at Phase 2 when the child "hand spells" /h/ /-ive /, hive; /h/ /-ole/, hole, /h/ /-ouse,/ house; /h/ /-ill/, hill; hearing the same beginning sounds, which are word parts long before she can read the whole words. Parts may come before wholes at Phase 3 when the child moves from inventing a spelling of BT for *boat*, getting the beginning and ending parts, to BOT, with a letter for each sound part. This word-part analysis may be happening even as the word *boat* is being read in context as a whole because it's easier to read words than to spell them (Bosman and Van Orden 1997), and it's easier to read words in context (Goodman 1965). Indeed, parts sometimes do come before, or with, the wholes, and approximations come before correctness. Interpretations of research such as the studies conducted by Liberman and her associates (1974) concluding that "83 percent of the kindergartners they tested could not analyze spoken words into phonemes most of the time" (Moustafa 1997, 12) seem off-base. Perhaps that conclusion applies to the particular task the kindergartners were asked to do in the study. But, one has only to go into any kindergarten classroom where children are writing and watch them joyfully analyze spoken words into phonemes over and over as they create authentic, wonderful writing in invented spelling. This happens long before they have fully broken the code and learned to read some of the words they are inventing. In these instances, the child who has not yet learned to read like a skilled adult reader *does* make sense of instruction in letter-phoneme correspondences. She is using parts even as she writes whole text.

The flaw in Moustafa's analysis, which was not the stance espoused by whole language practitioners and researchers such as Regie Routman who *did* include coding instruction from the outset, is found in Moustafa's introduction to *Beyond Traditional Phonics*.

Regrettably a body of research I do not report in this book addresses how children learn to write. Reading and writing are intimately related. Discussing reading without writing tells only half of the story. Just as we are making surprising, counterintuitive discoveries about how children learn to read, so we are making surprising, counterintuitive discoveries about how children learn to write. However, to provide timely information on our new knowledge about how children learn to read, I must limit this book to reading. (Moustafa, xvi)

So there's the rub. We may not have the prerogative to look just at reading or just at writing in either our research or our instruction. We *must* look at both reading and writing, as Marie Clay reminded us over twenty years ago. As Moustafa so eloquently reiterates in her introduction to *Beyond Traditional Phonics*, when we leave writing out, we only tell half the story. If we don't look at both, we are destined to make mistakes. We are destined to be blind to the obvious.

You Must Intervene During the "Tadpole" Phases of Writing and Reading

Paying attention to both reading and writing and following the Intervention Blueprint makes the writing/reading connection a reality, it takes advantage of writing and reading reciprocity, and it recognizes the need for intervention even as beginning readers, metaphorically, develop their reading legs and begin to hop away from the pond.

All tadpoles pass through identical phases of development as they metamorphose into froghood—they grow legs, lose their tails, develop lungs, and finally ingest insects. One might think of growing legs, loss of tails, development of lungs and ingestion of insects as marking points on the blueprint to froghood. Likewise, no use of letters, nonalphabetic use, partial alphabetic use, full alphabetic use, and chunking letters into phonics patterns are the markers for skilled reading and writing development. These phases will serve as the marking posts for our intervention. The intervention itself will engage the brain circuitry necessary for the child to move to the next higher level of development and help the child reach this level of functioning by a designated time at a particular grade level. In literacy development, the time that certain behavior is observed is important. Each phase or marking post will be clearly identified with a specific time when that level of functioning is expected to happen. If the specified phase of literacy has not been reached by the designated time, there is danger that appropriate development may not be occurring, because normally one would be observing that phase or level of functioning by the designated time. While accounting for the expected diversity and range in each child's language development, the Intervention Blueprint designates certain points in time as marking posts for when the child should have met the competency benchmark.

The competency benchmark may be reached by many children *much sooner* than the designated marking post, *but at minimum,* the phase or functioning should be observed by the specified time. If it is not seen, the child needs special attention—that is, *intervention.*

Seeing the phase development of each child is important. It's impossible to gain control over something, your bank account or a child's literacy growth, for example, if you can't see it. Consider your financial assets; if you don't have a budget and you don't know what you are spending, it's very hard to control what happens. Tracking literacy development is like keeping up with your budget; you can't just spend and hope everything is going to be all right. You have to know where your money is going. The same is true with taking control of successful literacy instruction. To be successful, you must have a correct vision of how certain aspects of literacy unfold and when these things should be happening. With literacy instruction you can't just herd children through a basal program or teach the book your district has selected for reading instruction; you have to know what each child is doing—how she or he is responding to print in your lessons. The Intervention Blueprint does just that, explicitly showing the literacy phase in which each child is functioning, when that phase is expected to happen, and what you should be doing for a child who is not meeting the minimal expectations outlined in the Intervention Blueprint.

In essence, the Intervention Blueprint is a very simple plan:

1. Identify the child's phase of development.
2. Check it against what is expected.
3. Intervene early whenever development is lagging behind.
4. Provide the right kind of instruction.

This is precisely how the Intervention Blueprint works. It charts the expected early literacy development for each child and shows you what to do if you see that a child is off track from what you are expecting to happen. Now you are ready to move forward with the Intervention Blueprint.

6

The Intervention Blueprint

What if you knew exactly when a beginning reader or writer is off track for learning literacy? What if you knew exactly what to do about it? While the Intervention Blueprint may seem overly simplistic, this profoundly insightful plan for early intervention with beginners will revolutionize and energize the teaching of any teacher who is not already seeing these phases as he or she works with beginning or struggling readers and writers.

The Intervention Blueprint Helps You Achieve Your Mission of Teaching Literacy

Success in the workplace can be spearheaded by a mission and values statement (Welch and Welch 2005). Let's consider a mission statement and values or behaviors that support our goals for teaching literacy:

A KINDERGARTEN AND FIRST GRADE TEACHER'S MISSION AND VALUES STATEMENT

I must teach each writer and reader in my classroom to break the English code. I accept this defining mission of every kindergarten and first grade teacher. I will be accountable for this mission and I will explain exactly why any learner is not following the expected path for breaking the code. If a child is off track, I will intervene early. I realize that the learner who does not read and write (decode and encode) by the end of first grade is at risk for a rocky academic future. Without learning to read and write in kindergarten and first grade, future academic growth may not happen.

With a clear mission focused on breaking the code, you are now able to establish what decoding-related behaviors you value and wish to see in the children you teach. The values are the behaviors that will accomplish your mission (Welch and Welch 2005). The Intervention Blueprint will help you establish straightforward values for code breaking by articulating the values needed at each of the phases of development due to reading and writing reciprocity. These values or behaviors must be applied to each child at each of the phases of writing and they will carry over into the child's reading development. Here are four behaviors you must value if you are a kindergarten or first grade teacher:

WHAT BEHAVIORS DO YOU VALUE AT A PARTICULAR PHASE OF WRITING?

1. Seeing a writer's phase of development.
2. Knowing when this level of functioning is expected.
3. Intervening to provide support when the child is falling behind.
4. Choosing the right tools to move the child forward.

Seeing a Writer's Phase of Development

Remarkably, you can see a child's phase of development by asking five easy questions about the invented spelling you see in a beginner's writing:

Question 1: Is this child using letters? If only scribbles, wavy writing, or loopy writing is used and no letters are present, it's Phase 0.

Question 2: Is this child using letters but not matching any of the letters to sounds? If letters are used but no sounds are represented, it's Phase 1.

Question 3: Is this child using letters and getting mostly beginning and ending sounds? If mostly beginning and ending sounds are represented but some sounds are missing, it's Phase 2.

Question 4: Is this child supplying a letter for each sound? If you can finger spell the invented words and get results similar to what you see in the child's invented spelling, it's Level 3.

Question 5: Does this child usually spell in chunks of phonics patterns? If you can see that the child is spelling in chunks of familiar phonics patterns, it's Level 4.

Knowing When Each Phase Is Expected

The Intervention Blueprint is based on minimal expected competency benchmarks that should be reached at five critical sign posts of beginning reading and writing development: (1) Pre-kindergarten and beginning kindergarten, (2) middle kindergarten, (3) end of kindergarten, (4) middle first grade, and (5) end of first grade. Your decision to intervene is always a child-based decision. You will base your intervention on what you observe the child doing as a writer and a reader. The observation methods are easily conducted in the regular day-to-day activity in classroom with very little outside testing. Additionally, the Intervention Blueprint is easy to follow and criteria for determining whether a child is on or off track is straightforward.

Here are the guideposts for when early intervention should occur:

MINIMAL COMPETENCY EXPECTANCY LEVELS

PHASE	COMPETENCY IS EXPECTED BY:
Phase 0—No letters	Pre-kindergarten/Beginning kindergarten
Phase 1—Letters without sound representation	Middle kindergarten
Phase 2—Beginning and ending sounds are represented	End of kindergarten
Phase 3—Finger spelling/A letter for a sound	Middle first grade
Phase 4—Spelling in chunks of phonics patterns	End of first grade

When half of the invented spelling in a volume of writing (or half of the spellings of a particular level of the Monster Test on pages 161, 166, 171, and 177) fits one of these five phases, you have identified the child's level of functioning. If a child is not functioning in the phase by the minimal expected competency level, you will be able to follow the Intervention Blueprint to provide precisely the type of instruction that will help move this child forward.

Intervening Early

There is a reason to intervene early. Neuroscientists tell us that from 5 percent to 17 percent of children may be prewired for reading failure (Shaywitz and Shaywitz 2001). These children may have a neonatal glitch in the brain circuitry that keeps a specialized area of the brain associated with automatic word reading from activating normally (Shaywitz 2003). The right kind of early intervention may enable these children to overcome this biological obstacle to decoding. Preliminary studies of beginning readers using new brain scan technology indicate that with early intervention during kindergarten and beginning first grade, when the child's brain is plastic and malleable, the faulty wiring can be fixed. It is critical to intervene early because the younger the brain, the greater the propensity for more adaptability. Some neurologists say that with early intervention, dyslexia may even be prevented (Shaywitz 2003). The same kind of intervention needed to prevent dyslexia is the kind of instruction that normally developing children need for breaking the code. So in addition to preventing dyslexia, this instruction, and early intervention, may keep children who have no neurological problems with reading from falling through the cracks for nonbiological reasons.

Choosing the Right Tools

Many of the tools needed to "fix" the brain are easily used in the context of teaching beginning writing. Due to writing and reading reciprocity, these same tools help "fix" a struggling reader's problems with reading if the struggling reader is functioning in the tadpole phases. These tools for writing likely activate the same brain circuitry used for reading and help the beginner or struggler develop the same underlying knowledge that beginning readers use. You simply need to use certain tools during certain phases of development, and the Intervention Blueprint shows when to use the right tool.

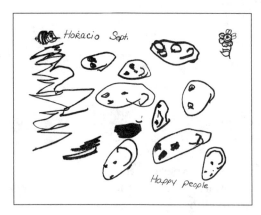

FIGURE 6.1   Level 0 Writing

Instructional Intervention for Phase 0 Writers

Let's start with *seeing* Phase 0. Level 0 writing is demonstrated in Figure 6.1. Notice that the writer is using no letters and is unable to write his or her name. If children are not using letters by the beginning of kindergarten, early intervention is necessary. The instructional measures recommended in the Intervention Blueprint are also appropriate for any normally functioning Level 0 writer (in prekindergarten).

Perhaps Level 0 is the easiest level to detect and the easiest to address when development is falling behind what is expected. If a child is not able to write her name when she enters kindergarten, teach her to write her name. Teach him to read his name (from memory or logographically) at the same time you are teaching him to write it. Recognize that the meaningful whole and the parts occur simultaneously.

Major intervention strategies for level 0

Name Writing. Teach the child how to hold the pencil (see Figure 6.2).

Next show the child how to place the paper for writing as demonstrated in Figure 6.3. These early demonstrations of proper handgrip for the pencil and proper placement for the paper build confidence and get kids off to a good start fairly easily. Now the child is ready to trace the letters in his or her name. Write the child's name with a yellow highlighter and show him or her how to trace over each letter. This process should be repeated frequently. Remember, the brain loves repetition (but not repetitious nonsense such as

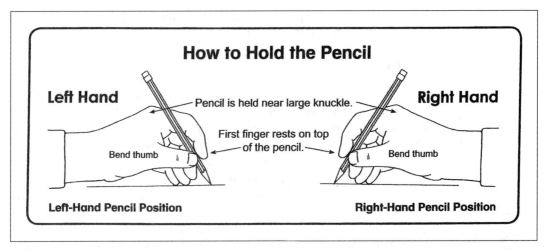

FIGURE 6.2 How to Hold the Pencil

FIGURE 6.3 Correct Paper Position

eighteen worksheets stacked on the child's desk for completion during the day!). Teachers should be modeling letter formation in group, interactive, and individual contexts. Teaching letter writing in kindergarten is hands-on and interactive.

Teach the Letters. Letters are the building blocks of alphabetic reading and writing. By learning to write the letters in one's name, the child makes a giant cognitive and psychological leap toward real literacy. Many teachers begin by having the child trace the letters in his or her name on a red highlight model from left to right. Show the child the proper letter strokes from the beginning as illustrated in Figure 6.4.

Begin Teaching the Alphabet. All beginning readers and writers should work with all twenty-six uppercase and lowercase letters of the alphabet from the outset of kindergarten. Remember, in every kindergarten classroom, children must read and write their names from the very first day. Since classrooms have children whose names range from *Antonio* to *Zachary* with every name in between, kindergarten children who are reading and writing their names use *all* the letters of the alphabet from the moment they walk into the classroom and pin on their nametags. It's fine to target a letter per week (Gentry 2004b), but targeting a letter doesn't mean all letters aren't in use! It simply means that a particular letter or sound is being highlighted for refinement—not being taught for the first time. The first letters to be taught are whatever letters appear in a child's name. If you are a kindergarten teacher, don't ever think that you don't teach a particular letter until November, when it is the focus of the lesson in the spelling book. You teach every letter contained in each child's name from the very first day of kindergarten.

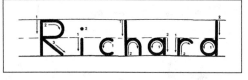

FIGURE 6.4   Proper Strokes for Tracing the Name "Richard"

Teach the Alphabet Song. Singing the alphabet song is one of the easiest ways to learn the twenty-six letter names by providing needed repetition and pattern recognition. (Don't forget that it's not unusual for a kindergartner to think that El-em-en-o-pee is one letter name!)

For children, learning twenty-six new letter names is much what it's like for a person who cannot speak Hungarian to walk into a roomful of twenty-six Hungarians with names like Gyöngyi (unless you speak Hungarian), and all of a sudden you are expected to know everyone. You begin reacting to some of the new faces and interact with some more than others. The ones you interact with are the ones you are likely to learn first. Remembering *W* or "double-u" initially may be just as complex for a kindergartner as remembering one of twenty-six Hungarian names and matching it with a face. It's not so easy! Learning the twenty-six uppercase and lowercase letters takes time. Sometimes children move from writing levels 0 to 2 before they have learned all the letters. This process may take weeks and even months.

Pair a child who knows the letter names and recognizes the forms that match them with a buddy who is learning the letters for the first time. Some teachers have team competitions and "letter name spelling bees" to see which teams can "spell" or say the name of the letter. Remember that intervention does not always have to be one-on-one and that children learn lots of literacy in joyful and playful interaction with each other.

Begin Teaching Sounds. Some sounds as word parts are easier to perceive than others, or in the words of researchers, are "psychologically more perceptible" (Goswami 1996). Shouting out the rhyming word in a nursery rhyme, as in "Jack and Jill went up the HILL," is fairly easy for many children, especially when the activity is done in unison in a whole group as a choral response. It's much easier for children to respond in unison than individually. Clapping syllables (An-to-ni-o/four claps) is easier than hand spelling onsets and rimes (/J/ with thumb up, /-ack/ with handshake position). Working with onsets and rimes is easier than working with phonemes (Goswami 1996). Start with rhyming words and syllables and work toward more sophisticated sound/word parts. Remember that phonemic awareness is not natural and is perceptibly challenging even for some adults. It is also important to recognize that when we exaggerate or stretch out sounds, we sometimes change them. For example, technically, stop consonants like /b/ can't be said in isolation because the consonant sound, made by a particular placement of the lips, is only realized when the following vowel rushes air through the articulatory structures of the mouth. Without the following vowel, or rush of air, there is no sound. The point is that when the teacher models the /b/ sound at the beginning of *boy,* he or she is actually saying /b/ followed by a short vowel. Care must be taken so that the sound is modeled as /b/ and not /buh/ (Wilde 1992).

Use Materialization Techniques. Materialization techniques (Bodrova and Leong 1998; Gentry 2004) such as clapping syllables, hand spelling, and finger spelling make it easier for children to perceive the targeted sound or word part. A materialization technique is any technique that uses a tangible object (the hand, fingers, stretchable fabric) and a physical action to represent a mental construct such as a sound or word part (Bodrova and Leong 1998; Galperin 1969; Gentry 2004). Materialization techniques grew out of Vygotskian theory and research (Bodrova and Leong 1998, Vygotsky 1978). Seven resourceful materialization techniques especially useful for working with tadpole readers and writers are shouting and "high-fiving" rhyming words, clapping syllables, hand spelling, stretching out the sounds in words with stretchable fabric, finger spelling, using sound and letter boxes, and word sorting with cards. To provide continuity and to help you see how to move progressively from easier to harder sound awareness, all seven materialization techniques are presented here in order from least to most sophisticated (easiest to hardest for children) with designation of what phase generally best matches with a particular materialization technique. Generally, only the first three are used with Level 0 writers and readers.

1. **Shouting Out the Rhyming Word with a High-Five.** Have children shout out the rhyming word in a nursery rhyme as they give a buddy the high-five when it's time to shout the word.

   > Jack and Jill went up the HILL.
   > (Kids shout out *hill* and give their buddy the high-five.)
   > Jack fell down and broke his CROWN.
   > (Kids shout out *crown* and give their buddy the high-five.)

   Use this materialization technique with Phase 0 and 1 readers and writers.

2. **Clapping Out Syllables** (syllabic awareness—an aspect of phonological awareness). Start out by modeling until pupils can clap out the syllables in names or target words in nursery rhymes or poems.

   > Bill (one clap)
   > Lo-is (two claps)
   > An-to-ni-o (four claps)

   Use this materialization technique liberally with Phase 0 through 2, but keep in mind that syllables may be extremely important through Phase 4 and even beyond for skilled readers when they try to figure out an un-known word. The way skilled readers store representations in memory may relate to ability to analyze words into their graphosyllabic constituents (e.g., *in-ter-est-ing*). In order to form complete connections between letters and sounds in words, syllable units such as *in-ter-est-ing*, may be extremely important for analogizing and decoding new words. Skilled readers (i.e., "frog readers") use the strategy of analyzing words into their graphosyllabic constituents. And while skilled readers use backup systems so that ulti-mately tehy cna raed txet fialry esaliy eevn wehn the wrdos aer msisepleld, readers who can decode these scrambled letters *are already skilled readers* who have learned to use the redundancy of the system. At the moment you were reading the scrambled spellings, you were aware that the spellings were incorrect. You were aware that they did not match the dictionary in your head even though you were able to read them. As a skilled reader you have developed a complex backup system for using syntactic information and for making sense so that you can read the scrambled letters. However, it's very unlikely that a beginning reader could learn to read using a scram-bled letter system. For example, research shows that students who try to read making only partial connections between letters and sounds often are not very successful (Bhattacharya and Ehri 2004).

   Some research studies call to question the reality of some of the con-ventional rules for syllable division at the end of lines of text and accept different ways of dividing words into syllables as long as each syllable con-tains one and only one vowel sound (e.g., *fin-ish* or *fi-nish*) and as long as the student's division forms a legal pronunciation (e.g., *sim-ple* or *simp-le* but not *si-mple*) (Bhattacharya and Ehri 2004, 337). I agree with this practice for instructional purposes for beginning reading. For example, while *rabbit* by conventional rule must be divided as *rab-bit* at the end of a line of text when syllable division might be required, children may perceive *rabbit* as *ra-bit* or *rab-it* to rhyme with *habit*. Use common sense and refrain from making the "divide between the double b's" distinction or trying to teach syllable juncture (a third-grade concept) to beginners. *Rab-bit*, *rab-it*, and *ra-bit* all demonstrate phonological awareness and developmentally appropriate knowledge of syllables for an early tadpole phase. When the teacher models how to break the word into chunks, of course one would model correct syllabication. For *rabbit*, one might say "the first syllable or word part is *rab* which works like *nab*, *cab*, *lab*, and *tab*. The next syllable or word part is *bit*, which works like *hit*, *kit*, *sit*, and *pit*." The point is that close approximations are desirable and appropriate in the early stages. It would not be appropriate to correct a child who was clapping and saying *ra-bit* or *rab-it* for *rabbit*, to insist upon *rab-bit*. That is too much complexity for a tadpole level of functioning. Teaching the intricacies of syllable juncture will come much later. Likewise, at Phase 4, RABIT is an acceptable invented spelling for *rabbit*. First-grade writers should not be expected to have mastered the intricacies of syllable juncture for spelling. Clapping out syllables may be used at all levels.

3. **Using Hand Spelling to Help Children Recognize the Onset or Beginning Sound.** I invented hand spelling for onsets and rimes modeled after finger spelling, a higher-level technique, that originated with Orton-Gillingham and consists of putting the consecutive phonemes of a word "on one's fingers" and then grabbing the word (Gentry 2004a; Orton 1964). Hand spelling, shown in Figure 6.5, begins with the pronunciation of a word such as *rat* represented by the hand held in a balled-up fist position (i.e., say *rat* and put out your fist). Next pronounce the onset, the sound that comes before the vowel, and hold up the thumb (i.e., say /r/ and stick up your thumb). Now pronounce the rest of the word—the vowel and everything that follows, which is called the rime—and extend the hand into a handshake position. Finally, pronounce the whole word again returning to the fist position symbolically pulling the onset and rime word parts back into the whole word.

Model this procedure with easy rhyming words such as *rat*, *cat*, *bat*, *fat*, and *mat*. The procedure is modeled *for* children and then done *with* and *by* them. Once children have learned the procedure, it's a wonderful technique for highlighting a targeted beginning sound such as hand spelling *h* words: /h/ in /h/ - /-ouse/, *house*; /h/ - /-ill/, *hill*; /h/ - /-ive/, *hive*; /h/ - /-ole /, *hole*; /h/ - /-ut/, *hut*.

Hand spelling is particularly useful with Level 0 through 2 learners to help them conceptualize beginning sounds. It may also be useful at Levels 3 and 4 to designate the rimes in words or to draw attention to spelling

FIGURE 6.5   Hand Spelling Symbols

word families or to spelling letter combinations and patterns for analogizing.

Higher-level materialization techniques include stretching out the sounds in words with stretchable fabric, finger spelling, using sound and letter boxes, and word sorting with cards. All materialization techniques appropriate for all phases of tadpole development are described in this section so that you can clearly see the progression of working from easier to perceive sounds, moving toward the conceptually more difficult to perceive sounds and word parts.

4. **Stretching Out the Sounds in Words with Stretchable Fabric.** Using stretchable fabric (or anything that stretches), have the child hold the fabric in front of himself or herself at book-reading level and slowly stretch out the fabric as both you and the child pronounce the word slowly exaggerating each phoneme. The idea is to help the child perceive the constituent sounds in the word as entities. Once the sounds in the word have been stretched out, allow the fabric to shrink back to its original position and pronounce the word normally to show that the word in its normal state is the same as the stretched-out word.

    Stretching out sounds is particularly useful for Levels 0–3.

5. **Finger Spelling.** Master teachers Judy Farley and Penny Jamaison taught me to how to do finger spelling, which they learned in Orton-Gillingham training (Orton 1964). Beginning with the thumb, each consecutive phoneme in a word is "put on a finger" in the order of thumb (first sound), index finger (second sound), third finger (third sound), and so forth. Keep in mind that finger spelling represents the number of *sounds* in a word, not the number of letters: *Bee* (/b/ + /e/) is spelled with two fingers; *eight* (/a/ + /t/) is also spelled with two fingers. Finger spelling designates the number of phonemes in a word as in the finger spelling *rat:* Put up the thumb for the /r/, the index finger for the short vowel sound /a/, and the third finger for the /t/. This materialization technique helps the child identify all the phonemes in a word and is particularly useful in helping a child move from Level 2 to Level 3. Children who finger spell successfully have full phonemic awareness.

6. **Using Sound and Letter Boxes.** Sound and letter boxes (also called Elkonin boxes) are borrowed from Reading Recovery training with an adaptation for writing a letter in each box for a sound. As shown in Figure 6.6, sound and letter boxes are drawn so that the child sees a box for each of the sounds in a word. The writer then spells each sound by placing a letter in the appropriate box, proceeding box by box until the constituent sounds in the word are spelled (Clay 1993; Gentry 2005). This technique works best to move Level 2 writers to Level 3 from partial to full alphabetic representation by showing the child how to put a letter in the box for each sound in the word being spelled. Sound and letter boxes are often useful with Level 2 children who get beginning sounds and ending sounds but leave out the middle sounds in the word being spelled. Some teachers have Level 4 writers use sound and letter boxes showing them how some sounds may be represented by letter combinations. I generally encourage teachers to dispense with the use of sound and letter

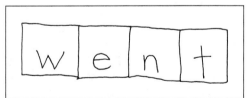

FIGURE 6.6 Sound and Letter Boxes for *went*

boxes once children are functioning at Level 3, and instead of spelling words sound-by-sound in boxes, help children move to attempts at spelling unknown words syllable-by-syllable, analogizing with chunks of phonics patterns while attending to graphosyllabic constituents. For many words, syllable-by-syllable processing is likely psychologically more real than letter-by-letter processing for skilled reading (Ehri 1997).

When modeling with children, use the materialization techniques 4, 5, and 6 together. Start by having the child stretch out the sounds in a word. Next have the child finder spell to determine how many boxes are needed. Make the sound and letter boxes to accommodate the appropriate number of sounds represented on the fingers. Then finger spell the word again, placing a letter in the appropriate box to match the sound designated for each finger immediately after the child says that sound. The sequence is (1) stretch out the sound, (2) finger spell, (3) draw the sound letter box for the number of fingers used, (4) supply a letter for each sound as you finger spell again.

7. **Word Sorting with Word Cards.** Sorting word cards into columns based on spelling patterns is conceptual, hands-on, collaborative, student-friendly, theoretically based, and supported by empirical research (Bear et al. 2000; Brown and Morris 2005; Gentry 2004; Zutell 1992a, 1992b). This instructional approach intended to develop automatic pattern recognition and improve analogizing and correct spelling, in my opinion, is one of the best brain-based strategies for developing word-specific knowledge for both reading and writing. Word sorting capitalizes on the brain's search for patterns and its propensity to respond to repetition. Sorting words on word cards is a wonderful hands-on instructional activity with a plethora of sorting options to keep the repetition interesting, including teacher-led sorts, individual sorts, buddy sorts, and speed sorts. A complete description of the word-sorting technique is provided in Chapter 7.

Now you are ready to consider three additional techniques that may be used effectively with Phase 0 learners, which also become important routines for writers at Levels 1 and 2: use of scaffolded writing, use of private speech, and adult underwriting. These techniques become the backbone of the beginning writer's writing workshop. They give tadpole writers early independence and directly connect writing and reading. In my view, scaffolded writing, private speech, and adult underwriting are key components of writer's workshop for Level 0–2 beginners.

Use of Scaffolded Writing. Bodrova and Leong (1998) define scaffolding as types of assistance "that make it possible for learners to function at higher levels" (4–5) and attribute the term *scaffolding* to Bruner (Wood, Bruner, and Ross 1976). The scaffold is a support necessary for the learner to complete a task at a level higher than the child's independent level of functioning. Once the student is able to complete the task independently, the scaffold is removed. Scaffolding resonates with the Vygotskian concept that what the learner can do today with assistance, he or she can do tomorrow independently (Vygotsky 1987).

Bodrova and Leong outline a five-step scaffolding technique for beginners:

1. The child chooses a topic and draws a picture. He or she selects words that go with the picture or tell a related story.

2. The child draws lines for each word in the message with a highlighter. Longer stories may be planned in sections with the child writing one sentence or phrase at the time. Often lines are longer for "longer words" containing more phonemes. For example, *elephant* gets a longer line than *bee*.

3. The child uses private speech: he or she rehearses the phrase or sentence to be written, matching each highlighted line with a word in the sentence by saying the sentence out loud and pointing to the line where the word will be written.

4. The child says the word that corresponds to a line in the message and then writes it on the line at whatever level he or she is able (i.e., using no letters, random letters, beginning and ending letters, a letter for each sound, or using chunks of phonics patterns). Sometime the child needs to go back and rehearse the message to figure out what word comes next in the sequence.

5. If the message has more than one sentence or phrase, the child highlights and writes one sentence or phrase at a time. Eventually the child will discontinue the use of the highlighted line and write independently without the scaffold. (1998, 9–10, reported in Gentry 2005, 123–24)

At Level 0 the writing scaffold may consist of a line for a one-word label or two or three lines for a two- or three-word phrase. The child draws the scaffold (e.g., three lines drawn with a yellow marker) and rehearses the message to be written, "reading" the words to be put down on the lines using private speech.

Use of Private Speech. Bodrova and Leong (1998) describe use of private speech as self-directed regulatory speech used by the learner to give himself or herself auditory directions to support the development of new mental actions, and they attribute the technique to Galperin (1969, 1992). Private speech serves as a temporary mechanism and is dropped once the process is internalized. One use of private speech by beginners is to internalize the correct spelling of a high-frequency word. For example, they are often observed to say something like: "Oh, I know that one, it's *the,* t-h-e, *the.*" Private speech is also in use when the child repeats the words to be written in the scaffold over and over until they are internalized. Once a child has decided to write *my truck goes fast,* he draws four lines for the scaffold and points to the line that matches each word as he repeats "My truck goes fast." He might repeat the private speech pointing to the appropriate line for each word several times—"My truck goes fast. My truck goes fast"—until the intended message is internalized and the child knows the line for the word's appropriate placement in the scaffold. Sometimes the child begins writing, for example writing the first two words, *My truck,* and then uses private speech to re-hearse—"My truck goes"—to determine which word comes next in his writing. I have found modeling the use of private speech to be extremely helpful in giving very early writers a sense of independence (Gentry 2005).

Adult Underwriting. Adult underwriting is a variation of an instructional read-ing technique called *language experience approach* originally developed by Russell Stauffer (1969, 1980) and R. Van Allen and Van Allen (1966). In a wonderful teacher's guide for teaching writing in kindergarten entitled *Kid Writing* (1999), Eileen Feldgus and Isabell Cardonick adapted aspects of language experience approach specifically for kindergarten writing workshop and labeled the tech-nique "adult underwriting." Adult underwriting is the corrected version of the child's writing, but as Eileen Feldgus would say, it's done "in a praise mode." I recommend writing the adult version at the bottom of the page below the full version of the child's writing as opposed to writing the adult version directly un-der each child's word, to keep the integrity of the child's version intact. Adult underwriting is not a "correction" of the child's piece but a readable adult ver-sion appearing on the page with the child's writing, which is important because many Level 1 and 2 samples of children's writing cannot be read, even by the writer, after a period of time. The teacher's version should have the same words on each line that the child used to make it easy for the child to do the voice to print match and to make it easier for the child to reread the adult version from memorization. In a shared-reading format, the teacher and child practice read-ing both the kid writing and the adult underwriting alternately with the teacher first prompting by saying, "Read the kid writing." Then the teacher prompts by saying, "Now try the adult writing" and offers encouragement such as "Wow, you are such a good reader!" Eventually most of the reading is from the adult version, which excites the child because he or she is reading from the "harder" version. The teacher encourages this behavior with prompts such as "My good-ness! You can read the adult writing!" This process connects writing directly with beginning reading instruction. Often the level of text in the adult under-written copy of the child's writing is a close match for the child's guided reading level. For example, a Level 1 or 2 writer might be placed in a guided reading Level A book such as *The Pancake* by Roderick Hunt. Characteristics of level A books are that there are usually three to five words on a page, a clear print to pic-ture match, often a repeated sentence stem, and the topic is an age-appropriate concept that children are familiar with, in this instance, "pancakes." These are exactly the same characteristics of typical samples of adult underwriting of chil-dren's writing samples at the early stages of writing, so the adult underwriting is excellent age-appropriate reading material for the child. Three examples of adult underwriting for samples of Level 0, Level 1 and Level 2 writing are pre-sented in Figure 6.7.

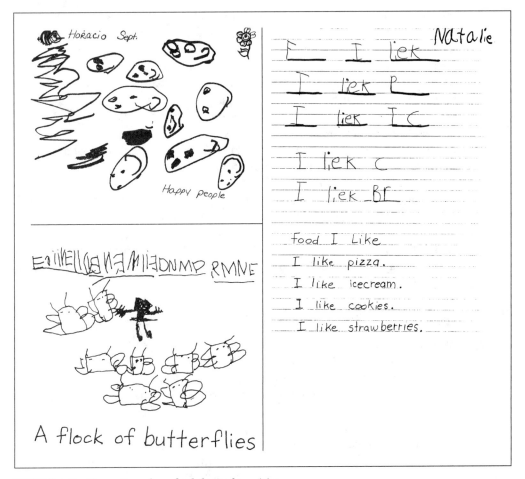

FIGURE 6.7 Three Samples of Adult Underwriting

When teachers use the terms *kid writing* and *adult writing* sensitively, they convey to children that children aren't expected to write like adults and give them confidence to do productions in "kid spelling." It is an affirmation of their work. Notice the agreement with this terminology and the brain research that suggests that there are two systems, or two distinct modulations in learning to read—first *beginning reading* (and writing) and later *skilled reading* (and writing). In the first "beginning readers must analyze a word"; in the second, "skilled readers identify a word instantaneously" (Shaywitz 2003, 78). Notice that the notion of "kid writing" versus "adult writing" is in perfect agreement with my tadpole versus frog metaphor for reading and writing, which is precisely why I think the Feldgus and Cardonic work was groundbreaking on a practical level in making the reading and writing connection in the classroom. In the first instance, *beginning*, the child activates slow and analytical circuitry. In the later instance, *skilled*, the child likely activates an area of the brain that accommodates automatic recognition. I believe activation of the automatic "word form" area coincides with the occurrence of breaking the code when a child is able to recognize many sight words and phonics or spelling patterns. Only then can the brain *see* the regularity in print by recognizing chunks of phonics patterns as well as over one hundred one-syllable, high-frequency "sight words," which also serve as models for analogues and syllable chunks in polysyllabic words. This theory is a good fit with neuroscientists' reports of activation of an area of the brain that reacts to whole words and patterns, an area that Shaywitz calls the "express pathway to reading" (Shaywitz 2003).

At beginning levels, it makes perfect sense for teachers to mediate children's writing by supplying the "skilled version" or adult written version of the child's written message for children who are writing at Levels 0–2 as a "reading" scaffold. When this is done, the child is able to read the adult underwriting over and over, ultimately being able to read what they wrote—in adult writing—from memory.

Instructional Intervention for Phase 1 Writers

As with the previous level, let's start by *seeing* Phase 1. Level 1 writing is demonstrated in Figure 6.8. Notice that the writer is using what seems to be random letters and that the letters do not match the sounds in the words being written. If children are not functioning as Level 1 writers by the middle of kindergarten, early intervention is necessary. The instructional measures recommended in the Intervention Blueprint are also appropriate for any normally functioning Level 1 writer in kindergarten.

Level 1 is important because the child now uses the building blocks of reading and writing, namely, letters. The critical aspect of your instruction is to show the child how letters in alphabetic languages represent sounds.

FIGURE 6.8   Level 1 Writing

Major intervention strategies for level 1

Depending on the Level 1 writer's level of sophistication, all of the intervention techniques recommended for Level 0 that have not been exhausted may further develop the Level 1 writer. So glance back at the Level 0 list and note any intervention strategies that seem appropriate to move the Level 1 student forward. Many of the techniques such as the materialization techniques extend through several phases. Major Level 1 intervention strategies include a continuation of teaching letters, sounds, and more sophisticated scaffolding and adult underwriting. It is important to increase the volume of writing and to provide for independent reading of adult underwriting.

Continue Assessing Letter Knowledge and Teaching the Letters. Level 1 writers exhibit varying degrees of alphabetic knowledge. One of my all-time favorite examples of Level 1 writing is a grocery list, written by Dan in precommunicative spelling presented in Figure 6.9. Dan started his list using environmental print he knew from memory—*7-Up*. Sometimes I ask teachers to guess what he listed in the remainder of the list (see Figure 6.9). Often they guess *eggs, fish,* and if they are clever they may think the fourth word in the list is *mousse,* a product Dan might purchase at the grocery store for his hair. Of course, none of these guesses are correct because Dan is at Level 1 and does not yet match letters to sounds. In actuality, Dan's Level 1 grocery list says *7-Up, milk, Raisin Bran,* and *doughnuts.* Dan didn't know all of the sixteen letters needed to make his grocery list: *u, p, m, i, l, k, r, a, s, n, b, d, o, g, h,* and *t.* (More importantly, he didn't know how to match letters to sounds.) He did know how to make *O's, S's, E's* and *I's* and he demonstrated a preference for uppercase lettering, which is typical of beginning writers. The uppercase letters are easier to form with fewer con-

FIGURE 6.9 Dan's Grocery List

figurations such as dots or crosses, and uppercase letters are much more frequently seen in the child's world of environmental print. Adult underwriting would have exposed Dan to some new letters and would be an appropriate contextual teaching opportunity in a short writing conference. Once the teacher did the adult underwriting, in addition to having Dan read the list, she might query, "Dan, how many of the letters that we have used in the grocery list can you name? I'll get you started, here's a *U* and a *P* in *7-Up.* Let's see how many letters you know in both the kid writing and in the adult writing."

Continue Teaching Sounds and Sound Parts of Words. At Level 1 work continues with rhyming words and syllable clapping, but emphasis may be placed on beginning sounds for which hand spelling is particularly useful (see the Use Materialization Techniques section for Level 0 on page 53). Once a child can say several words that rhyme with a particular easy, high frequency spelling pattern such as *cat: bat, fat, hat, mat, pat, rat, sat*—have the child contrast the beginning sounds of these words by finger spelling them. First pronounce *cat* with the hand held in a balled-up fist position, then hold up the thumb and say the beginning sound /k/—the onset. Extend the hand into the handshake position for the rime, /-at/. Then reach out and grab the sounds and bring them back into the word as you say "cat" again. Repeat this hand spelling procedure with the other -at words drawing the child's attention to the changes in the beginning sounds of *bat, fat, hat, mat, pat, rat,* and *sat,* for the letters b, f, h, m, p, r, and s, respectively, pronouncing each beginning sound with the thumb held up. Once the child is successful hand spelling words in the same word family, try hand spelling targeted sounds such as the sounds in "h" words as in *house, hill, hive, hole, hand,* and *hut.*

Word Sorting with Word Cards. Sorting picture cards into columns based on beginning sounds is an excellent instructional and intervention strategy for Level 1 learners. Figure 6.10 shows a picture sort of word cards used to contrast the beginning *h* and the beginning *u* sound, which was presented contextually with the learning of the nursery rhyme "Jack and Jill."

Scaffolding Writing, Using Private Speech, and Adult Underwriting. Of course scaffolded writing, private speech, and adult underwriting are indispensable tools for intervention with Level 1 writers. Figure 6.11 shows a Level 1 writer's work with which these techniques have been employed. Chapter 7 will provide a full explanation of how these techniques are used with a Level 1 learner.

FIGURE 6.10   Picture Word Sort for Beginning H and U

Instructional Intervention for Phase 2 Writers

As with the previous level, let's start by *seeing* Phase 2. Level 2 writing is demonstrated in Figure 6.12. The giant cognitive leap achieved by Level 2 writers is that they begin to match some letters to sounds in their invented spelling. In essence, this is their first actual use of the code as an alphabetic system: it's the first time they are matching letters to sounds. Most of their initial attempts to write and spell in this phase involve getting the beginning and sometimes ending sounds or other "prominent" sounds but they do not get all of the sounds. The harder middle sounds are often missing, which is to be expected because often these are vowel sounds that are represented by complex patterns—*sail* or *sale,* for example. Representing this kind of patterning is very sophisticated and comes later.

Sometimes correct letter-sound correspondences at Level 2 are interspersed with random letters as the child transitions out of Phase 1 into Phase 2, so BCFYT might spell *boat.* In Figure 6.12, Michael demonstrates that he knows the correct spelling for *my,* but it is the invented spelling that guides us to understand what he is able to do with the alphabetic system as a Level 2 writer. He represents the compound word *motorboat* as two words: *motor* and *boat.* I might tend to go with his notion of treating them as two words in the adult underwriting (usually adult writing is presented conventionally), simply because teaching compound words seems over his head at this point, or beyond his zone of proximal development (Vygotsky 1978). Notice that he gets the beginning and prominent /m/ and /t/ sounds in *motor* and the beginning and ending /b/ and /t/ sounds of *boat.* This is a fine example of Level 2 writing. If children are not functioning as Level 2 writers by the end of kindergarten, early intervention is needed. The instructional measures recommended in the Intervention Blueprint are appropriate for any normally functioning Level 2 writer.

Level 2 is important because the child matches letters to sounds in partial alphabetic representations. The critical aspect of your instruction is to show the child how to make *full* alphabetic representations. The move is from partial phonemic awareness to full phonemic awareness, which signals the move into Level 3.

FIGURE 6.11 Scaffolded Writing and Adult Underwriting with a Level 1 Writer

FIGURE 6.12 Level 2 Writing

Major intervention strategies for level 2

Many of the instructional and intervention techniques used at previous levels are extended into Level 2. You will find occasions to teach unknown letters, unknown letter-to-sound correspondences, occasions to highlight rhyming words or in some instances syllables, and you may sometimes start out with hand spelling to highlight onsets and rimes with Level 2 writers. But your main coding instruction and intervention will be to move the Level 2 writer to represent *all* the sounds in a word. You will be nudging the child to produce a letter-for-a-sound invented spellings. The move will be from MT BT to MOTR BOT. The most useful techniques for making this critical move with Level 2 writers is to stretch out sounds in words, finger spell, and use sound and letter boxes. You will also be moving to greatly increase the volume of writing if you aren't already getting good volume, because the more the child writes, the more he or she engages the brain circuitry in the critical brain areas for literacy. In this context, you will continue to use scaffolded writing and adult underwriting to great advantage.

Stretching Out the Sounds in Words with Stretchable Fabric. Look again at Figure 6.12. Suppose you want to nudge Michael to move from BT for *boat* to BOT—from partial to full alphabetic spelling. Start by having him hold the fabric in front of himself at book-reading level and slowly stretch out the fabric as both you and he pronounce *boat* slowly exaggerating each phoneme: /b/ (stretch), /ō/ (stretch some more), /t/ (fabric is fully extended). Then say "boat" and allow the fabric to go back to the original position signifying that the stretched out word is the same as the normal pronunciation of *boat*. Then you might ask Michael how many sounds he heard. If he says "three," you would say, "Great, now let's finger spell *boat* on three fingers." If he gives you an incorrect response say "Let's try it again: /b/ is the first sound, /ō/ is the second sound, and /t/ makes the third sound." While stretching the fabric again and exaggerating the three sounds the teacher would say, "/b/, /ō/, /t/—one, two, three!"

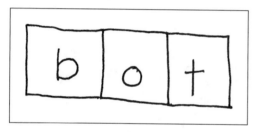

FIGURE 6.13   Sound and Letter Boxes for Boat

Finger Spelling. To finger spell *boat*, put each sound "on a finger" by holding a finger up each time the sound is spoken starting with the thumb. "*Boat.* OK, Michael, what's the first sound?" /b/—hold up the thumb. "What's the next sound?" /ō/—stick out the index finger. "What's the next sound?" /t/—put out the third finger. "Now reach out and grab the sounds!" "Boat!" Now you are ready for sound and letter boxes.

Sound and Letter Boxes. Figure 6.13 shows the completed sound and letter boxes for the spelling of *boat*.

Here are the procedures and commentary:

Teacher: Michael, since we used three fingers to finger spell *boat*, let's make three boxes for our spelling. It looks like this. (She draws three contiguous empty boxes.)

Teacher: Let's finger spell *boat* again, only this time we will choose a letter to place into the appropriate box to spell each sound. OK, hold up your thumb. What's the first sound?

Michael: /b/

Teacher: How do you spell /b/?

Michael: With a *b*.

Teacher: OK. Put a *b* in the first box.

Teacher: What's the next sound?

Michael: /ō/ (He holds out his index finger as he says /ō/.)

Teacher: How do you spell /ō/?

Michael: With an *o*!

Teacher: OK. Put an *o* in the next box.

Teacher: What's the last sound?

Michael: /t/ (He holds out his third finger as he says /t/.)

Teacher: How do you spell /t/?

Michael: With a *t*.

Teacher: Great. Put a *t* in the last box. Say Michael, that's a great kid spelling for *boat*. You got all the sounds! You are really a good kid speller!

FIGURE 6.14   Level 2 Writing After Scaffolding, Private Speech, and Adult Underwriting

Scaffolded Writing and Adult Underwriting. Scaffolded writing, private speech and adult underwriting continue to be indispensable tools for intervention with Level 2 writers. Figure 6.14 shows Michael's Level 2 sample after these techniques have been employed. Chapter 7 will provide a full explanation of how these techniques are used with a Level 2 learner.

Instructional Intervention for Phase 3 Writers

As with the previous level, let's start by *seeing* Phase 3. Level 3 writing is demonstrated in Figure 6.15. The Level 3 writer crosses the threshold into full phonemic awareness using a new strategy for inventing a spelling by supplying a letter for each sound in the word. By this time in development, it is not unusual for many words in the child's writing to be correctly spelled, as is the case in the three little pigs story in Figure 6.15. But most of the invented spellings are spelled by supplying a letter for a sound, as you see in the sample: MUTHR for *mother*, OT for *out*, WOD'S for *woods*, LITL for *little*, BUNDL for *bundle*, UV for *of*, CTRO for *straw*, SED for *said*, and GIV for *give*. Of course, English orthography, for the most part, works in chunks—not a-

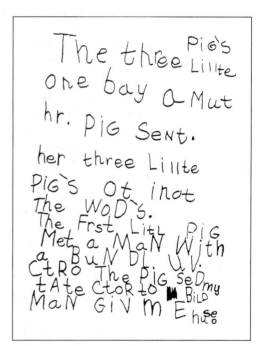

FIGURE 6.15   Level 3 Writing

letter-for-a-sound. So the major instructional goal for coding instruction at Level 3 is to help the child recognize chunks of phonics patterns. You must move him or her to spell to use chunks, to spell by analogy to known spellings, and to recognize and correctly spell lots of high-frequency one-syllable sight words, which are often used as phonics chunks in polysyllabic words.

Major intervention strategies for level 3

Word walls, hand spelling the rime, and word sorting with word cards are particularly useful instructional and intervention techniques for Level 3 writers. At the same time you will be dropping the writing scaffold and dropping the adult underwriting, but continuing to increase the volume of writing. Using a comprehensive research-based spelling book to provide a curriculum for word-specific knowledge to the rest of the literacy program is also paramount to assessing the Level 3 learner's literacy growth.

Word Walls. Word walls are opportunities to highlight high-frequency words using materialization strategies such as clapping and chanting the spellings to commit the words to memory. I view the word wall as a big classroom dictionary and its function is to expose children to the words often enough through repetition to transfer these words into automatic sight recognition in the dictionary in their brain. The goal is accurate, automatic word recognition. Word wall work begins in kindergarten (see Chapter 8) generally with about two words being added each week, and becomes a prominent part of the first-grade curriculum stepping up to five words per week. Typically, many children are at Level 3 at the end of kindergarten and during the first half of first grade. At the end of thirty weeks, theoretically, first graders would have had repetition and exposure to word wall words to the extent that they recognized over 150 words on sight (five words per week multiplied by thirty weeks). I believe recognition of over one hundred words on sight is a huge factor in breaking the code and activating the word form area or Area C (occipito-temporal area) of the brain.

Pat Cunningham has written extensively about word walls in *Phonics They Use* (1995) and she collaborated with Richard Allington on the topic in a wonderful book entitled *Classrooms that Work* (Cunningham and Allington 1994). I did a synthesis on word walls in *The Literacy Map: Guiding Children to Where They Need to Be (K–3)* (Gentry 2000b). Each of these sources may extend the overview provided here.

Select a wall in the classroom with space for displaying the letters of the alphabet in alphabetical order including space under the letter for displaying high-frequency words alphabetically by first letter in columns. (See Figure 8.3.) Some teachers like for word walls to be low enough for children to detach the words and always large enough so that they may be seen easily seen from anywhere in the room.

Each week new high-frequency words for reading and writing are gleaned from the literacy activities the children engage in—generally two words per week in kindergarten and five words per week in first grade. The teacher focuses attention on these words using materialization techniques such as write, clap, and chant to help the children commit the words to memory. The word wall grows throughout the year and children constantly refer to it. While the major intent and easier challenge for children is to learn to read the words automatically, the word wall also serves as the child's first dictionary for writing. Many children learn to spell many of the word wall words perfectly. The teacher conducts word wall practice daily following certain routines.

1. Pronounce the word distinctly.
2. Present the word in context.
3. Have children say the word and clap and chant the spelling.
4. Conduct ten-minute practice sessions.

Various practice strategies are used for about ten minutes each day such as the following:

Clap, Chant, and Write. After the teacher calls out a word a student finds it on the wall. Then everyone pronounces the word, and claps and chants the spelling. "Cat, c-a-t, cat." It's a version of the ancient ABC method of learning to read that was practiced in the American colonies!

Letter and Rhyme. "Write the word that rhymes with *fig* and begins with *p*."

Guess the Missing Word. The teacher holds up prepared sentence strips and uses cloze procedure to have the children write the missing word in sentences such as "Little pig, little, pig _____ me come in!" Sometimes he/she gives a sound or letter cue.

Word Wall Sentences. After about forty-five words are on the wall, the teacher can dictate short sentences made up of word wall words such as "this little pig went home."

Read My Mind. Children number a sheet of paper from one to five. The teacher selects a secret word and gives appropriate clues highlighting beginning letters, chunks, vowel patterns, rhymes, or semantic and syntactic clues. After five clues everyone should have guessed the word. (Adapted from Cunningham and Allington 1994)

In my view, word wall work is certainly a brain-based activity allowing for the kind of repetition and engagement that leads to automatic word recognition, and along with pattern work (working with phonics chunks) eventually plays an important role in helping children break the code.

Hand Spelling the Rime. This is a variation of the hand spelling activity described on page 53 adapted for more advanced learners who are being nudged to pay attention to the chunking patterns in rimes. The activity begins by focusing on the rime in the handshake position and having children spell the rime chunk in words such as /d/ /-ay/, *day;* /b/, /-ake/, *bake;* and /n/,/-ail/, *nail;* in this instance, drawing attention to three chunking patterns for the long *a* sound.

Sample Long Vowels   able—flame—bay—mail

Cut the word study sheet into word cards. Sort these words into four columns: words like *able*, words like *flame*, words like *bay*, and words like *mail*.

able	afraid	bay	flame
gray	mail	main	paint
ray	spray	wait	place
cage	cape	table	fable

FIGURE 6.16   Word Study Sheet for a Second-Grade-Level Long *a* Sort

Word Sorting with Word Cards. Level 3 learners start with easy first-grade level patterns such as high-frequency word families, short vowels, and eventually perhaps a few short vowel and *e*-marker contrasting pairs. The word study sheet in Figure 6.16 is an example of a second-grade-level pattern sort appropriate for Level 4.

Sorting activities include a pretest to determine if the child knows the pattern being studied, teaching the sort by calling attention to the attributes of the pattern (teacher-led sort), and practicing the sort.

In the word study sheet in Figure 6.16, the teacher would first call out the sixteen words in a pretest, before the child sees the word study sheet. If he or she spells a high percentage of the words correctly, he or she knows the pattern. The target or instructional level is about 50 percent correct. (This only works if you are working from a researched-based word study sheet for which the words have been selected based on word frequency and word use studies.) If the child scores a low percentage on the pretest the sort is too difficult and a lower-level sort would be chosen.

The word study sheet will be cut into sixteen words for sorting. Much like the *to*, *with*, and *by* shared reading technique developed by Don Holdaway (1979) in which the reading is modeled *to* the children, then done *with* the children, then done *by* the children, the word sorting procedure works the same way. The sorting is modeled *to* the children, then done *with* the children, then done *by* the children. The teacher-led sort is an opportunity to teach the pattern, to show how the pattern might contrast with another pattern, and to model how the sort is done. In the second-grade-level sort to be conducted from the word study sheet presented in Figure 6.16, the teacher might begin by hand spelling the words to focus on the chunk that has a pattern for spelling long *a*:

Bay /b/, /-ay/ (hand spelling). What pattern makes the /ā/ sound in *bay*?

Answer: -ay

Mail /m/, /-ail/ (hand spelling). What pattern makes the /ā/ sound in *mail*?

Answer: -ai (VV) (two vowels together)

Flame /fl/, /-ame/ (hand spelling). What pattern makes the /ā/ sound in *flame?*

Answer: VCe (vowel consonant silent *e*)

Once the teacher points out the patterns explicitly, the group shares in the sorting of the words under the direction of the teacher so that he or she may draw attention to important pattern elements. Words are sorted into the four columns, words like *able*, words like *flame*, words like *bay*, and words like *mail*.

When the children understand the concept for the patterning in the sort, they are ready to cut the word study sheet into sixteen word cards and sort on their own. They may conduct individual sorts, buddy sorts, and speed sorts with one partner doing the timing. Word sorts are written in column formation in the pupil's individual spelling journal to keep a record of which sorts have been studied and to provide practice writing the pattern in column formation. The second-grade-level sort modeled in Figure 7.16 on page 87 would be appropriate for a Level 4 writer.

If children are not functioning as Level 3 writers by the middle of first grade, early intervention is necessary. The instructional measures recommended in the Intervention Blueprint are appropriate for any normally functioning Level 3 writer.

Level 3 is important because the child matches letters to sounds in full alphabetic representations and its signature is that Level 3 readers and writers have moved to full phonemic awareness. The critical aspect of instruction at Level 3 is to show the child how to make the move to reading and spelling in chunks of phonics patterns so that instruction should move them to full phonemic awareness and eventually to chunking, which signals the move into Level 4.

Instructional Intervention for Phase 4 Writers

As with the previous level, let's start by *seeing* Phase 4. Level 4 writing is demonstrated in Figure 6.17. The giant cognitive leap achieved by Level 4 writers is that they abandon the letter-for-a-sound strategy and begin to spell in chunks of phonics patterns. This is the final giant step toward breaking the code. It's the first time they are matching sound parts of words to chunks of English spelling patterns. The move is from a spelling such as UNITD for *united,* to YOU-NIGHTED. The spelling of *boat* might move from BOT to BOTE, analogizing with *note.* The move is from full phonemic awareness to recognizing that the regular patterns in English print are a complex system of chunks of letters that correspond to sound parts of words. Note the following chunking exemplars and other examples of word-specific knowledge in the Level 4 sample in Figure 6.17:

Good THING to Eat

I like STRALBARES and i like ORRANGE.
I like tomato SUPE and I like PECHIS.
I like apples and I like BROCLE.
I like COLEFLAWORE TO, you know.
I like corn and I like green BENES.
I like FRIDE CEKEN and I like BARBO Q CEKEN TO.
But most of all I like HO MAED SPOGATE.
THOSS things are good for you.
That's why I put them down.

FIGURE 6.17   Level 4 Writing

- Many first-grade-level words are correctly spelled automatically.
- A number of sophisticated spelling patterns—*oo* in *good*, *ea* in *eat*, *-ike* in *like*, *kn* in *know*, *or* in *corn*, *ow* in *down*, are correctly spelled.
- The contraction, *that's* is correctly spelled.
- Some polysyllabic words such as *tomato*, and *apples* are correctly spelled.
- Liberal use of chunks of acceptable phonics patterns appear in invented spellings: STRAL-BAR-ES (perhaps dialect influenced), OR-RANGE, PE-CHIS, BRO-CLE (perhaps reduced to two syllables in her dialect), CO-LE-FLA-WORE, and SPO-GA-TE.
- The CVCe long vowel pattern is amply used in invented spellings such as SUPE for *soup*, WORE for the last syllable of *cauliflower*, BENES for *beans*, and FRIDE for *fried*.

Major intervention strategies for level 4

All of the instructional and intervention techniques used at Level 3 are extended into Level 4 with increased emphasis on word sorting and explicit spelling instruction. The idea is to expand the child's word-specific knowledge once the child is recognizing patterns and analogizing. Your main coding instruction and intervention will be to move the Level 4 writer to increase the number of phonics patterns and high-frequency words in his or her repertoire and to begin to recognize which of the phonetically acceptable patterns in English are conventional, correct spellings. The move might be from MI MOTR BOT (Level 3) to MY MOTUR BOTE, consolidating the correct spelling of a high-frequency word such as *my*, analogizing, and spelling polysyllabic words in syllables with chunks of acceptable phonics patterns. The most useful techniques for making this critical move with Level 4 writers are to engage in a number of spelling and chunking exercises such as word sorting, making and writing words, chunking columns, chunking drills, and of course, explicit spelling instruction. You will also continue to move to greatly increase the volume of writings and reading, because the more the child writes and reads, the more he or she engages the brain circuitry in the critical brain areas for literacy.

Word Sorting. The word sort presented in Figure 6.16 is actually a Level 4 sort. Word sorting extends the Level 3 levels of sorting by broadening the patterns and moving up a degree in sophistication. While a Level 3 sort might contrast the CVC words with different short vowels working with words such as *cap, hat, pet, hen, bit, rip, hop, got,* and *cut* or *pup*. The Level 4 sort might move to contrasting these patterns with the comparable e-marker long-vowel pattern such as *cap* and *cape, pet* and *Pete, bit* and *bite, hop* and *hope,* and *cut* and *cute*. Word knowledge grows by degrees and at each grade level the patterns being sorted will grow in sophistication.

Chunking Columns (a version of making and writing words). I made up a game called "chunking columns" tailored somewhat after *Making Words* Cunnningham and Cunningham 1992) and *Making and Writing Words* (Rasinski and Oswald 2005). Chunking columns focuses on important patterns in words that come out of the books or writing that is happening in class. I start with easily recognized patterns but move to very sophisticated use of the same pattern in much more sophisticated polysyllabic words. It goes something like this:

Teacher: If you can write *ho, ho, ho,* you can write *so!* (Student writes *so.*)
             If you can write *so,* you can write *no.* (Student writes *no.*)
             If you can write *so,* you can write *so long.* (Student writes *so long.*)
             If you can write *no,* you can write *no-tice.* (Student writes *notice.*)
             If you can write *so* you can write *so-lu-tion.* I help the student with the chunks such as *-tion* in *solution* if a chunk other than the target chunk is unknown. Then we practice reading the list in column formation until the student reads the words quickly and accurately:

ho, ho, ho

so

no

so long

notice (no-tice)

solution (so-lu-tion)

Here's another example of what a final chunking column might look like:

ton

money (mon-ey)

Monday (Mon-day)

son

person (per-son)

personal (per-son-al)

personality (per-son-al-i-ty)

I find that Level 4 writers love this activity and that it gives them great confidence as readers and writers along with a feeling of accomplishment with really big, mature words.

Column Drills. I find that sometimes when students and I encounter words in reading or writing, it's great to decontextualize the word at the end of the authentic reading or writing activity to practice a chunk that might have been misidentified. For example, the following column drill grew out of a reading in which the student miscued on the words *bit* (CVC) versus *bite* (CVCe) and is based on the respective short- and long-vowel patterns.

hop	hope
at	ate
pet	Pete
bit	bite

Sometimes I have the student write the words and sometimes I write them. Then we drill until we can read them quickly and with accuracy.

Explicit Spelling Instruction. I have written extensively about the need for explicit spelling instruction in *The Science of Spelling: The Explicit Specifics That Make Great Readers and Writers (and Spellers!)*. Spelling instruction is to frogs as coding instruction is to tadpoles; that is, it's just as imperative to teach spelling to "frogs" as it is to teach phonemic awareness and phonics to "tadpole" readers and writers. In effect, explicit spelling instruction is the natural continuation of coding instruction. Teaching spelling is complex, multifaceted, and important. It is grossly underrated in most American schools and many of the resources teachers receive for teaching spelling are inadequate. Correct spelling is something all teachers must teach. Once writers reach Level 4, the importance of teaching spelling explicitly becomes exceedingly apparent. If we don't teach correct spelling and expect children to grow in degrees of word specific knowledge throughout elementary school, THAY MAE STEEL BEE RIGHTING LIEK THAY ROTE WHIN THAY FERST MOOVED TO LEVUL 4.

7

Five Phases of Intervention, Support, and Instruction—Up as Close as You Can Get

If I want to see what five-year-old kindergartner Michael knows about writing and reading in October, I look at his writing as shown in Figure 7.1. If I want to see what he knows a month later, I look at the sample pictured in Figure 7.2.

These simple little kindergarten productions probably tell me more about Michael's literacy learning than any neuroscientist could discern from two brain scans administered on the respective days that he wrote them, which speaks to their power. If we peeked inside of Michael's brain with a computer and a magnet—which is what the neuroscientists do—we could not say much about what is happening. By studying his writing samples, a knowledgeable kindergarten teacher can tell you volumes. Michael's writing lets us see what's happening inside his head when he writes, and if he reads it back and talks about it—in terms of finding out what's going on in his brain—you can't get much closer than that!

Observing writing, reading, and listening to children talk about what they are thinking are all wonderful ways to get way up close to what's happening inside a child's brain with literacy, especially when we pay attention to the Instructional Blueprint as we watch and listen to what they are saying. For example, the Jensens made a delightfully surprising discovery regarding their five-year-old prekindergartner, Connor, as he demonstrated remarkable growth in word knowledge one Friday night at the mall. The family was sitting together each enjoying a drink called an "icee." Ro emailed me the following vignette.

We were at the mall tonight, and we bought each of the kids an ICEE. So we are sitting there enjoying our treats and talking, and Connor says, "Hey, this word says ICEE."

Rick and I looked at each other in amazement. We asked him, "How do you know?"

"Look," Connor says, "the Letter I says /ī/, and the C-E-E spells "see." It spells IIIIICEEEEEE—but sometimes the *i* has the short *i*, /ĭ/, sound."

I'm telling you, if you met him, you'd be astounded.

FIGURE 7.1 Michael's Writing in October

While all children don't have Connor's advantage of literacy from birth in the household of a gifted former first-grade teacher, they all will amaze you if you watch them read and write and listen to their conversations about it.

In this chapter I want to show you what some teachers and I see when we look closely at a child's writing and talk with them about it. We will look together at writers at each of the phases of development to see what understandings we might glean. I'll show you how studying their writing gives me ideas to further support their literacy learning and guide them to higher levels. I'll show

you how, ultimately, teaching into what they do as writers is a clear pathway for helping them break the code as readers. We'll look together at Phase 0 through Phase 4 writers, but first let's look back at Michael.

While the writing samples in Figures 7.1 and 7.2 are only tiny samples, when the two are juxtaposed, they are powerful indicators of how his knowledge of literacy was growing in just one month. (Can you imagine what we would know if we were watching Michael in the production of lots and lots of volume, day by day in school?)

The sample from Halloween in Figure 7.1 showed that Michael had learned to write his name mostly in all caps. Writing first in uppercase is quite predictable—"STOP" and the other signs he most

FIGURE 7.2 Michael's Writing in November

likely has noticed in environmental print show up much more frequently in all caps. Additionally, uppercase letters generally have fewer elements—no dots (*i*, *j*) fewer crosses (*t*, *f*)—so they are generally much easier to make.

The most noticeable feature of Michael's Halloween sample is his mirror writing—he started on the right side of the page and moved toward the left. (If you hold it in front of a mirror, it looks perfectly correct.) Whenever I see mirror writing, I'm reminded that whether writing goes left to right, right to left, top to bottom, or in some other direction, it's merely a convention. In Michael's case, it certainly was no cause for alarm, or as some might have you believe, a signal of brain dysfunction. A proper response would be to show Michael which direction to go when he is writing in English. Otherwise, he may befuddle himself much like I do when I find myself driving down a one-way street in the wrong direction. Left undetected, I suppose mirror writing might cause an accident. When I watch kids write in the classroom and see them going in the wrong direction, I simply tell them to turn it around. "Hey, Michael, you are mirror writing. Start here. It goes this way . . . M-I-C-H- . . . you finish it." That usually takes care of it.

One month later in the Thanksgiving piece presented in Figure 7.2 the mirror writing was all cleared up and Michael was growing in letter knowledge mastering his name with the capital *M* and perfect lowercase lettering. He even got the capital *P* of his last name. The juxtaposition of pieces written over time—even pieces as tiny as these two renditions of Michael's writing of his name, can often be powerfully informative.

Intervening, Supporting, and Teaching a Level 0 Writer

The sample in Figure 7.3 shows Horatio's production in August near the beginning of kindergarten. He came to school unable to write his name. His teacher might start by praising his picture and his writing approximations, which she refers to as "wavy writing," in their conversation. "You are ready to write your name!" she explains as she models and pronounces his letters. She might show him where to start and watch him trace it.

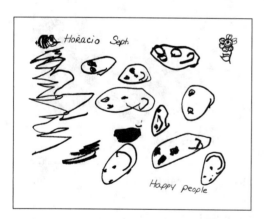

FIGURE 7.3   Horatio's Level 0 Writing

But then she sees other opportunities. Perhaps she will clap out the syllables in his name: *Ho-ra-ci-o, Ho-ra-ci-o* for sound work with phonological analysis. Perhaps she will place the adult underwriting at the bottom of the page after Horatio tells that his wavy writing says "happy people," and together they will practice reading words and phrases, *Horatio*, and *happy people*, by echo and repeated readings while fingerpoint reading. Perhaps she will stretch out the beginning sounds of *Horatio* and *happy*, respectively, and show that "Wow, /h/, /h/, these start with the same sounds! Can you hear the /h/ at the beginning of *Horatio*? Can you hear the /h/ at the beginning of *happy*? It's the same sound!" She might do this in a conference or perhaps with Horatio beaming in front of the whole class as she walks through the possible learning opportunities in his name. Perhaps she will show how the two sounds are spelled with an *H*. Perhaps she will ask how many of the letters in *Horatio* he can name. Perhaps they will explore the concept of what a word is. "Can you find the word *Horatio*? Here's a hint, it starts with the letter *H*. Show me the *whole word*. Where does it start? (The term *whole word* is important because it conveys that words have parts—beginning parts, ending parts, and middle parts. These are important concepts that eventually play a role in code breaking.) Let me spell it for you as you point to the letters. *Horatio*, look at all the letters you will know when you write your name!" These little conversations are exercises in metalinguistic awareness as Horatio begins to build a register for words and concepts about language such as *word, letter, sound, syllable, beginning sound, whole word, spell, write, read,* and the like. There are wonderful opportunities to teach, support, and nudge Level 0 writers forward each and every time that they write, and as you can see, a plethora of teaching and learning opportunities grow out of Horatio's first attempts at writing.

Intervening, Supporting, and Teaching a Level 1 Writer

Leslie's teacher listens as Leslie gives an elaborate verbal account of her trip to her grandmother's house in the country, where she took a walk in the pasture and was suddenly surrounded by a "flock of butterflies." "Let's write about that!" Her teacher exclaims, "A flock of butterflies. You can write it on these lines." Then picking up a yellow highlighter the teacher draws four consecutive lines for each word separating them appropriately for word spaces, making the "butterflies" line the longest since it is a long word with many letters, and finger pointing as she "reads" the highlighted lines saying the word that Leslie will be writing on each line for "<u>a</u> <u>flock</u> <u>of</u> <u>butterflies.</u>" The teacher might have Leslie re-peat the phase as she points to each line matching it with the appropriate word in her mind as she says it out loud—"a flock of butterflies, a flock of butter-flies" an exercise in private speech and scaffolded writing. The lines show that individual words are separated by spaces in print. Now Leslie is ready to write on her own—"a flock of butterflies"—making decisions about what letters to use and how to take it from this point. Her Level 1 writing is shown in Figure 7.4.

As with Level 0, Level 1 writing presents a pleth-ora of possibilities for teaching into the writing. One of the greatest possibilities for significant liter-acy growth to come out of a piece such as this is to return to the piece after the Level 1 writing is completed and make a reading-writing connection

FIGURE 7.4 Leslie's Level 1 Writing

through adult underwriting. The teacher-student dialogue might go something like this:

Teacher: Leslie, this is very nice "kid writing." Now I'll put it in "adult writing" and we'll see if you can read it! OK, you wrote "a flock of butterflies," watch as I write it and think about it out loud. "A flock of butterflies." I'll start with the *A*. It's right here, the first letter on your alphabet strip. *A* . . . a flock. Flock is *f-l-o-c-k*. There you have it . . . a flock. Read that part for me.

Leslie: A flock . . .

Teacher: That's great. Read it again as I point.

Leslie: A flock.

Teacher: Good Leslie. Let's do the rest. A flock of . . . *of* goes here. *O-F.* A flock of . . . what comes last?

Leslie: Butterflies!

Teacher: That's right! Butterflies! That's a long one isn't it? Here we go. B-U-T-T-E-R-F-L-I-E-S, butterflies! (The teacher may or may not choose to repeat the letters as he or she writes.) Now we have the whole thing. A flock of butterflies. You read it.

Teacher and Leslie together with fingerpoint match: A flock of butterflies.

Teacher: Read it again.

Leslie: *A flock of butterflies.*

Teacher: Read it fast!

Leslie: *A flock of butterflies!*

Teacher: Leslie, you are a great reader and writer! Look you can write and you can read the adult writing. I want you to practice reading this. We'll see if you can read it tomorrow! What does it say? Read it and point to the words.

Leslie: *A flock of butterflies!*

Of course, this dialogue is not a script. It's just the gist of a real conversation with the child as the teacher supplies the adult underwriting. The interaction provides opportunities to go in a number of directions. Teachers who know the Instructional Blueprint develop a good feel for how to proceed, sensitive to the specific needs of a child with just the right instruction and timing. Some children will need more repetition and some less. Some pieces will be longer and some may simply be a label. One critical accomplishment at Level 1 is that the child makes the voice-to-print match.

At times, opportunities arise to teach a sight word or focus on a sight word that may later become the model for a chunk for writing. A great deal of attention will be placed on beginning sounds with some of the words used in a Level 1 writing sample. Perhaps in this sample the teacher will bring attention to the *fl* "sticky letters" at the beginning of *flock* and *flies* (in the *fly* part of *butterflies.*) Perhaps Leslie's next drawing and label will be "My close-up of a butterfly—by

Leslie." —a whole sentence that she can learn to read; and the *my, by* and *fly* chunks may lead to the reading of

my

by

fly

A hand spelling activity might spin off from these words to focus on the beginning sounds /m/-/ī/, *my*; /b/-/ī/, *by*; fl/-/ī/, *fly*; and these words might be practiced for sight-word recognition and perhaps put on the word wall. "My close-up of a _____, by _____" might become a "close-up studies" writing model for everyone in the class after Leslie shares her work during the sharing time in writing workshop; so now any child could choose a detail in a previous drawing and do "a close-up." "My close-up of a _____, by _____." Now everyone is learning *my,* and *by,* which are great selections for a kindergarten word wall—and the community of learners explores the world of authentic literacy together in a fluid, spontaneous, and a natural language use that makes it all interesting and fun for everyone.

Intervening, Supporting, and Teaching a Level 2 Writer

Figure 7.5 shows a piece of Level 2 writing that is all ready for adult underwriting. Moments later, the piece looks like the version in Figure 7.6 and there is lots of reading and rereading of it. The adult underwriting properly provides the conventional form, which is much better for reading. And while the child is encouraged to invent spellings in writing, he is exposed to conventional English from the very beginning, a fully wholesome and age-appropriate example of the reading-writing connection.

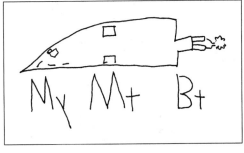

FIGURE 7.5   Level 2 Writing Ready for Adult Underwriting

In a conference or whole-class mini-lesson, many opportunities for teaching, extending, and supporting this Level 2 writer present themselves. For example, the teacher may decide it's a good time to nudge Michael to create more volume:

Teacher (*after Michael can read the adult underwriting on his own*): Well, Michael. Tell me something your motorboat can do.

Michael: It goes fast!

Teacher (*pointing to the first three words and then scaffolding by making two yellow highlight lines*): My motor boat (*goes*) (*fast*). (The

FIGURE 7.6   Level 2 Writing After Adult Underwriting Is Added

teacher leaves the last two lines blank for Michael to write and recognizes that if Michael can write a phrase he can write a sentence. Now that he can write the sentence, he can expand his story.) What else can your motor boat do? (If he can tell more, he can revise and write a whole story about something that happened with the motor boat—with a beginning, a middle, and an ending.) There are wonderful options for expansion, elaboration, adding detail and for creating volume.

The piece in Figure 7.6 might also present opportunities for instructional support for decoding:

Teacher: Michael. Let's stretch out the sounds in *boat* (holding the stretchable fabric). Here we go. /b/-/o/-/t/. How many sounds did you hear? *Michael shakes his head indicating that he's not quite sure.*
Teacher: Well, let's fingerspell it.

Together, they start with the thumb and match three sounds with three fingers. Then the teacher recommends that they try sound boxes, and they end up with the revised invented spelling for *boat* in Figure 7.7.

A comparison with the adult underwriting allows the teacher an opportunity to praise Michael's move from a Phase 2 to a Phase 3 spelling:

Teacher: Look, Michael, your new spelling had all three sounds—the beginning, the middle, and the ending sounds. It's almost just like the adult spelling and that's great. *Boat* is a pretty hard word for kindergarten. It's a second-grade word. Look, you have the *b,* and the *o,* and the *t* just like the adult spelling. Michael, that's very good kid spelling!

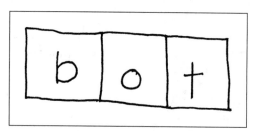

FIGURE 7.7   Letter Boxes for *boat* After Finger Spelling

Michael will read both the kid writing and the adult writing and eventually he will depend more on the memorization of the adult underwriting for reading (because it has more cues). Perhaps he'll learn to read the word *boat* on sight, and he may even learn to spell it. It's perfectly normal for kindergartners to read many more words than they can spell, because spelling the word is harder. The decoding growth for this Level 2 writer has come in small increments—from Michael's original Level 2 attention to beginning and ending sounds to his trying for the sound in the middle with a full alphabetic representation. This will be a giant move toward breaking the code and will lead to the brink of chunking and later full decoding knowledge and correct spelling. But for now, spelling BOT for *boat* is a very significant move forward.

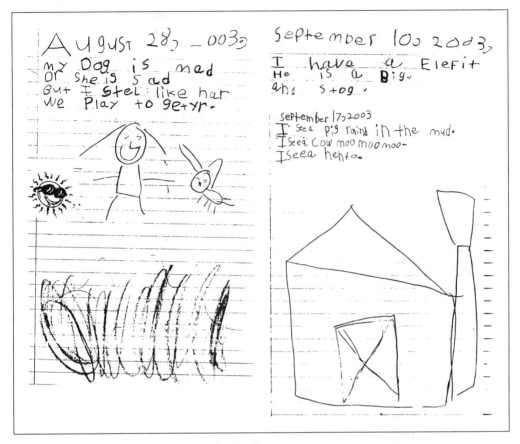

FIGURE 7.8   Sarah's Stories with Level 3 Spelling

Intervening, Supporting, and Teaching a Level 3 Writer

Sarah was exactly on grade level when I met with her in September. She had volunteered to be interviewed in front of about fifty teachers and administrators and I showed them the writing samples pictured in Figure 7.8, all short, three- or four-line stories with almost pure Level 3 invented spellings: STEL for *still*, HAR for *her*, TOGETTR for *together*, ROLIND for *rolling*, TO for *too* (Level 4) as well as ELEFIT for *elephant* and STOG for *strong*—these last with the preconsonantal nasal omission of the *n* (i.e., no *n* before a consonant), a Level 3 phenomenon.

Sarah read a selection from her basal fluently for me in front of our audience of teachers and from all signals appeared to be functioning exactly as expected on beginning first-grade level. As bright as she appeared, I thought it might be nice to model an instructional intervention for the group—not

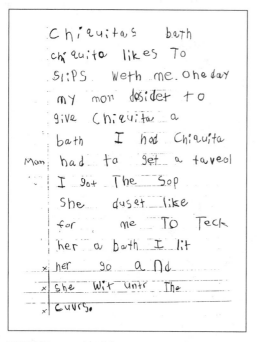

FIGURE 7.9   Sarah's Longer Story

intended to remediate, but simply to challenge her and take her one notch higher. I decided to start with writing and I intended to model the powerful writing-reading connection. Having bonded with Sarah and having discovered that she was enthralled with her little dog, Chiquita, we chatted at length in front of our audience about Chiquita—what Chiquita ate, where she slept; and when I asked Sarah to tell us a very funny story about Chiquita, she told the story of Chiquita's Bath. Writing in front of the audience of educators, I guided Sarah through a first-then-next-last framework, and in a few minutes she completed the wonderful fourteen-line story shown in Figure 7.9. Sarah had moved from three-line stories to a fourteen-line story right in front of our eyes. This production gave her brain a workout with fifty-one words for writing and reading as compared to her usual fifteen-word average. Not only was the coding volume enhanced as she coded many more words, the longer, more elaborate story full of voice and creativity was much better writing.

To further demonstrate the power of the writing/reading/spelling connection, we treated the audience to a spelling test as I checked Sarah's spelling of many of the CVC words from the basal unit—*nap, mat, hug,* and *sad*—and she spelled them all correctly. I chose to highlight the one sentence in her writing for the audience, "I let her go and she went under the covers," because it showed how Sarah was still developing control of the Level 3 preconsonantal nasal signaled by her omission of *n* before a consonant. (She spelled *went,* WIT.) And while she controlled short *a* and perhaps short *u,* short *e* was still a Level 3 phonetic spelling (i.e., WIT for *went,* LIT for *let.*) The sentence that I chose to highlight for working with these Level 3 coding issues is presented in Figure 7.10.

To work on the inclusion of *n* in the preconsonantal position (*went,* in this piece and *strong,* and *elephant* in the samples in Figure 7.8), I simply demonstrated stretching out the sounds of *went* with fabric, hand spelling, and moving to sound boxes. As pictured in Figure 7.11, with the finger-spelling and sound-box mediation, Sarah spelled *went* correctly.

We tried the same routine for *let* and Sarah's spelling is presented in Figure 7.12.

To nudge her forward, I simply showed her that the correct spelling for the short *e* sound in words

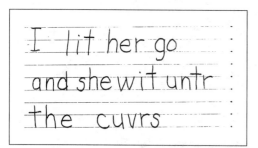

FIGURE 7.10   Decontextualized Sentence for Working with Coding Issues

like *let* is l-et, as in *bet, get,* and *pet,* and Sarah dazzled both her audience and me as we hand spelled and then word sorted the *let, bet, get, pet* word family. Then Sarah spelled these words as presented in Figure 7.13.

At the end of the session a teacher from the audience told me that our session was the best demonstration of the writing-reading connection and coding instruction that she had ever seen. I told her that once she followed the Instruction Blueprint, it would become second nature in her own classroom.

Intervening, Supporting, and Teaching a Level 4 Writer

Once writers start chunking, coding instruction goes in all kinds of directions. It's a time for more formal spelling instruction, continued word wall work for first graders, and great opportunities for word sorting. Children's writing often shows the teacher exactly what patterns need practice or verifies which of the patterns that have been taught and assessed in spelling lessons are not yet consolidated or transferred into the child's independent writing. Figure 7.14 shows the writing of a beginning second grader, Tameka, whom we can celebrate because Tameka has definitely broken the code.

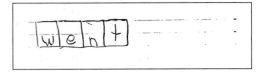

FIGURE 7.11 Letter Boxes for *went*

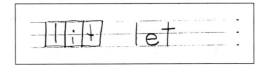

FIGURE 7.12 Letter Boxes for *let*

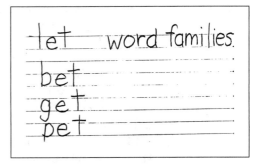

FIGURE 7.13 Sarah's Word Family Spellings

Good THING to Eat

I like STRALBARES and i like ORRANGE.
I like tomato SUPE and I like PECHIS.
I like apples and I like BROCLE.
I like COLEFLAWORE TO, you know.
I like corn and I like green BENES.
I like FRIDE CEKEN and I like BARBO Q CEKEN TO.
But most of all I like HO MAED SPOGATE.
THOSS things are good for you.
That's why I put them down.

FIGURE 7.14 Tameka's Level 4 Writing

While the piece is not particularly elaborate writing and shows dialect diversity and a few vocabulary constraints (i.e., *thing* instead of *things; orange* instead of *oranges; ho maded* instead of *homemade*) those would provide opportunities for learning in the writing revision. The sample demonstrated Tameka's high level of word knowledge and her use of a chunking strategy for invented spelling. Only about one-fourth of the words were misspelled, which is good compared to typical beginning second graders who may misspell one-third of the words in their independent writing (Gentry 2000b). The words Tameka spelled correctly included a number of sophisticated spelling patterns—*oo* in *good, ea* in *eat, -ike* in *like, kn* in *know, -or* in *corn, -ow* in *down.* She knew the contraction, *that's* and she spelled some polysyllabic words such as *tomato* and *apples* correctly. But the remarkable display was her liberal use of invented spellings in chunks of acceptable phonics patterns: STRAL-BAR-ES (perhaps dialect-influenced), OR-RANGE, PE-CHIS, BRO-CLE (perhaps reduced to two syllables in her dialect), CO-LE-FLA-WORE, and SPO-GA-TE. She had reached the point where good explicit spelling instruction would dramatically increase her word knowledge and writing (and reading) precision. Her liberal use of the *e*-marker pattern for long vowels in SUPE, WORE for the last syllable of *cauliflower,* BENES for *beans,* and FRIDE for *fried* amply demonstrated her readiness to master a plethora of correct choices for a myriad of patterns. She had broken the code, and now she needed the volume of reading and writing and the challenge and joy of word study and spelling to propel her to the stratosphere of "frog" reading and writing. For "frog" readers and writers who have broken the code, decoding spirals into spelling and word-specific knowledge, and like Tameka, "frog" writers who have just broken the code should be pretested in a second- and third-grade-level spelling curriculum such as the one presented in Figure 7.15, and happily challenged with the word-sorting activities such as the one she started in Figure 7.16.

Given a developmentally appropriate word study sheet in the word sort such as the one presented in Figure 7.17, one would begin by pretesting Tameka on the sixteen words in the sort. If she got most of them correct, it indicates that she knew the pattern, but if she missed about half of the words (carefully selected based on word-study research), the pattern is on her *instructional level,* and through teacher-led sorts, individual sorts, buddy sorts, and a little additional spelling study and word work, she would master the pattern and add to her repertoire of specific word knowledge (Gentry 2004). Tameka had broken the code and with explicit instruction, her word knowledge and use of the English language would soar. She would be on her own and on her way as a writer and reader. With more years of word study in elementary school, Tameka would master English print with potential to use language gracefully, powerfully, and eloquently as a lifelong reader, for her own benefit and perhaps for yours and for mine.

Spelling Curriculum for Grade 2

Revisited Patterns and Concepts Applied to New Vocabulary

Short-Vowel Patterns (CVC becomes solidified and is applied to a growing grade 2 sight vocabulary.)

Blends: *st, tr, dr, br, pr* (applied to a growing grade 2 sight vocabulary)

Digraphs: *sh, th (ch, wh, dr, nd, nt, ng)* (applied to a growing grade 2 sight vocabulary)

New Spelling Principles—Major New Learning

In second grade, short-vowel patterns introduced in first grade are revisited a second time, adding expanded second grade vocabulary. The major new learning in second grade is the discovery of pattern relationships in spelling, specifically, the basic CVCe and CVVC patterns for long vowels in single-syllable words. Children leave second grade having mastered myriad one-syllable vowel patterns. They learn that vowel sounds and the pattern of letters used for spelling the vowel sounds within a one-syllable word or a single syllable are related. Some high-frequency two-syllable words are introduced.

Basic One-Syllable Patterns for Each Long Vowel

    CVCe for each long vowel

    CVVC for each long vowel (*nail, bean, peep, pie, boat*)

Introduction of high-frequency two-syllable words such as *funny, mother, happy*

Fine-tuning the Grade 2 Curriculum

-aw, -ow, -ight, -ind, -ood, -ook, -ound, -own

-art , -ore

Double-consonant patterns *ff, ll, ss* (*puff, hill, grass*)

Compound words are introduced (*birthday, into*)

Homophones are introduced, such as *see, sea*

Inflectional endings *-s, -ed,* and *-ing* are introduced

FIGURE 7.15   Spelling Curriculum for Grades 2 and 3 (continues)

Spelling Curriculum for Grade 3

Revisited Patterns and Concepts Applied to New Vocabulary

Unusual Short-Vowel Patterns, as in *bread, healthy, weather*

Basic One-Syllable Patterns for Each Long Vowel

> CVCe for each long vowel (applied to a growing grade 3 sight vocabulary)

> CVVC for each long vowel, including *ai, ea, ee, ie, oa* (applied to a growing grade 3 sight vocabulary)

/s/ spelled *s* or *c*, as in *seven, city, circle*

r-controlled vowels, as in *hair, cheer, earth*

Contractions such as *didn't, weren't*

Spellings of /aw/ in *long, bought, lawn, because,* and *walking*

Ou, ow, oi, oy, as in *found, flower, oil, joy*

W, wh, as in *word, which, where, wheel*

New Spelling Principles—Major New Learning

By third grade, children have developed a large repertoire of correct spellings. Even by the beginning of third grade, over two-thirds of the words they use in writing are typically spelled correctly. Most one-syllable short vowels are spelled correctly and long vowels are spelled with a legitimate long-vowel pattern, albeit not necessarily the correct one. The important principle of meaning constancy is major new learning for grade three (Henderson [1985]1990). Students learn, for example, that *too, two,* and *to* or *by, buy,* and *bye* are allowable patterns for the respective homophones with consistency in spelling once the particular spelling pattern has been affixed with meaning. Meaning constancy is also solidified as they learn that a suffix such as *-ed* is a meaning unit that is always spelled "ed," even though it may be pronounced /t/, /d/, or /id/ in words such as *jumped, dodged,* or *traded.* They learn to expect meaning constancy in prefixes and suffixes and that meaning and letter patterns are related.

New learning includes the following:

Homophones such as *there, their, sent, cent*

Compound words such as *football, grandmother*

Prefixes and suffixes for word building such as *unhappy, preheat, repaint*

Changing *y* to *i* and adding *es*

Plurals *-s* and *-es*, as in *lips, cages, glasses*

Contractions

FIGURE 7.15   (continued)

A second major new principle for grade three is an inchoate understanding of how English spelling works at syllable junctures—particularly, when to double, or not to double, a consonant in two-syllable words.

Double consonants in two-syllable words such as *kitten, rabbit*

Consonant doubling and *e*-drop principle: *hopping* versus *hoping*

Consonant doubling with *er, est,* in words like *hotter, reddest*

Fine-tuning the Grade 3 Curriculum

Stress pattern relationships are introduced

Unstressed syllables *-er* and *-le* are introduced

Spellings for the reduced vowel, schwa, in unstressed syllables are introduced

Capital Letters in words such as *Wednesday, Thursday, March, June*
Unusual spellings of sound, such as /s/ and /j/ as in *circle, pass, giant, join*
-tch, as in *hatch, watch, patch*
Consonant blends *scr, spr, str, thr,* as in *scratch, throw*

FIGURE 7.15 (continued)

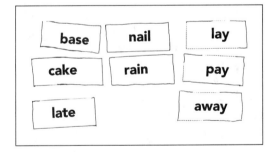

FIGURE 7.16 The First Stages of a Word Sort

Sample Long Vowels   able—flame—bay—mail

Cut the word study sheet into word cards. Sort these words into four
columns: words like *able,* words like *flame,* words like *bay,* and words
like *mail.*

able	afraid	bay	flame
gray	mail	main	paint
ray	spray	wait	place
cage	cape	table	fable

FIGURE 7.17   Study Word Sheet for a Word Sort

8

Reforming Kindergartens by Teaching Writing—Visions and Voices from the Pioneers—Plus Learning About *Love*

Connor's mother, Rosemarie Jensen, a former first grade teacher, captured an important moment and shared it with me in an email:

> Connor totally surprised me today. We were making a card for his friend and he wrote:
>
> ### HAPE BRFDA BUDE
>
> But here's the best part. He looks at me squinting out of one eye with a gesture evoking total seriousness and confidence, then lowering his voice he whispers, "I know how to spell *love*."
>
> "Really?" I said.
>
> "Yes," he says, "L-U-V-E."
>
> Then he writes it:
>
> ### LUVE Connor.
>
> I was so surprised and so proud. I tell you because so few people can appreciate it. He surprises me daily. I guess Rick and I are doing something right!

Everyone—especially parents and educators—should appreciate what Connor can do. This five-year-old, who starts kindergarten in three months, can write and he can read what he has written. Connor is on the verge of breaking the code.

When Connor enters kindergarten, he will have a repertoire of stories and nursery rhymes that he reads from memory along with a history of being read to and of celebrating books. He will enter kindergarten with accomplishments far beyond ability to write his name, and he'll be intrigued and interested in writing and reading. He will know a lot about letters and sounds and will do the voice-to-print match. Letter-sound matches will already characterize his invented spellings. He will enter kindergarten only one level away from breaking the code—fully a year ahead of many of his classmates. Connor will have other interests too; while he has growing interest in writing and reading, he would rather do anything that involves running and a ball. Will Connor find the support that will continue his personal journey to literacy once he goes to school? I suspect his parents will insist upon it. And if he enters a kindergarten classroom where the teacher is teaching writing and supporting young writers—his classmates will all learn to do what he can do, and he will be one of their teachers. Writing in kindergarten provides good literacy preparation for all children. Kindergarten classrooms where children write every day provide opportunities for children at all the tadpole levels to thrive. Whether they come as advanced as Connor, or are just beginning to grow by writing their names for the first time, early writing will provide the foundation for their literacy learning. The tadpole writers in kindergarten will be readers by the end of first grade—with many of them becoming skilled readers even sooner.

I believe we are in the midst of a writing reformation in kindergarten classrooms. Interest in bringing independent writing into kindergarten classrooms needs to be more than a hot topic in literacy education. It needs to be more than something relegated to a few gifted kindergarten teachers—it needs to be standard practice. In the highly influential report on how best to teach children to read, *Preventing Reading Difficulties in Young Children* (Snow, Burns, and Griffin 1998), the committee compiling the report recognized the merit of writing in the kindergarten but failed to see that writing is actually imperative. In the section on instructional strategies in kindergartens, the report cited important findings about kindergarten writing:

> Scanlon and Vellutino (in press) found that, of all the various foci of language arts instruction observed in the kindergarten classroom, only the proportion of time that was devoted to analyzing the internal structure of spoken and written words reliably predicted differences in reading achievement at the end of first grade. (186)

In the next few paragraphs they go on to report:

> Another kindergarten activity that promotes both letter knowledge and phonological awareness is writing. In many kindergarten classrooms, children are encouraged to compose and write independently. Interestingly, in the aforementioned Scanlon and Vellutino study, writing was the context in which word analysis most often took place, typically as using phonological analysis in the service of "figuring out" the spelling of words. At the earliest stages, writing may consist of scribbling or

strings of letter-like forms. If opportunities to write are ample and well complemented by other literacy activities and alphabetic instruction, kindergarteners should be using real letters to spell words phonetically before the school year is out. (187)

But did the report go far enough? What has become clearer since that publication is that in kindergarten classrooms that are organized for writing, where teachers teach and support writing explicitly, the kindergarten "accomplishments in reading" go far beyond those listed in the report such as writing names, most of the letters, some dictated words, and expressing meaning in invented spelling (Snow, Burns, and Griffin 1998). The "reading accomplishments" in kindergarten classrooms where ample writing occurs include many first-grade accomplishments such as creating written text for others to read and "real" reading itself. While the report is full of powerful recommendations, it falls short in not making the reading-writing connection explicit, only reporting the tip of the iceberg. In the final analysis, appropriate focus on writing combines attention to breaking the code with attention to constructing meaning and developing fluency. It's the whole package. Writing in kindergarten is the secret to the reading-writing connection and the solution to successful beginning reading instruction in today's schools.

In this chapter we listen to the voices of experts. I did not find the pioneers of teaching writing in kindergarten so often among academics or neuroscientists as I found them in kindergarten classrooms all across America. I found a grassroots movement promulgated by one of America's most powerful unsung resources, a core of smart, self-directed, reflective, continually learning, highly professional, dedicated, passionate, intelligent guardians of true educational reform—teachers who respond to the needs of children. They may be overworked and underpaid (Eggers and Moulthrop 2005) and still lack the universal respect they deserve, yet many teachers read the research and continue to learn, and some of them spend a lifetime growing in expertise behind the closed doors of their classrooms even as they rise up to meet the demands of teaching the children in their midst. It is kindergarten teachers, such as the voices you hear in this chapter, who have ushered writing reform into American kindergarten classrooms and discovered the reading-writing connection. These harbingers of curriculum reform, many of whom stepped into unhinged kindergarten curricula teetering on the brink of disaster, were reading the research and doing sensible things even before the university academics, neuroscientists, and state and federal governments joined in the effort to shore up reading curricula. Notably, two of the most prominent were career professionals in the school district of Philadelphia, Eileen Feldgus and Isabell Cardonick, where Isabell still teaches kindergarten.

In the mid-1990s Eileen Feldgus sent me the manuscript of a book she and Isabell had written with a request to read and give them some feedback. I was also asked to provide a blurb for the cover. What I found was the beginnings of a movement. From the moment I read the book I recognized that these two teachers in Philadelphia (Eileen had moved to the Central Office and by then had a doctorate in education from the University of Pennsylvania) were issuing in a paradigm shift in American kindergarten education by making the reading-writing connection. I hoped their book, *Kid Writing* (1999), would change a nation of kindergarten teachers. To me, they were answering Marie Clay's 1982 call to find the writing connection to reading instruction, that is, to capitalize on the potential for beginning writing to complement the early reading program. In *Kid Writing,* I could see the reading-writing connection explicitly laid out in the work they were doing. Not only had they found it, they were watching it unfold by monitoring the changes they saw in beginning writers with the use of my Monster Test, a quick assessment of reading and writing phases explicated herewith in the Instructional Blueprint (see the Appendix). Taking the Monster Test far beyond a simple measure of children's growth in invented spelling, they were using it as an easy way to monitor children's writing and reading growth, and growth in phonics. They were tracking children's progress in breaking the code.

I think their story is somewhat remarkable. Working side-by-side as kindergarten teachers beginning in 1980 and later with the collaboration of other teachers in the Philadelphia Writing Project, they developed a writing workshop format for kindergarten, which they describe in their book. *Kid Writing* made writing a mainstay of the kindergarten experience and provided teachers supportive structures so children were joyfully writing and reading all day long—meaningfully, in response to literature, in documenting science observations, in writing notes to solve social issues, and in scores of other meaningful writing opportunities. Feldgus and Cardonick discovered for themselves that for many children, "writing is the gateway to understanding how reading works" (1999, 6). But their work did not grow out of a vacuum. Over the years they had synthesized Regie Routman (1991), Vygotsky (1978), Bruner (1981), Dyson (1989), Graves (1983), Calkins (1986), Atwell (1987), Fountas and Pinnell (1996), Harste, Woodward, and Burke (1981), McKenzie (1986), Fletcher (1993), Gentry (1985, 2000b at that time "in press"), and many others to provide a deep theoretical and research-based synthesis to their practical experience. In their forty-five-minute writing workshop they made invented spelling the key to independent writing. Without knowing it, perhaps, the most powerful element of their program was their addition of adult underwriting, which connected the child's writing to real reading. By adding the adult version to multiple opportunities for children to write and read their short takes on their meaningful experiences, these teachers provided a rich context for personal attention to each child as the child demonstrated to them his or her level of literacy accomplishment. They let the children's writing tell them what the children knew (or did not know) and they responded to the developing tadpole with good teaching. The following simple framework emerged for a kindergarten writing workshop.

   I. Drawing

  II. Writing in invented spelling (with teacher support for the "stretching through" process—writing with support and modeling)

 III. Adult underwriting (an adult written version at the bottom of the page where the teacher writes the child's story using conventional writing while praising children's approximations)

 IV. Mini-lessons—appropriate literacy instruction growing out of the writing

  V. Reading and rereading with teacher help

 VI. Sharing

Children started writing from the first day of school, keeping a writing journal, and soon they were writing all across the curriculum: book writing, riddle writing, class books, math experiments, tally surveys, results of the weighing station, story murals, story comparisons, with all kinds of science, math, health, and social studies connections. They adapted what they called a "Phonics Inventory Assessment" from Gentry (2000b), which connected directly to the reading curriculum and made the Monster Test (Gentry 1985) and my stages of developmental spelling a centerpiece for monitoring each child's literacy development. They even found the system remarkably useful for teaching underprepared children to write and read. As they report:

> A strength of using a developmental (writing) scale for assessing children's writing is that the teacher can visually show a child's progress in a way that is understandable to children and parents. Teachers can, at a glance, determine appropriate learning goals for children. Actually assessing and entering the information on the scale requires minimal teacher time and can be done at the conference as the child, parent, and teacher look at the writing sample together. Using a developmental scale also allows the teacher to determine the child's progress and the progress of the class in relationship to a district's expectations, thereby serving a data collection function. (125)

A typical school day followed the schedule presented in Figure 8.1.

Isabell Cardonick recently provided the following description of a typical school day in her classroom today:

> In a typical day, we work with groups of children who've completed enough of their drawings to anchor their story ideas. Moving from one child to the next and back again, using the moving target, we help them—and they help each other—to hear the phonemes, chunks, and blends, which we call sticky letters, needed in their writing. Once they are able to use sensible phonetic spelling, they may write independently.

The number of children who complete a journal entry each day is a function of the number of students, the proportion of students who are

8:45–8:50	Attendance board, calendar, and schedule check
8:50–9:40	Writing workshop
	Guided or independent writing
	Adult underwriting
	Minilessons
	Minisharing
9:40–10:15	Integrated curriculum unit (focus science or social studies)
	KWL (teacher modeling of writing and interactive writing)
	Observations of science projects
	Dramatization of process
10:15–10:30	Playground
10:30–11:15	Reading workshop
	Read-aloud
	Shared reading (stories and/or songs or poetry on charts)
	Independent reading (paired or independent reading; four to five children may be involved in a guided reading group)
11:15–12:00	Mathematics
	Model lesson
	Small groups or individual exploration
	Meeting on carpet to share and record
12:00–12:45	Lunch
12:45–1:00	Meeting/message time (teacher modeling of writing and interactive writing)
1:00–1:30	Choice/center time
1:30–2:00	Literature study/dramatization
2:00–2:45	Gym, music, health, other specials
2:45	Preparation for dismissal

FIGURE 8.1   Feldgus and Cardonick Sample Schedule

independent writers, the number of volunteers, and the amount of time allotted to writing workshop. In my full day program with 30 students and 1 or 2 adult volunteers, about half of the children complete their writing each day. But this is not "down" time for the other children. They are also learning by listening and helping while drawing their own detailed pictures for the next day's writing workshop. Of course, with additional volunteers or with smaller class size, every child can complete a journal entry every day. And, because it is such a joyful experience, many children opt to kid write during choice time. (Personal communication July 2, 2005)

In retrospect I believe it is unfortunate that *Kid Writing,* which is as fresh today as it was in 1999, grew out of the era of the reading wars and was presented as an alternative to packaged phonics programs. It more aptly should be presented as a framework for making the reading-writing connection and as a mainstay of kindergarten reading instruction. Early writing is, for many

children, the best way to become familiar with the structural elements and orga-
nization of print, a recognized goal for fostering literacy (Snow, Griffin, and
Burns 1998, 179). Early writing has the added dimension of motivating children to be literate and enabling them to feel successful as literacy learners. That
said, the systematic presentation of phonics instruction in *Kid Writing*, based on
assessment of children's continuing growth, is still very relevant as part of the
professional conversation.

Other groups were recognizing the power of teaching writing from the beginning, notably, the Teachers College Reading and Writing Project in New York
City under the leadership of Lucy Calkins. Years of collaboration and intense
staff development led this group to develop a yearlong writing curriculum. In a
schedule that supported forty-five minutes to one hour per day of kindergarten
writing, kindergarten children and teachers followed Calkins' (2005) common-
sense philosophy:

> When we teach someone to do anything—whether it's to play the oboe,
> to swim, to make pottery—the learner needs to be doing the thing, and
> we as teachers, need to establish structures within which learners do the
> work. (60)

Starting with the notion that the learner "should be doing the thing," Teachers
College Reading and Writing Project developed month-long units of study
where children learn to write within a particular genre or learn aspects of the
writing process. To paraphrase Calkins, children are nudged toward writing with
expected stamina and volume (33), and they do it in a setting where minilessons, conferencing, and assessment guide the learning. A simple set of basic
routines comprises a scaffold for the Teachers College Reading and Writing Project framework:

1. Teachers assign writing spots and send children off to write.
2. Writers write their names on the paper and date each day's work.
3. They choose a topic.
4. They write it.
5. They revise or confer with the teacher. Much of the learning and teaching
   happens during the conference and in minilessons.
6. They put the paper in a finished work section.
7. They begin a new piece.
8. Children are expected to do about two pieces per week.

In their writing workshop, children often sit next to a long-term partner,
with higher- or lower-level writing ability for the advantage of the lower-level
writer. Both tables and folders are color-coded. Writing folders are kept the
entire year serving as a vehicle for assessment. There's a writing toolbox and table monitor. Pencils are sharpened before the workshop begins and there is a

writing center where paper and writing materials are stored. The volume of writing increases by the end of kindergarten with expected volume over the kindergarten year following templates such as the one in Figure 8.2.

What I find most appealing in frameworks for beginning writing in kindergarten is the power for teaching all aspects of beginning literacy through the reading and writing connection that teachers discover in the craft of beginning writing. Good things happen in kindergartens where writing is connected with reading. Early writing not only complements the reading program, it ensures early reading success.

A Glimpse into Writing-Reading Kindergarten Classrooms

What does it look like to walk into a kindergarten classroom where the reading-writing connection is powerfully in evidence? I asked a few of the experts to invite you in for a look and to share some of their favorite ideas.

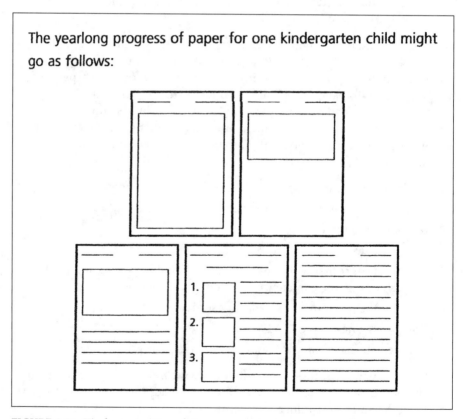

FIGURE 8.2   Kindergarten Templates

Shelly Bromwich—Iowa

I asked Shelly to describe the opportunities she uses for making the reading-writing connection and to tell about special opportunities she finds for teaching writing. A look at Shelly's daily schedule shows the concept of kindergarteners "joyfully reading and writing all day long." She sent me the following schedule.

Shelly Bromwich's Pre-K/Kindergarten Schedule

8:20–9:00 Center Time. All centers are open. Children choose from various centers around the classroom—unit center, math center, science center, literacy center, social studies center, dramatic play loft, blocks, painting, doll house, puppets, and Legos. The kids think the science centers are awesome! There they will find the pendulum, water activity, cooking, ramps, target ball, bubbles, and an activity for blowing with straws. Activities for discovery about the forces of air are the science centers that we have been doing lately. I use a vacuum cleaner that blows air out instead of in and children have been levitating all sorts of things!

The children write about what goes on during our center time. They love writing about their experiments. I also take photographs of children at center time and at the same time, I write notes on what the children said and what interactions they had with the materials. After developing the photos, I have the children look at them, and ask them to write and share with me any other ideas about what they are doing in the picture. The photo and commentary allow for the creation of documentation boards where standards and benchmarks are listed and documented. The documentation board documents writing progress as well. Lower-level writers label a "P" for the "pendulum" while at a center, while those that are more advanced write descriptions of their experiments. It is a great way to integrate literacy into all aspects of our classroom!

My students choose whatever center they would like to visit, though we have regulations and expectations. Often the class comes up with particular center rules if we find it necessary. Involving children in making the rules fosters self-regulation and promotes better behavior in the classroom.

9:00–9:30 Group Time. We start every day with the "Name Game" (described later). After our classroom meeting and discussion on topics of interest, I love to sing and read stories that correlate with our theme. We do "sharing" through "show and tell" during group time following a schedule, which allows several children to be responsible for share time each day. (In a note from Eileen Feldgus she reminds us that creating units around themes is powerful. "Teachers often rely on basal anthology themes that are boring rather than real inquiry/explorations such as spiders, skyscrapers, nighttime, flowers, oceans, or reptiles.")

9:30–10:00. Specials

 Monday—Music Class

 Tuesday—Library

 Thursday—Guidance (Our school counselor comes in and talks about feelings and important social issues.)

 Friday—Swimming (We are lucky, our school has a pool!)

 Friday—Art

10:00–10:10 Snack Time.

10:10–10:30 Recess.

10:30–11:00 Literacy Activities. We work in large and small groups on various literacy lessons and activities. I love using language experience charts to share student ideas with the class. Using various questions to "provoke thought" that go with each theme we study, I write the questions at the top of chart paper, and invite each child to express his or her ideas. I hang the language experience charts all over the room and children love to revisit these charts to see what they said, or to see what their friend said. They read them and read them and read them. Parents love to come in and read the charts too!

11:00 Pre-Kindergarten goes home.

11:00–11:15 Math manipulatives. Children experiment with various math manipulatives to expand their math knowledge and creativity.

11:15–11:30 Kindergarten sharing.

11:30–12:00 Recess.

12:00–12:30 Lunch.

12:30–1:00 Quiet Reading/Writing Time. During this time, I try to sit by each child and have them read to me. I do one-on-one whisper reading, take running records, and use various reading strategies with my students. This is also a wonderful time to do adult underwriting, sitting quietly with one or two students, which offers a powerful opportunity for differentiated, explicit, direct instruction. It's time for me to observe individuals read and time for them to practice.

(Monday and Wednesday) **12:45–1:00 Phonological Awareness.** Our speech teacher comes into our room and teaches various phonological skills through games and activities. (This may be construed as the day's minilesson for the beginning of writing workshop.)

1:00–1:25 Writing Workshop. All children write for twenty minutes each day. I do conferences, minilessons, and sharing. At the beginning of the year the minilessons focus on "Letter People" for teaching letters and sounds.

1:25–1:30 Snack

1:30–2:00 Math. I use an excellent balanced math curriculum for delivering math concepts using hands-on manipulatives.

2:00–2:30 P.E. We have physical education every day except Thursday, when we have swimming for kindergarten students.

2:30–3:00 Center Time. All centers are open (as listed above). I think it is important to start the day and end with day with children being able to choose what they want to do. Children need choice in their lives, and allowing them to make choices helps them enjoy learning. Since we write about our activities in centers, kid writing and adult underwriting are prominent aspects of the center activity.

3:00 Dismissal

The Name Game. Perhaps the most important thing that I can do for my Pre-K/Kindergarten students is to give them the skills and confidence needed to succeed with literacy. One vehicle I find extremely useful is the "Name Game," which I have played in my classroom for several years. I print out all of the children's names on $1\frac{1}{2}$-inch-by-1-inch name cards, laminate them, put magnet strips on the back (found at a super mart or craft store), and stick these name magnets to an $8\frac{1}{2}$-inch-by-11-inch cookie sheet. Since I teach a multiage looping Pre-K/Kindergarten, I use a separate cookie sheet for each group. The cookie sheet may be placed on the ledge of an easel and easily moved anywhere in the room. At group time, I tell the children that we are going to play the Name Game. When I hold up each child's name, the children love to try to be the first to shout out a name. I sing various tunes, rhymes and rhythms to spice up the game. For example, when we do a nursery rhyme unit, I substitute a name for "Jack": "Tarrel be nimble, Tarrel be quick, Tarrel jump over the candle stick." Then I have a real candle stick that the child jumps over holding his name tag or substituting it for "Jack" in the chart. By the middle of the school year, or earlier some years, every child can read all of their friends' names. When the children are able to recognize their classmates' names, I cover the entire name except the first letter. I may ask, "Whose name do you think this might be?" Children quickly learn to recognize their own and others' first initial letter and beginning sound. By the end of the year we may we working with high-frequency spelling chunks in the names. I continue challenging them and changing the Name Game to fit their needs, keeping them guessing and excited about learning and reading.

Over the years I have found that children love the Name Game. "Wow, do you realize that all of you are readers!" I say to them at the beginning of the year. "If you can read your own name, you are a reader!"

Last year I had a child who seemed sad on the second day of school. I said, "You look sad, what is the matter?" She explained that she thought she was going to learn how to read in kindergarten, and that it was the second day of school, and she did not know how to read! We gathered and had a group talk about how she was feeling. I told her everyone is smart when they come to school, so no one should be worried. "We are all smart here," I said, "and we already know how to read because we can read names in the Name Game!" She looked up at me and smiled, and the sadness melted away from her face. "We'll only become smarter as the year goes on," I promised, "so no one should worry!"

The Name Game magnet board can be used for many purposes, allowing children countless meaningful opportunities to read the names over and over until they recognize many names and word parts automatically. I use these magnet name cards for attendance ("here" and "absent") and for lunch count activity. Each morning when the children arrive, they find their name card and put it in a column for "hot lunch" (lunch bought at school) or "cold lunch" (lunch brought from home). This valuable early childhood literacy activity also teaches responsibility, and since the board is often used for voting purposes, it provides an early civics lesson on democratic principles. For example, I may have the students vote for what book they would like me to read to the class on a particular day. They come up, find their name, and use their magnetic name card to vote for the book of their choice. The original idea to use name cards came from my mentor and friend, Dr. Rheta DeVries at the Regents' Centers for Early Developmental Education at the University of Northern Iowa.

Isabell Cardonick and Eileen Feldgus—Philadelphia

When presenting some of their favorite techniques, Cardonick and Feldgus reminded me that literacy activities change over the year, and certainly, by midyear, guided reading is happening in many kindergartens and becomes prominent in the schedule.

Word Walls. Word walls are powerful. They are multimodal, often with clapping and chanting the spellings, and the repeated attention to a few high-frequency words provides the repetition that the brain needs to commit these words to memory. We find that many teachers have questions about effective use of word walls. Eileen and I feel that color-coding provides a crutch, which keeps the children from exercising their own problem-solving strategies. Secondly, we believe only high-frequency words—not names—should be included. Adding names dilutes the word wall, making it more difficult and time consuming to find the high-frequency words. We do understand the value of names in teaching phonics. When names are together in one place in the classroom—on a sign-in board, a name wall, or a block graph—children can locate names much more quickly. Names are so important, in fact, that I strive to keep nametags on children all year long. We find that clear plastic nametags with swivel clips work best. Chunks, blends and digraphs can easily be highlighted on these nametags as they come up in minilessons. When I get my new class list, I check the names to look for phonics opportunities! I'm always happy to get an Austin for the *au*, or a Shane for the *sh*. I'm not as excited about the name Christine because it confuses the *ch!*

Of course, we need to teach letter and sound correspondences explicitly. I use my alphabet chart to head up my word wall as shown in the photo in Figure 8.3.

We follow the chart as we do a phonetic alphabet song every day, so the children are very familiar with the chart. I start by posting only one word under any particular letter. The children help me figure out where to place the word. If they own the process of creating the word wall, they are more likely to know

FIGURE 8.3   Isabell Cardonick's Word Wall

how to use it. I teach the children how to find the word by listening for the first sound, identifying the corresponding letter, and finding that letter on the wall. When a new word is added and there are already one or more words under that letter, I model (through a think-aloud) how to differentiate between the words. For example, suppose the word *could* appears in someone's writing journal and I decide to add it to the word wall. Suppose that the words *can* and *come* are already there. I would first ask the children where I should post *could*, pointing out that if I put it under a letter other than *c*, it will be hard to find when needed. I then might say, "Hmmm. Now we have three words under the letter *c*. If I write the wrong word, then my story might not make sense. Let me think about how I can tell them apart. First, I think I'll listen for the ending sound. *Could*. I hear a /d/ at the end. That sound is made with a *d*. So it must be this word" (pointing to the word *could*). If there are two words with the same beginning and ending sound, I would point that out and explain that we have to think about other features of the word—perhaps a blend or a chunk. (By the way, I call blends "sticky letters." It seems to really help the children understand the concept and get beyond placing a vowel or *schwa* sound in the middle, such as *ber* instead of *br*, for example.) Even beginning writers are much more fluent once they know some words from memory, so we add about two words per week and give them lots and lots of practice.

Moving Targets. We find that kids really benefit when we use a "Moving Target" process during the kid writing. We emphasize (louder and longer) the sound that we're up to in the word, keeping it in the context of the word, and refer to this target sound as a *moving target*. We do not separate the sound. Much like Richard Gentry recommends when he suggests that good teachers must attend to the appropriate type and timing of instruction for particular phases, we only emphasize the sounds that we think the child we're working with has a chance of figuring out. That's why the target keeps moving. It may be beginning or beginning and ending sounds, a medial sound, or eventually the target may be recognition of a chunk. As we pause at each sound we decide to emphasize, we say, "Write what you think you hear." We do not tell the child what letter to write. In using this process with the children, we teach them how to do the stretching themselves. It's just like holding their hands when they're first learning to walk.

Teaching Chunks. I also teach the children how to figure out spellings through analogies to word wall words. I might say something like, "If you can spell *look*, then you can spell *cook*." Or "What word can I use to figure out how to spell *toy*? Hmmm. Since *toy* rhymes with *boy*, I'll use that."

I love making Word Family Houses for teaching chunks, an idea that Eileen and I developed presented in Figure 8.4.

FIGURE 8.4   Making Word Family Houses

Tape together 9-by-12-inch pieces of cardboard accordion style to make a free standing display. Draw a house on each section and write a rime (-*ill*, -*ell*, -*at*, etc.) on each roof. Have children list words that rhyme in each house as the words arise in reading and writing.

A great way for taking teaching chunks a step farther is to make the roof of the house be a Dr. Seuss hat. When kids give nonsense rhyming words, we call them "Dr. Seuss words" and kids write them on the hat. Conceptually, this separates the "real words" from the "nonsense words."

Another wonderful way to teach high-frequency chunks is to highlight them on the nametag when they appear in a child's name. Figure 8.5 shows my own highlighted nametags which are used for teaching -*ick* (in Cardonick) and -*ell* (in Isabell).

The Monster Test. Eileen and I made the Monster Test a centerpiece of our assessment. The pictures in Figure 8.6 show how easy it is to track each child's progress. Of course we track other aspects of writing growth, but for breaking the code, the Monster Test is easy to use and powerfully informative.

Rosemarie Jensen and Dot Solenski—Florida

Dot Solenski was my friend, colleague, and collaborator long before this extraordinary kindergarten teacher taught my daughter in kindergarten. When I

FIGURE 8.5   Teaching the *-ick* and *-ell* Chunks

was teaching first grade alongside her several years ago, we searched for authentic ways to motivate beginning writers. One of our best projects was Memory Photo Albums.

Memory Photo Albums. First we make each child a Memory Photo Album and then we take photos in the classroom of each child to be pasted in the album. The child looks at the picture and writes captions or stories about what he or she was doing in the picture. It's a wonderful memento at the end of the year not only of the activities that the child participated in, but also for seeing the progression of each child's spelling and writing development. For this project, we enlist the help of parents by asking them to donate one roll of film and to sign up to develop the roll. We ask them to order double prints because most pictures have several children in them and can be placed in more than one child's book. I three-hole punch paper and place the pages in Duo Tang folders to make my albums. Dot pastes her class pictures in black composition books. Figure 8.7 shows photos of my daughter Danielle's album, completed while she was in Dot's kindergarten.

Little Book Publishing. Publishing is an important part of the writing process and we found that beginning writers loved to be published. We began Little Book Publishing in our kindergarten and first grade classes ten years ago and found that publishing empowered even beginners as writers and readers. Sometimes used in addition to underwriting and sometimes in place of it, we make a computer-generated adult-written version of each child's story using conventional writing that the children can read, a version of Language Experience Approach. We see power in handing our students their stories the very next day after they are written in class. These little books can be put in their book boxes and read over and over—to themselves, to each other, and to their buddies in other

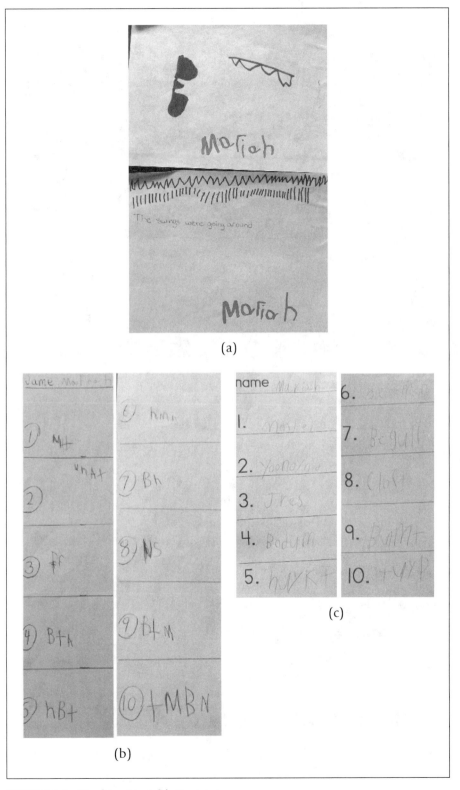

FIGURE 8.6 Tracking Mariah's Progress

(a) Baseline sample; (b) December Monster Test; (c) June Monster Test; (d) September Monster Test; (e) May Journal.

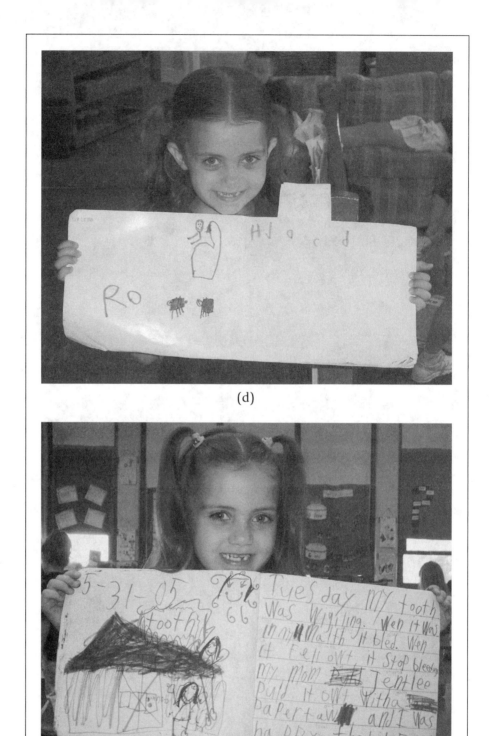

(d)

(e)

FIGURE 8.6 (continued)

classrooms, building their confidence as writers and as readers. While little book publishing without a doubt is a lot of work, we made it easier on ourselves by enlisting the help of parents. Parents premake the books so that all we do is add the writing and then the child makes the illustrations. The process involves stapling several sheets of blank white paper into folded construction paper covers. Using an IBICO binding machine, we train one or two parents to bind several sheets of paper between oaktag covers. At the end of each day, students who finish working on a piece at our guided writing tables may bring them for publishing. We simply type their stories into the computer in single line sentences, print them, cut them out, and paste the sentences on each page. Sometimes parents come in early to help. The booklets are treasures. Figure 8.8 shows one of my favorite books created by Danielle in Dot's classroom.

There are now hundreds of kindergarten teachers creating reading/writing classrooms like the ones these extraordinary teachers have shared in this chapter. It's the kind of classroom into which all kindergarten children should be invited—a nurturing environment for learning, an environment for breaking the code, and an environment that will spew forth children who are readers.

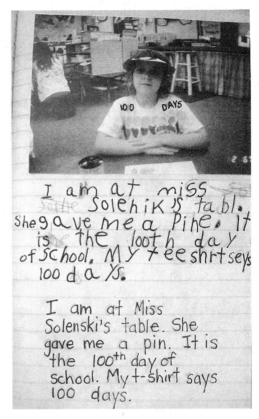

FIGURE 8.7   Danielle's Photo Album

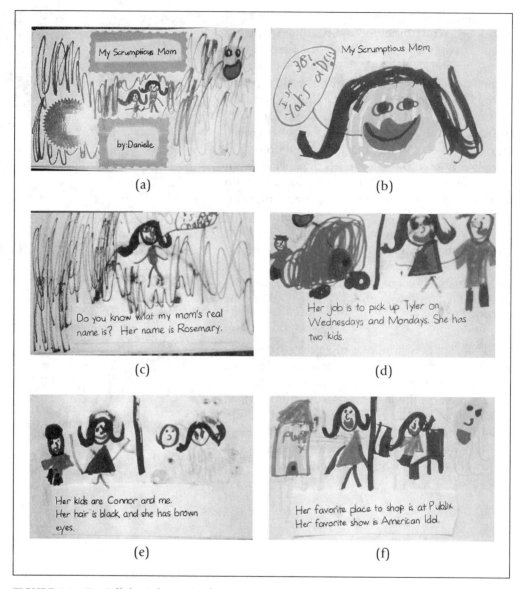

FIGURE 8.8   Danielle's Little Book After Publication

(a) Title Page: My Scrumptious Mom, by: Danielle (b) Page 2: My Scrumptious Mom (in bubble "I'm 38 YARS old!") (c) Page 2: Do you know what my mom's real name is? Her name is Rosemary. (d) Page 3: Her job is to pick up Tyler on Wednesdays and Mondays. She has two kids. (e) Page 4: Her kids are Connor and me. Her hair is black and she has brown eyes. (f) Page 5: Her favorite place to shop is at Publix. Her favorite show is American Idol.

FIGURE 8.8 (continued)

(g) Page 6: She can be really fancy sometimes. My mom's dad is our grandpa. (h) Page 7: Ro drives a van. Ro is afraid of cockroaches. (i) Page 8: She likes to date my dad. She is a tremendous mom. (j) Page 9: She the most important job in the world that is taking care of us. (k) Page 10: Mom used to be a teacher and I really love her.

9

"The Remedy Should Be Applied Where the Evil Commences," Otherwise We're in Trouble!

"The remedy should be applied where the evil commences," is a quote about early intervention. I found it in *McGuffey's Fourth Eclectic Reader*—page ten. I had spent the last seven months thinking about the findings of neuroscientists and revelations of brain scan technology. Now I was attempting to bring to bear my thirty-some-year career of research and practice regarding what might be important to include in a book for reading teachers about teaching beginning readers and writers to break the code. One day in the last month of my writing with three-fourths of my work completed, I was searching for a book in my downstairs office and I happened upon seven antique books that I have standing between bookends at the end of an oversized desk. They were put there to be inspirational and decorative. Some of the books belonged to my great-grandfather and to my grandmother who were both reading teachers. Now I found myself leafing through these books my ancestors had used in their teaching. It occurred to me that since both my grandmother and great-grandfather had been reading teachers in the 1800s, there ought to be something in the books they used to teach reading that connected to what I was currently doing. Brain scan technology notwithstanding, the brains in the children they taught over one hundred years ago probably were just like the brains of children today. I should find some evidence of what I was recommending for today's reading teachers resembling aspects of what they had done, because I knew they had been successful. Grandma had told me they were. It occurred to me that I was cross-referencing my own work and brain scan technology with history, and I wondered if there might be a connection. There was.

I picked out my favorite for closer inspection, an 1857 edition of *McGuffey's New Fourth Eclectic Reader: Instructive Lessons for the Young*, by W. H. McGuffey. The cover page is inscribed by my great-grandfather, Solomon O'Briant, a schoolmaster in a one-room schoolhouse. On the blank page before it, peeking out from what remains of the front cover is my grandmother's name, Rosa Bella O'Briant. I think her name was written there by her father and dated March 25, eighteen ninety-something—the last number being obliterated so that I can't quite make out the date. I'm guessing the date was when he presented the book to her and taught her to read from it. She might have used this book to teach when she became the youngest teacher ever to be commissioned in the state of North Carolina, at the age of seventeen.

There were other personal connections to this ancient tome that I have loved since Grandma showed me the book when I was a little boy. It was already marked with the rich patina of age, faded, musty, tattered, and since my earliest memory in its current imperfect state with half of the front cover missing. The book's author, William H. McGuffey, LL.D., was the namesake of The McGuffey Reading Center at the University of Virginia, where I received my Ph.D. in reading education. Professor McGuffey, who taught there more than a century before I enrolled in the program he founded, was, of course, the author of the famous *McGuffey Readers*, thought to have ushered American teachers into the new age of reading instruction. What would I find that connected William H. McGuffey, Great Grandpa Sol, and my beloved Grandma Rosa in whose house I grew up, whom I loved dearly, and whose hand I had held and forehead I kissed as she drew her last breath—the same one who called out my spelling words. What connected them to the venerable educational theory and research and the brain research that was shaking reading education over one hundred years later? I found plenty!

What I found front and center—literally—are lessons in chunking. I found code instruction and meaning coexisting. I found appeals to the teacher to do what in the pages of the present book I have described as brain-based instruction. Placed right up front in the introductory pages on page 10, for example, is a section written in all caps entitled ARTICULATION. Here I found Professor McGuffey's venerated instructions to reading teachers: "Distinct and correct ARTICULATION lies at the foundation of all excellence in reading, conversation, and public speaking," he had written, and to follow were *nineteen pages of chunking lessons!* Chunking was the foundation, or as I had stated earlier in the already written pages of this 2006 edition, the important lowest level of processing. McGuffey had placed chunking and coding instruction right up front. Sensibly he had combined it with meaning and, I think, with writing. Here he had single syllable and polysyllabic words presented in practice exercises so students might practice reading with the goal of *seeing them in the brain*. The kind of instructional lessons for fourth graders Bhattacharya and Ehri were calling for in their research paper entitled "Graphosyllabic Analysis Helps Adolescent Struggling Readers Read and Spell Words" (2004). He called them *articulation exercises* but the focus was clearly sounds and chunks of spelling patterns and reading "multisyllabic words by analyzing and matching their syllabic constituents to pronunciations" (Bhattacharya and Ehri, 345). By my imperfect count, there were some 2,388 words or spelling chunks in all to be practiced. And then to follow McGuffey's brain-based admonition: "Repeated and persevering practice is necessary, but will, with great certainty produce the desired result," reminding us that a learned craft requires practice and guidance (28). There they were—chunks and chunks of English spelling patterns: "man, ran, pan, tan, can, van, fan, shall, back, hack, mat, cat, bran, stand" to "go, gad, gig, gaf," to "throb, thrum, thrush, thrust, throng, three, thru, thro, thrive, thrice" to "rhet-o-ric, res-o-lute, in-do-lent, op-po-site, croc-o-dile, com-pro-mise, anch-o-rite." The exercises included commentary such as "Let the *sound* of each letter be given, not its *name*. After articulating the *sounds*, each word should be pronounced distinctly. Silent letters are sometimes omitted, that the *sound* alone may occupy the mind" (13). Chunks of letters and sounds alone should occupy the mind indeed, and according to my thinking, they should occupy the occipital-temporal lobe by grade two. McGuffey was wielding sound instruction directed specifically to activate the occipito-temporal area of the brain and while he called it "articulation" and Bhattacharya and Ehri, 147 years later, were calling it "graphosyllabic analysis," it was the same thing. What I was seeing were chunking lessons—vocabulary and spelling instruction—that he had made central as part of the basis of his system. His wonderful collection "The Reading Lessons" was also included, "drawn from a great variety of sources," he commented, and "of enduring interest to all Americans." It reminded me of how reading theorists such as Ken Goodman "demonstrated that children use their knowledge of spoken language as well as their knowledge of the letter-sound system to read" (Moustafa 1997, 6). Reading is *both* converting print into spoken language *and* making sense of print in wonderful texts such as "The Reading Selections."

Professor McGuffey was comprehensive in his approach. He also included "Exercises in Spelling and Defining," and placed them in his words "at the head of the lessons" (10), confirming my own life-long commitment to the importance of spelling. I found the section where Professor McGuffey recommends "a mutual exchange of slates" for a spelling lesson. "This impresses upon the mind the *appearance* as well as the *sound* of words, and will form a useful auxiliary to the Spelling-book; though there can be no *substitute* for that *indispensable drill*" (180). I was delighted to learn that McGuffey had not thrown out the spelling book and I still wonder why most of America has thrown it out and replaced good spelling instruction with busywork worksheets or with nothing at all (Gentry 2004a). I was thrilled that Professor McGuffey agreed with me on the importance of spelling. This brilliant reading educator from the nineteenth century recognized that the word's *appearance* had to be impressed on the brain—at least in one in five learners who develop the usual left-brain reading system and who show no signs of neurological glitches. He believed that exposure, explicit instruction, and practice had something to do with the extent to which word-specific knowledge may be impressed. I interpreted the good professor's reference to drill to mean, in my own words, "lots of repetition" because as I had already written in this book, "the brain loves repetition." After a career of studying literacy instruction and seven grueling months in the arduous task of writing this book, I inadvertently picked up McGuffey and found that over one hundred years ago he, Great Grandpa, and Grandma were all doing much of what I was advocating, and they were getting the same good results. I am not recommending that we go back to nineteenth-century reading instruction, but I did feel great confirmation—almost spiritual affirmation. In the nineteenth century reading teachers were giving the brain a workout that activated the same brain circuitry that we must activate today. They were doing a fairly balanced comprehensive program connecting writing and reading. They were teaching literacy explicitly. I judged them to be doing it rather nicely.

Figure 9.1 shows the faded pages of Lesson XVII of my great-Grandpa's antique reading book. Notice the chunking exercises to help the child with

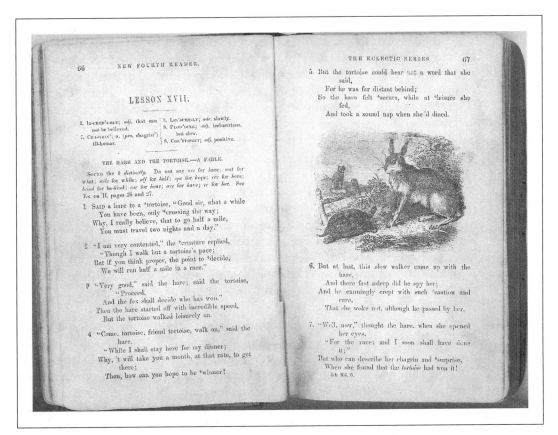

FIGURE 9.1 McGuffey's "The Hare and the Tortoise"

unknown reading vocabulary: *in-cred-i-ble; cha-grin; lei-sure-ly; plod-ding; con-fi-dent*—McGuffey has placed them right up front before the reading—"The Hare and the Tortoise."

Can the Trouble Be Avoided by Early Intervention? Four Fourth Graders Who Struggled

For a child, not learning to read is insidious. What if our instruction is not right from the start? What if we don't do code instruction within a balanced program? What if we teach the reading program and not the child? If we do not intervene or provide explicit instruction early, what will eventually happen to children who do not break the code? Why do some seem to struggle no matter what we do? I have worked with four students this year whose experiences have bearing on these questions. None of their stories is pleasant in telling. There are victories and triumphs to be sure, extraordinary breakthroughs and successes, but at what great a toll. Sadly, a thread that connects the case study and experiences of struggling readers or struggling spellers reported in this chapter is a common experience of frustration and even hostility emanating from their school experience—meted out by teachers, administrators, even a principal. All good people, I'm sure, who really have no intention in harming children; but from my perspective, many of the key players in these children's academic lives lacked an understanding of beginning literacy and reading or spelling disability, and fell far short in compassion for struggling readers and writers. Decisions were being made that ranged from unwise to devastating. Parents were given bad advice. Children were left behind. And while I believe most educators have positive energy, they love children, they are compassionate and giving, and they want to do the right thing, I have decided to include a glimpse into a darker side of reading disability with the hope that these glimpses can be instructive. I am taking on something that is untouchable: Even people with integrity can make bad decisions when they are uninformed. These case studies are real, there is authenticity here, and without wallowing in adversarial thinking, sometimes I think if we get the wind knocked out of ourselves we can get up, keep going, and we do better. I hope this is what you will do if you find remnants of your own actions in what I perceive to be the misguided actions of some of the educators who worked with this struggling foursome. The case study and three reports are intended to be agents for change.

Missteps in beginning reading instruction and the negative experiences some children have learning to read can be devastating. Even a spelling disability can cast a shadow on a child's whole academic career. The school experience of the children in this chapter pitted parents against teachers. Confrontation, anger, disappointment, hostility, suicidal ideation, crushing inferiority, resentment, lying and cheating, repression of voice and dignity—a full range of negative human emotions surround the stories of these four third and fourth graders who failed at reading or spelling because they did not break the code in first grade. There was also heroism: parents who would not give up; struggling mothers who devoted hours every night to tutoring; a persistent teacher who followed her gut instinct and continued to provide compassion and support when everyone else blamed a "lazy" child; and even a brilliant reporter who revealed to the world that there are extremely successful writers who still cannot spell.

The negativism associated with the four case studies in this chapter is the stronger thread that binds the experiences of these struggling children. Each of them came to me this year while I was writing this book—by email, in a tearful session with my hair stylist, from a teacher in my seminar in a faraway state—and I think these case studies are instructive, compelling, and they need to be shared to help us all see the urgency for some change in what we do when we teach reading. One of the needed changes is earlier intervention. Another needed change is to always treat children who struggle with literacy with compassion and respect whatever they can or cannot do.

There is too often a gravitational pull of negativism surrounding children who do not learn to read—"she's just being lazy"; "everyone else passed the test in my class, why couldn't he?"; "you need to get her a private tutor"; "she needs to try harder!" Too often it's an expression of frustration because the educator may not know what to do. She may be a new teacher who, through no fault of her own, has not been well trained to teach reading. She may be a third grade teacher with a first-grade-level reader. She may be a kindergarten teacher who was trained to teach "frogs" but not "tadpoles." She may be a principal who is overwhelmed with annual yearly progress mandates and enervated by district demands that no child who fails the test be promoted. These caveats notwithstanding, all educators need to be aware of the gravitational pull of negativism toward struggling readers, and we need to fight it.

Daniella: Meeting in the war zone—the school team is the enemy

Daniella is the most extraordinary case study of beginning reading I have ever witnessed. I taught her to read in nine non-stop two-hour lessons. She came to me hating reading and we struggled, we bonded, and we endured. I'm sure her unbelievable progress is as much a result of her brilliant mind and her mother's perseverance as it is to my teaching. She also received help at school when my schedule made it impossible to devote the amount of time necessary for a beginning reader to be successful. Credit is due to the special reading teacher who worked with Daniella on a daily basis throughout much of third grade. Credit is due to the principal who made the third grade intervention possible. Credit is due to Daniella's third grade teacher, who bonded with Daniella and whom I truly believe wanted to help her.

The hero in Daniella's story is her mother. Working two jobs, this devoted, intelligent, wonderful, loving mother, who is an English language learner herself, spent hours at night trying to help her academically ailing daughter to whom she is totally devoted. Daniella's stepfather, a world-class musician and also an English language learner, stepped in whenever he could. What strikes me is the extraordinary effort and time it takes to rescue a struggling reader. Indeed, to borrow from Hillary Rodham Clinton, it does take a village. Not only does it take many people working together to effect the rescue, it takes time. There is a cumulative effect in the hours of beginning reading instruction, and reading practice, that must be made up. The hours and days that drifted past Daniella when very little literacy learning was happening in kindergarten, first grade, and second grade when no intervention was provided had to be recaptured two or three times over in hours and hours of special help that this child would require later. Taken by itself, the time element alone for reading remediation justifies early intervention. Professor McGuffey was wise, indeed, to suggest that "the remedy should be applied when the evil commences," that is to say, as soon as the child is falling behind. In Daniella's case, early intervention not only would have eliminated hours and hours of struggle, frustration, anger, failure, and humiliation for the child, it would have eliminated these same negative human emotions in the adults who surrounded her. Early intervention is not an option, it is a necessity.

I can document Daniella's advancement in reading from beginning first-grade level to fourth-grade level in ten months. In thirty years of teaching, I have rarely seen such remarkable advancement. Daniella broke the code and went from cueing on beginning and ending letters (Phase 2 partial alphabetic reading) to reading on grade level ten months later. Remarkably, she made this progress in spite of the fact that she remained a reluctant reader throughout the entire ten-month period and retained deep-seated negative associations with reading. She began making progress when I began tutoring sessions in the last week of July following her second-grade year. By the end of the following April her performance on the Jerry Johns Basic Reading Inventory (1997) was on fourth-grade level. Long before our tutoring began in the summer the gravitational pull of negativism was in motion: the school had already decided its course. The second grade teacher's parting words to Daniella's mother, after announcing that Daniella was too tall to be held back in second grade, were that "This child will fail third grade!" Our intervention and determination to prepare Daniella for promotion would lead us into hand-to-hand-combat with the school team.

When Daniella's mother and I first met with the school team in November of Daniella's third-grade year, exhilarated to report her remarkable progress over the summer and early fall, we were shocked to meet negative resistance. It seemed the new third-grade team, including a first-year teacher, a new principal, and ultimately even the reading specialist who would meet with Daniella daily from our November conference forward, were determined that Florida's rigid third-grade promotion requirements were more important than the child's remarkable personal journey. In my view all three key players on Daniella's third-grade reading team at school seemed fearful and anxiety-ridden by the rigid regulations and mandates of the No Child Left Behind Act and the state test score requirements that grew out of it. Ironically, *leaving some children behind became the solution.* It was easier to leave children behind than to rescue them. "I still think Daniella would do better if she were retained in third grade," the third grade teacher announced in our last parent conference—even after I had demonstrated that *Daniella now read on grade level!* The teacher wanted Daniella to fail third grade regardless of the fact that Daniella had passed the required state reading test. "She only scored a 2," she told us, "that's passing but below grade level." She did not mention that Daniella had scored a 4 in math on the same test, high above grade level! It was as if the negative gravitational pull could not be released. "She still struggles with some of her assignments in school," we were told. Even after we showed the grade level reading test results and invited independent testing—the state test had been given two months earlier—the hostile team sitting across from Daniella's mother and me wallowed in negativity. "Yes, but we know there are some gaps in her functioning. Maybe she can read well for *you,* but she has to be able to read for *others* and to do well on the test!" I could not believe what I was hearing. As we sat there facing the enemy across the table in the principal's conference room, I knew that Daniella could read for anyone who believed in her. After the teacher left the room, the principal told us that Daniella *would* be promoted to fourth grade.

The parent conferences that I started attending in November were hostile. Perhaps I was partly to blame because by then I knew that the school had failed this child and I went into the first conference insisting that they do their part to rectify their missteps. Her mother and I insisted that the school provide Daniella instructional intervention. As Daniella's advocate I felt this was my obligation. While being firm and making our position clear, I did try to work cooperatively with the school team. Here is part of the text of the letter I sent to the principal the day after our first conference:

> Dear (Principal):
>
> Thank you for meeting with (Daniella's mother) and me in yesterday's conference regarding efforts to continue Daniella's reading improvement. Thank you especially for demonstrating your willingness to pursue some collaborative efforts to meet this very special child's educational needs. When I recommended that (Daniella's mother) schedule a conference with (Daniella's teacher), I asked her to request that the principal also participate because I feel that the urgency regarding some special help for Daniella may go beyond what her teacher, alone, might be able to provide. It also may go beyond what her parents and I can provide. You were open and gracious as well as insightful and professional, and I am most optimistic that with a team effort, we will be

able to plan and provide the kind of intervention needed to save this very special child from falling through the cracks. As we both know, all children are special and, as you said in yesterday's conference, you have the responsibility of meeting the needs of *all* the children at (your elementary school). What I believe makes Daniella's situation different is that the solution to her reading problem is within our grasp. She has made excellent progress in her work with me this summer—making a one-year gain in reading level in just a few months. More importantly, she has broken the code and for the first time crossed the threshold from *beginning reading* to *skilled reading*. What she needs now is continued work at her current instructional level and lots and lots of practice. Every time Daniella reads or rereads a book independently or with support at her instructional level, she is moving further towards fluency and the automatic recognition of words, which is the signature of skilled reading. She can now leave the slow and analytic process of beginning reading behind. With enough practice, I believe she can move to levels needed to be successful at third-grade level. But I soon begin a heavy national travel schedule, and her parents have limited English language skills—even though (her mother) reads with Daniella for thirty minutes every night. They do not have the financial means at this time for expensive tutoring. We need the school's help!

One absolutely critical need for Daniella is to increase her volume of reading—not being read to, but reading material that is easy for her. Every time she reads a word correctly it reinforces the word and the spelling pattern in her brain eventually leading to automatic recognition. When she first came to me, this child had done very little reading and rereading of easy books and in essence she didn't have enough automatic sight-word recognition of easy patterns so that she could read skillfully. As (her teacher) pointed out, she would see "police" and say "cop," totally ignoring the spelling chunks. She was nowhere near beginning second-grade level, which should mark the end of memorizing a book such as *Brown Bear, Brown Bear, What Do You See?* and mark the initial move to skilled reading with automatic pattern recognition.

I am impressed with (Daniella's teacher) mainly because she has already, to some degree, bonded with Daniella—Daniella really likes her. We both know the teacher-student bond is important. I do disagree with one point Daniella's teacher made in our conference. On the practice state reading test, the one on which Daniella scored Level 1, she thinks that Daniella finished too quickly and perhaps "didn't try hard enough." Imagine if you or I tried to read that same material in Hungarian. Knowing we couldn't read Hungarian, we would probably do exactly what Daniella did—go directly to the questions and guess. If one can't read, guessing is a very sensible test-taking strategy as

Daniella's mother insightfully pointed out in the conference—"She just guessed."

To get Daniella ready for the test this year, we have to improve her current reading level by meeting her where she is and moving her forward. We can't just give her more third-grade-level practice test sheets and tell her to "try harder" or "take more time."

In the rest of the letter I suggested that there may be a need for staff development for the principal's elementary school's beginning reading teachers and I offered to provide a workshop for free. I never had a response from the principal, or even acknowledgment of receiving the letter, which I know she received because I backed it up with an email copy.

Daniella's mother and many English language learner parents are intimidated by school conferences. While she fully understood the dynamics of Daniella's personal academic tragedy, her voice would not have been heard by the principal or teachers without an advocate. It was difficult for her to understand or respond to the jargon on the report card. Words like *"criteria,"* for example, and esoteric phrases such as *"estimation and mental math"* (isn't all math mental?) *"justifies inferences," "organizes information for a variety of purposes,"* and even "SCIENCE/SOCIAL STUDIES/HEALTH"(she asked me what "science/social" was)—all presented here as they appeared on the grade three district report card, were confusing to this wise, intelligent immigrant, who is a tax-paying American citizen. It was often difficult even for me to interpret the report card comments or the information we received about state testing, and I have a Ph.D. in reading education. We were repeatedly told Daniella was scoring a 1 and she needed a 2 to pass and I found the obfuscating number jumble infuriating. If the goal was promotion to grade 4, why did the calibration indicate that the goal was a 2? Why not report the test scores in grade levels? Shouldn't third graders need a 4 to pass into fourth grade? Sometimes I think test scores are designed to give teachers and administrators power to obfuscate and hide behind fake numbers. "She needs a 1198 but she made a 1172 in reading," we were told. It became evident that the test numbers were more powerful than the school team's ability to assess reading improvement. On May 13, near the end of the year, we were finally given information describing how the Florida Comprehensive Assessment Test (FCAT) is scored—information we should have been given in November. There are five levels. A score within the 1046–1197 range is Level 2, which is considered passing but is below grade level. The Level 3 range begins at 1198. While only *passing* the reading section, Daniella scored at Level 4 in the *high, above-grade-level range* in math. Regardless of these passing and above-grade-level scores in April, the teacher thought retention was the solution to Daniella's academic problems.

The teacher's comments on the next page in the "Conference/Interim" form were often evasive and contradictory.

8/25/04 Conference: "Daniella works very hard in my class. She loves art and tends to draw during a lesson. She does stop when asked to do so. She shows lots of interest in math and she's doing quite well."

11/22/04 Interim Report: "To move on to 4th grade, your child must score a 259 or higher on the FCAT. Daniella scored a 207 on her practice test during the week of November 8th. Please encourage her to read at home." [I do not know why these scores do not comport with the numbers we were given in May. Apparently the practice tests use a different scoring scale.]

2/11/05 Interim Report: "Daniella has improved dramatically since the beginning of the year. She puts a lot of effort into her work. Her data Point Score from January was a 250, which is a Level 1. A Level 2 is needed to pass 3rd grade. Daniella needs to score a 259 in order to pass. I feel that Daniella has worked very hard and has a strong will to do well! I enjoy having Daniella in my class." [The school team seemed oblivious as to how to move Daniella nine points higher to meet the magical 259. "Just do it!" was their expectation—the failing score was Daniella's fault and pulling it up was *her* responsibility.]

3/3/05 Conference (Principal's comment): "Mother and Mr. Gentry very concerned about promotion. Promotion criteria shared. Parent and Mr. Gentry want it noted that they will take it higher if she is retained. Attendance and tardies [a school bus issue] were discussed."

4/28/05 Interim Report: "Daniella's social studies grade is currently a 60%, which is a 'D.' This grade is due to very poor grades on social studies assignments. Daniella's reading has improved dramatically since the beginning of the school year!" [No problem with social studies assignments was reported to Daniella's mother and me during the grading period even though we had requested that any unfulfilled assignments be reported to me by email. We later learned that a consent form was required from the parent so that someone might email me, Daniella's tutor, when assignments were overdue. But neither the teacher nor the principal told us about the consent form requirement when we requested emails regarding late assignments. They simply chose not to respond to our request. I considered this a gross affront to our genuine effort to work cooperatively with the school team and I truly found this lack of cooperation unimaginable.]

5/25/05 Conference (Principal's comment): "Daniella has strong comprehension skills. She still needs help with sight recognition and word patterns." [Gentry's comment] "Report card to be changed to reflect accurate instructional levels in reading."

Contradictory to written comments on the interim report that Daniella's reading had improved dramatically during the school year, her third official report card indicated that Daniella's instruction level had remained at the exact same level—2.5, middle-second-grade instructional reading level all year long. Her mother and I found this ludicrous. We had struggled to teach Daniella and had seen incredible improvement and we simply were not prepared to have the school team place inaccurate information in her Cumulative Record indicating that she had remained at the same reading level all year long. When asked for clarification as to why the report card indicated that Daniella's instructional level was not advancing, we were told that she was still being instructed in the same 2.5 level materials and had not moved out of them. My testing during tutoring sessions throughout the year, including the individually administered Seventh Edition *Basic Reading Inventory* by Jerry L. Johns with both reading passages and graded word list showed a dramatically different story. Not only had she move out of 2.5 level materials, she had moved far out of them. Both comprehension and sight-word recognition scores indicated that accurate instructional levels for the four marking periods in third grade advanced from grade level 1.5 at the beginning of the year to 2.5 in the late fall, to 3.0 in mid-winter, to 4.0 by the end of third grade. The principal agreed to adjust the instructional levels for the last report card—thus giving Daniella credit for making some reading progress at school in third grade. In fact Daniella had advanced from first grade level to fourth grade level.

Daniella's school team seemed under extraordinary pressure to hold kids back even though district policy clearly allowed accommodations for children under special circumstances and explicitly stated that no child was to be retained due to a single test score, a policy they were reluctant to follow. It became apparent that the school team and Daniella's mother and I had a different focus and different goals. Their focus was a test score in April; our focus was demonstrated performance by the following August. It was as if the school team was too busy, or perhaps too intimidated by superiors, to deal with exceptions. Wouldn't it be better to spend the year helping this child, praising her, building her confidence and self-esteem, and providing instruction on her level, rather than constantly reminding her that she still couldn't pass the state test? She was required to fail time and time again on the practice test exercises. We were expected to acquiesce to expectations of failure. I suspect no interventions would have happened without our insistence. "She has to meet the standard," we were told, "she can't just read the easy stuff." Daniella experienced "teach the test" *de rigueur!*

In third grade, Daniella was expected to do third-grade things that she couldn't do without support or mediation. She would be given homework assignments that she could not read and her parents were unable to help her due to their own English reading limitations. She would be drilled on test preparation passages, and instructed in the same set of materials all year with no adjustments for her progress. She would be graded down because she didn't do assignments that were too hard for her to complete alone. The school was demanding that she *be* a third grader, but they hadn't taught her to be one. They were demanding that she *fit* into a program of third-grade instruction but they never prepared her for it. When she improved and *did become* a third-grade reader they didn't recognize it. Remarkably, Daniella's school was an "A" school for preparing most kids to pass the state test, but when Daniella failed to fit the mold, she was a problem for them. I suspect there was worry that she might bring down the overall school scores or have negative impact on annual yearly progress. Daniella was messing up their numbers! Rather than help her, some of the school team seemed to look for excuses to blame Daniella for her inadequate academic progress—poor test scores, "not trying hard enough," "too many tardies," and a "D" in social studies for not completing assignments, which I suspected was petty vindictiveness because we insisted upon intervention. The school not only had expectations for failure, they created the justifications for it. Their actions throughout third grade were their own self-fulfilling prophecy.

Daniella's mother and I were not obsessed with Daniella's promotion, we just wanted what was in her best interest. She had made tremendous progress and we strongly felt she would be successful in fourth grade. She had passed the reading test and was in the high range in math. Furthermore, we thought it would be devastating to her self-esteem to fail in the year that she had progressed three grade levels in reading in only ten months. We only advocated promotion because we knew she had made this tremendous progress, and ultimately, we were sure Daniella met the criteria for promotion. Not to promote simply did not make sense.

Our experience with Daniella's school team is not simply a story about bad retention policies. It is a story about the school's failure to intervene early. It is a story about children who are left behind even in schools that meet mandates for high test-score performance. It is a story about the school's failure to teach a perfectly normal child to break the code because some beginning reading teachers do not know their practice. It is a story of how the school's failure to teach a child to read led to trouble for a lot of people and exposed an unexpected dark side of reading failure. As Daniella's mother and I got out of the car for the March conference, the principal drove into the parking lot and parked next to us. At first I didn't recognize her; I had seen her only one time five months earlier. She got out of the car and didn't speak to us even though Daniella was standing there holding her mother's hand. No "Good morning." No "Welcome to our school!" No greeting or acknowledgment whatsoever. Sensing the awkwardness of the "good morning standoff," Daniella said, "That's the principal," so I smiled and said, "Good morning. We are glad to be here with Daniella."

I have visited hundreds of schools all across America but I have never received such an inhospitable welcome. It was at that moment that I realized I was an intruder representing the parent. In this school I was the enemy. In becoming Daniella's advocate, I had crossed over to the bad side. Eventually I realized that Daniella's mother and I had been the enemy from the moment in November when I announced that we intended for Daniella to pass third grade. The battle lines had been drawn from our very first meeting.

The next chapter recounts the remarkable and happy story of Daniella's successful tutorial program. But first, let me share glimpses of three other struggling readers, writers, and spellers that illustrate the need for early intervention and the need to fight the negative forces that often surround them.

Reading, Writing, and Spelling Disabilities Are Real

Unlike Daniella, not all reading and writing problems are due to poor teaching. There is a neurological basis for both reading (Shaywitz 2003) and, I believe, for spelling disability (Gentry 2004). It has been estimated that one in five readers across cultures suffer from some form of dyslexia (Paulesu et al. 2001; Shaywitz 2003). Many dyslexic children who do learn to read are left with residual mild to severe spelling disability (Gentry 2004). Some children who read extraordinarily well and learn to read with ease cannot spell or write. While brain scan studies have not been conducted to fully substantiate the existence of a neurological basis of all spelling and writing disability, research using brain scan technology with dyslexics, many of whom are notoriously bad spellers in English, does establish a neurological basis for their functioning (Gentry 2004; Paulesu 2001). On a personal basis, as I report in *The Science of Spelling*, spelling disability is a reality for me and for many other writers. One of them is Steve Hendrix, a brilliant young writer for *The Washington Post*. He provided a fascinating confession of his personal struggles with spelling in an article entitled "Why Stevie Can't Spell (After More Than Three Decades of Mangling Words, a Mortified Writer Sets Out to Get Some Answers)" that appeared in *The Washington Post Magazine* (2005). Steve had called me before the December holidays for a phone interview in preparation for his article in which he planned to try to discover and reveal some of the mysteries of severe spelling disability. I found it rather remarkable that a world-class journalist who traveled to places like Thailand to report on the tsunami, or Alaska's Arctic National Wildlife Refuge to report on backpacking, would be gutsy and honest enough to tell his own humiliating story of being, in his words, "the world's worst speller." Over the next several weeks we had extensive phone conferences and email exchanges as I tried to guide Steve through the mysteries of spelling disability and the baffling peculiarities and inconsistencies of what elementary schools do with spelling. In a delightfully insightful report, this father of a second-grade spelling genius portrayed what it's like to be a professional writer with neurologically based spelling disability. "I read tons. I have a robust vocabulary. I just can't spell"

(Hendrix, 28) he wrote and he went on to describe how his atrocious spellings were "little land mines" powerful enough not only to embarrass and humiliate but to jeopardize careers. In Steve's words:

> Ours is a Gordian knot of a language, a tangled skein of threads pulled from dozens of alien dialects and balled into the richest, most expressive and downright maddening lingo on the planet. There's plenty of blame to go around—curse you, Greeks, Saxons and Normans—for the fact that *oven* doesn't rhyme with *woven, laughter* does rhyme with *rafter* and *colonel* is identical to *kernel.* (42)

I suggested that Steve contact Professor Sally Shaywitz, the Yale neuroscientist who is best known for her research in brain scan technology and reading, to schedule a brain scan, and I boldly suggested that they would find a compensatory reading system. They did.

Steve writes about the results of his fMRI at Yale:

> "Well, you're really smart," says this eminent authority on brains (Sally Shaywitz). "On our vocabulary tests, you scored about as high as you can possibly score. Also on the reasoning part, you're way, way in the superior range." I wonder if she could put that in letter form, addressed to: All Editors, *The Washington Post.*"
>
> The MRI confirms it. The Shaywitzes see the lights go on in the usual reading areas of the left hemisphere. But they also find an unusual level of action on the right side of my brain, in the areas where dyslexics tend to build new pathways to make up for misfires in the normal ones.
>
> "It all fits together, our clinical exams and our neurobiological exams, Shaywitz says. "You had the underlying threads of dyslexia, but you've compensated for it really, really well. When you have time, you do well. But when you have to do things very quickly, it's not automatic. Your autopilot, for spelling and for reading just isn't there."
>
> As a youngster, Shaywitz says, I was probably getting just enough information and pleasure from reading to push through some amount of dyslexic drag. And the more I read, the more compensatory tricks my brain wired into itself until I became fluent, at least under relaxed conditions. It's only when the heat is on that my reading goes a little wobbly and, even more often, my spelling collapses in a heap. (44)

Brain scan imaging is really in it's infancy. The tasks subjects are asked to do for the imaging are very, very simple—like responding to rhyming words—and most of the findings are based on patterns from groups of subjects. Neuroscientists are limited in what they can say about a single subject's image results. All of this notwithstanding, to my knowledge, Steve's article is the first brain scan report specifically related to neurologically based spelling disability, which, before Steve, had not been looked at directly. One hundred years from now, I would be pleased if it was recorded that Steve Hendrix's brain was the first brain where spelling disability was discovered definitively. It's only fitting that spelling disability be discovered to reside in such an extraordinarily fine brain! As Steve reports "Some people, even geniuses, just can't spell. . . . Science has spoken" (44).

When one considers the agony of reading, writing, and spelling problems, Steve Hendrix and Daniella's mother are not alone. Each year I receive scores of emails and letters from frustrated parents whose children are struggling. The following email came in from Minnesota:

> Dear Dr. Gentry:
>
> I recently read an article written by Steve Hendix in *The Washington Post.* The article dealt with the author's struggles with spelling. Your research was referred to throughout the article. Mr. Hendrix's struggle with spelling sounded exactly like my ten-year-old daughter Michelle, who has been struggling with reading since kindergarten. Michelle was tested last year, by the public school system, and was finally diagnosed as having a learning disability. Her testing showed a disability in the area of spelling and to a lesser degree in reading. I found none of this surprising, as I had fought with the school since kindergarten to have her tested.

The mother ended her email with heartfelt emotion:

> I am desperate for a way to help my daughter. I am so afraid that she will turn away from reading and learning because of all the frustration she is feeling.

In February of the child's third-grade year, after three years of parental pleading for intervention, the school finally referred Michelle to the school psychologist for testing. They found Michelle to be within the high average range in intelligence. Remarkably she was scoring on grade level in reading, largely, I believe, due to her parents' work at home and due to Michelle's high intelligence. She was also in the high average range in general knowledge in science, social studies, and humanities. Yet spelling skills for this third grader had tested at mid-first-grade level. Michelle's errors included "ran" for "rain" and "cookt" for "cooked." Comments on Michelle's second-grade report card that indicated problems with decoding words in reading were noticed at least two full years before the intervention in fourth grade. In the evaluation, the school psychologists wisely came up with appropriate eligibility status qualifying Michelle for intervention:

> According to Minnesota State eligibility criteria for Specific Learning Disabilities, a student must demonstrate all three of the following: a Severe Discrepancy, Severe Underachievement, and Processing Difficulties. Michelle meets state criteria for a Learning Disability in the area of Written Expression.

Regrettably, the evaluation team and the school struggled to come up with an effective intervention program. Some of the well-intentioned recommendations were ludicrous. But in my mind, what stood out most was one unspoken question: Why hadn't educators seen what was apparent to an observant, intuitive mother who had noticed the child's problems in kindergarten? The school intervention was finally happening when the child was in fourth grade—a year after the test results and two years after problems were reported on the second grade report card. I believe this mother and daughter's experience is a clarion call for early intervention. Had her kindergarten teacher followed the Intervention Blueprint, she would have received help in kindergarten.

In American schools, as Michelle's case so vividly illustrates, most learning disabilities are not identified soon enough. According to Robert Pasternack, the 2003 assistant secretary for Special Education and Rehabilitative Services, "The majority of students who get identified with learning disorders get identified between the ages of 11 and 17, and that's too late" (Gorman 2003). While Michelle's intelligence and devoted, persevering parents have probably rescued her, what a difference there may have been if the mother's plea for early intervention had been answered in kindergarten. Would Michele have overcome her disability? According to Shaywitz (2003), with early intervention, the brain may be able to "fix" itself! Whether this proves to be the case or not, there is no question that early intervention will ease the burden for children who struggle and turn school into a place for more joyful learning and greater academic success.

Michelle's experience illustrates that a school district discovered the problem too late. When they did admit that Michelle had a learning disability, the discrepancy was so great that it was very difficult to know how to ameliorate the problem. They needed an early Intervention Blueprint and an earlier response.

Every human brain is different and every child learns to read differently. Brains are like fingerprints; no two are exactly alike. Many will say that Daniella's, Steve's, and Michele's cases are unique. While each case *is* unique, they share similarities. It is interesting to note the unusual blips on each of their screens. Daniella jumped from Level E to Level J in a few weeks, for example. That's unusual. Perhaps Daniella had a lot of unconnected knowledge about words and once the code was plugged in, she may have made remarkable, fast, and unexpected progress—like finding the plug that's not connected in the Christmas tree, plugging it in, and the entire top of the tree lights up!

The human brain is a remarkable organ. One thing I learned from working with struggling readers and writers for over thirty years is that teachers and parents must never give up. The successes reported in this chapter all are due to someone's persistence. Each story gives hope to all kids who struggle.

"There is no such thing as a spelling disability"

I received an email from a mother in St. Louis who was baffled because her third-grade son, Christian, had severe spelling problems but was above grade level in everything else. "His written work suffers," she had written "and I think that's partially because he has so much trouble spelling." I found this statement intriguing because it was the exact thesis of a research article I had just submitted to a professional journal (Gentry, Nanez, and Benavides, in press). *Many children struggle with writing because they can't spell*—it was as if she had taken the words right out of my mouth. Then she came out with the statement that I have found mind-boggling for years and years: "His school has not been able to help him as they say *'there is no such thing as a learning disability for spelling.'*" I have written three books on spelling disability (Gentry, 1987, 1997, 2003) and I marvel that schools still just don't get it. Remarkably, Christian, who is in the gifted program and who has had a private tutor, is spelling on grade level—until one looks at his spelling in writing. This spelling-disabled child wrote the story in Figure 9.2 the same year he was able to spell on fourth-grade level on an informal spelling inventory.

My question is this: How can anyone look at this sample, from a gifted student who reads on grade level and who has had private tutoring and devoted parents who have worked with him individually, and not suspect some kind of processing difficulty? How could they tell the parent, "There is no such thing as a learning disability for spelling"? I would love to know *their* explanation. And why had someone written on his paper "Your spelling could be better"? We don't tell people in wheelchairs that there is no such thing as being crippled. We don't tell them it's better to walk. Christian already knew that his spelling could be better. He had been living with his spelling handicap for four years.

Upon close inspection one can see the unexpected spellings in Christian's sample that characterize the spelling of someone with a neurologically based spelling disability. You see a conglomeration of Phase 1, Phase 2, Phase 3, and Phase 4 spellings, and often what you see is unusual and not predictable. The first thing I noticed in the writing samples that Christian's mother sent me is that he misspelled his own name, rendering it *Christiain*, on one of his third-grade writing samples. Sometimes I think the brain of the severely disabled speller seems to be playing tricks on the speller. Even though Christian can spell on grade level on a spelling test, one can see scores of unusual below-grade-level spellings in the third grade. He spelled *said* five different ways: correctly, *siad*, *sand*, *sad*, and *siand*. *Tinkerer* is misspelled four different ways: *tinker*, *tincer*, and *tinke*. Some very basic patterns that Christian spells correctly on tests are misspelled in his writing such as *mate* for *met*, *rop* for *rope*, and *lat* for *let's*. High-frequency first-grade-level words often come out wrong: *go* for *good*, *all* for *I'll*, and *wat* for *want*. He renders *perfect* as *purfick*, *pursitk*, and *porfick* in the same two-page writing sample. *Can't* is *ca'nt* and *didn't* is *din't*. The teacher who told Christian's mother that "there is no such thing as a learning disability for spelling," is mistaken. Christian has one.

It's interesting to note that Christian's spelling looks a lot like mine did when I was in elementary school. Figure 9.3 shows one of my fifth-grade samples with misspellings such as *the* for *they*, *to* for *too*, *ben* for *been*, *befor* for *before*,

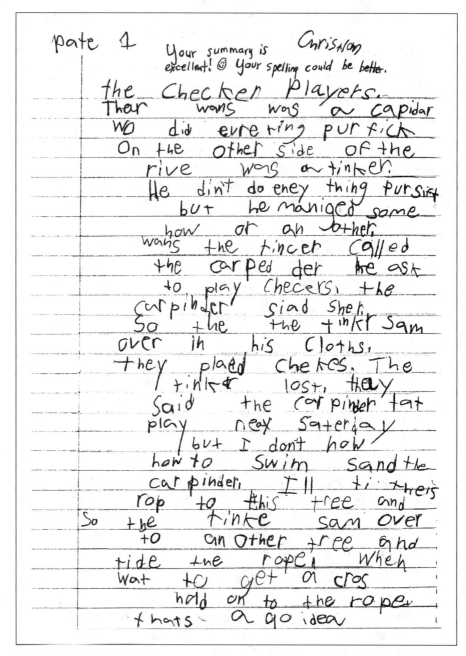

pate 1   Your summary is   Christian

excellent! ☺ your spelling could be better.

the Checker Players.

Ther wans was a capidar

wo did eurering purfick

On the other side of the

rive was a tinker.

He dint do eney thing pursift

but he maniged some

how or an other.

wans the tincer called

the carped der he ask

to play checers, the

carpinder siad sher,

So the the tinkr sam

over in his cloths,

they plaed chekes. The

tinkr lost, they

said the carpiner tat

play neax sateriay

but I dont how

how to swim sand the

carpinder, I'll ti theis

rop to this tree and

So the tinke sam over

to an other tree and

tide the rope, when

wat to get a cros

hold on to the rope,

thats a go idea

FIGURE 9.2   Christian's Story

p at 2   Christian

the cheaker players
how did you think of that?
it   just pop in my hads
sad the tinker, next sade
they   nat   this time
the   tinker   won,
let   met   hafe way
a   cros   the river'
fine said the tinker
you have your chorkss
all   have mine, but
I   can't swim well poo
hod bulld a boat,'
fine siand the carpinder
they   mate the tinkers
boat ways ok the carpde
was porfick. jus- then-
a gust of wind came
out of no wer and
the   Boat flipt,
help! crid the carpinder
I   coont swim. I'M
coming siad the tinker,
he drad him on shore
then   the bilt a boat
to   geinther a spant
many after hos to gath
The end,

FIGURE 9.2   (continued)

My 4-H Steer

My daddy sold me my calf. My brother had a calf with mine. We kept them in a pen and fed them every morning and night. At first my calf was wild. As we worked with them the became tame.

In the winter it was to cold to wash him. When it got warm he was not as tame as he had ben. He would run away every time I got him out, but after several weeks of work I had him tame.

A few days before time to take him to Durham Mr. Smith came out to the house to help me sheer my calf. The next day we washed them up and got them ready for the show.

When we got to Durham we had to wait to get him weighed Whild I was waiting a man took my picture with my steer and put it in the newspaper.

Fri. night we had the showing. They gave out the Blue ribons and then the red ribons and came down to me and stoped! Oh I wanted one so bad. But that was that.

Sat. night we sold them and then came the worst time of all leaving my calf! But I had made a good profit and was happy.

Richard Gentry

FIGURE 9.3   The Author's Fifth-Grade Writing Sample

weighted for *weighed, whild* for *while, ribons* for *ribbons,* and *stoped* for *stopped*—all words I had previously studied and mastered for a spelling test (Gentry 1987, 41–44).

As shown in Figure 9.4, I read the word *selected* on a 4-H project "Summary" questionnaire and within two seconds immediately misspelled it as *sollected* when I answered the question in writing. As for the gifted third grader from St. Louis, I told Christian not to give up. Lousy spellers can become writers.

When late intervention has to happen, the remedy is often complex. Here's an email outlining what might have to happen when the application of the remedy is too late. It's part of an email report I made to parents of a child I suspected had neurologically based processing difficulties. Over the years the child had apparently been rescued from disaster by persevering parents and by one extraordinary teacher who would not give up. The teacher, who had faith in this child, brought Janey to my attention.

> Dear (Janey's parents):
>
> Here are my reflections and recommendations for Janey's Individual Education Plan (IEP). You may share this with the school team if you wish.
>
> I have never met with Janey, I have only evaluated her work and relied on reports from others for insight. In my opinion, however, Janey is likely a dyslexic who remarkably, and to her credit as well as to the credit of those who have persisted in working with her, has learned a compensatory system for reading. Based on recent brain scan studies with dyslexics, it can reasonably be hypothesized that Janey activates different areas of the brain than many normal readers who use a left brain reading system. For example, she may have greater activation in areas such as the left frontal lobe and perhaps activation in the right hemisphere. She likely has less activation in the occipito-temporal area of the left hemisphere thought to be the express pathway for automatic reading and theorized to be an area activated for expert spelling (Shaywitz, 2003; Gentry, 2004). Of course Janey has not had a brain scan nor does she need one. Scanning will not fix the problem. But if this hypothesis is correct, it is appropriate to speculate that her different brain activation for reading likely matches

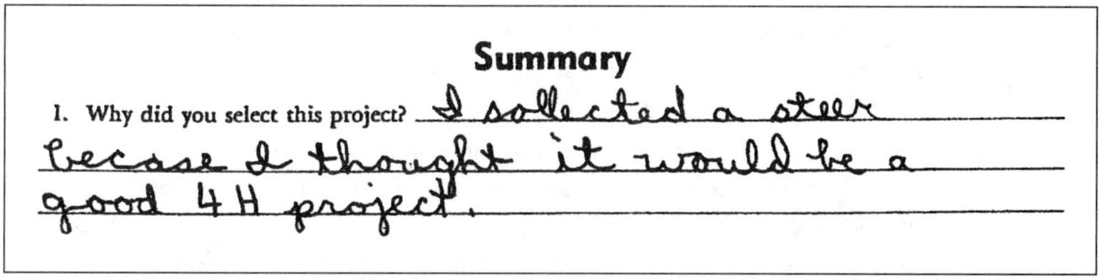
Summary

1. Why did you select this project? I sollected a steer becase I thought it would be a good 4H project.

FIGURE 9.4 The Author's Spelling of *selected*

the type of activity that is found in many successful dyslexics who *do* learn to read, but whose reading may have variations from normal reading. For example she may be slower in rate and, as with most dyslexics, she may have a history of difficulty learning to read.

Dyslexics (and perhaps Janey) who learn to read using different than usual areas of the brain sometimes develop *stronger* than usual levels of reading skill, some with particular strengths in comprehension, problem solving, reasoning, critical thinking and deriving meaning (Shaywitz, 2003). All of this is to say that the prognosis for Janey's success as a reader is quite good. She has already accomplished the hard part—beginning reading and breaking the code. I would consider Janey to be a huge success as a reader. She very likely overcame tremendous obstacles in learning to read and this child, whose recent WAISC-IV IQ scores are all in the average range, now reads almost on grade level! Remarkably for her, spelling, a residual deficit in almost all dyslexics, is only about one year below grade level. Instead of being identified as "the only third grade student in her school who did not score proficient in math and language on the NJASK (The New Jersey reading test)," she should be identified as a child with a learning disability who is doing extraordinarily well. Her parents, her teachers, and the tutorial team should praise Janey for her accomplishments and make her feel good about her academic success. She is a gold medalist in the Olympics of reading and if she continues to improve, through hard work, she will be competitive with anyone.

Janey likely will continue to need extra support to reach her potential as a reader, writer, and speller. But regardless of the anticipated extra work, one goal should be to make the journey as enjoyable and pleasant as possible. Academic rigor should not be imposed upon her at the expense of her self-esteem, which seems to have suffered. She may likely continue to experience difficulties as a speller, but teachers should be sensitive to her disability, perhaps cut her some slack at times, and not constantly penalize her with red marks and points off for misspelled words. She shouldn't be told she is lazy unless there is other evidence to back up this statement. Simply show her where she made errors and help her fix them. Show her ways to adapt—learning to write on a keyboard and to use the spell check might help in the future. Computers notwithstanding, the real solution is to continue to help her gain confidence, improve her skills, and increase her volume and enjoyment of reading and writing. An appropriate teacher role might be that as her "editor,"—one who helps a writer fix misspellings and learn from them—as opposed to the role of the error-finding demon who grades her down.

Janey's IEP should encompass comprehensive literacy skills including reading and writing but with particular emphasis on development of word specific knowledge or spelling. A teacher/tutor might help her select chapter books of interest to her at her present fourth-grade instructional level. Self-selection of books she's interested in along with support for selecting good children's literature is important. Some selections should be easy for her and others more challenging. One major goal should be to increase her volume of reading.

I recommend that the teacher/tutor read passages or chapters silently with Janey and have probing discussions about the content. Make predictions about what might happen then reread sections to confirm or change the original predictions. Probing should include analysis, evaluation, synthesis, and delving into the esthetic or emotional content.

Janey probably needs work with oral fluency. I recommend dramatic reading of short selections or reader's theater. Janey might enjoy repeated reading of favorite passages, or songs, or poems that she practices over and over until she can read them orally with wonderful expression. These activities should be designed to build reading fluency and confidence.

Janey's IEP word study component might focus on word sorting including teacher-led sorts, individual sorts, buddy sorts, and speed sorts. Once the pattern is introduced by her teacher and Janey recognizes it, she should sort the pattern over and over and write the sort in column formation in her individual spelling journal. The journal might also include a list of high-frequency first-, second-, or third-grade-level words that Janey frequently misspells in her writing and gleans for further study. The teacher should help her find these words.

Based on Janey's spelling pretests, I designed a spelling program for Janey focusing on patterns and word sorting.

Apply the Remedy Early

Early intervention is important. Some kids *do* have dyslexia and there *is* such a thing as a spelling disability. There are too many children in America who need earlier intervention than they are currently receiving. The examples I report here are just a sampling that I come in contact with every few weeks. Let's remember to heed Professor McGuffey's admonition, "The remedy must be applied before the evil commences" (McGuffey 1857). When we don't, we face the negative gravitational pull and a much more difficult task of remediation.

10

Come See a Miracle

Within ten minutes of working with Daniella in our first meeting—her mother and stepfather sitting across from us at a large dinning room table in my home—I knew Daniella's problem. She simply had not broken the English code. Daniella had not learned to recognize the printed word with ease and speed. The rapid, seemingly effortless word recognition of a skilled reader was not within her grasp. She was smart, bilingual—speaking both Hungarian and English fluently—and she caught on fast. There were no signs of processing difficulty or dyslexia. She could analyze, synthesize, make inferences, and think critically responding to books read aloud with excellent comprehension. The art that accompanied a couple of her writing samples spoke to creativity and artistic talent. Her English language learning deficits were minimal beyond requiring an occasional explanation for unknown vocabulary, such as the noun, *rifle*, a word she would later encounter in one of our reading selections. English language learning was never the root of Daniella's problem. Her problem was a lack of understanding of the English spelling system. She didn't understand the code or see the regular patterns in it. No one had taught it to her or showed her how it works. I was shocked in the first session to discover that this bright, perfectly normal third grader was functioning at beginning first-grade level. She could not read the *Foot Book* by Dr. Seuss, a mid-first-grade-level book. I could see in her writing and spelling that she didn't know basic first-grade spelling patterns.

When Daniella saw an unknown word she tried to decode it by cueing from the first and last letters, which resulted in errors in accuracy. *Foot* could be "feet," "foot," or "float." She overused context clues. While she recognized some beginning level patterns, she didn't know how to use them, often guessing as she struggled to make sense of the text. She didn't analogize. I noticed all of this within the first ten minutes of working with her and by thumbing through her second-grade notebook, which Daniella brought to our first tutoring session.

Once I had identified Daniella's level of development, I intervened with the type of instruction that Level 2 tadpole readers need—basic, comprehensive, first-grade reading and writing instruction following the Intervention Blueprint. I started by meeting her at her instructional level with the right kind of instruction—something that had not happened previously with Daniella in two and one-half years of schooling. I designed a comprehensive tutorial program of reading, writing, and word study that would be appropriate for any child who, like Daniella, was a Level 2 tadpole transitioning into Level 3. I didn't include anything fancy, just the basic common sense stuff: good children's literature and lots of authentic reading and writing, appropriate repetition and fluency work, lots of guided practice, and work with spelling, sight words and chunks. It was the type of instruction any parent should expect their child to receive in first grade. The only problem was that Daniella was getting it one and one-half years too late.

I looked at Daniella's past and present performance in light of the tadpole phases as I planned appropriate instructional intervention. It was difficult to determine what she had accomplished in first grade although her Stanford Achievement Test score (ninth edition) from that year indicates that she scored at the 23rd percentile in reading and the 82nd percentile in math. The evidence of her second-grade experience was clearer. Daniella brought her second-grade notebook to the first tutoring session, a green looseleaf notebook with 127 pages of mostly copy exercises interspersed with occasional math seatwork. The notebook spoke volumes. Daniella must have spent hours and hours in second grade filling it up with copy work—mostly inappropriate grammar exercises, which she could not read. Copying must have occupied a great deal of her time. The notebook was full of something called Daily Oral Language (D.O.L.), spelling exercises, subject and verb agreement exercises, and spelling patterns that were far above grade level for normally functioning second graders but in the stratosphere for Daniella. It was work that was over her head. The exercises were teaching her to plagiarize and to pretend that it was her work. Daniella was probably very clever at masking her lack of understanding, assiduously copying the seatwork that she couldn't read. I suspect she spent two years faking it and no one really noticed. *Why hadn't anyone noticed?* It saddened me that Daniella's kindergarten-, first-, and second-grade teachers apparently had no Instructional Blueprint guiding their work with children. Two sample pages from Daniella's second-grade notebook are presented in Figure 10.1.

Here is what I found: There were spelling words, such as the list in Figure 10.1, but Daniella had not been taught the word-specific knowledge that would enable her to take advantage of these lessons. At the same time that she was painstakingly copying spelling words that she could not read such as *laugh, cough, enough, paragraph,* and *petroglyphs* in the notebook, one could see *wet* for

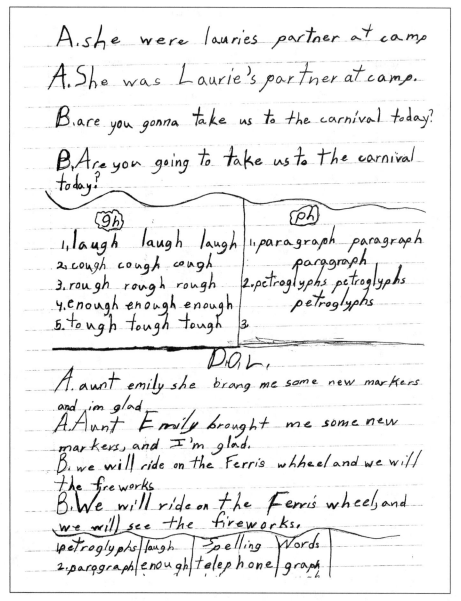

FIGURE 10.1 Two pages from Daniella's Second-Grade Notebook

with, *send* for *sand*, *kek* for *kick*, and *hat* for *hot* in her independent writing. *Cough*, *enough*, and *petroglyphs* are not appropriate spelling words for second graders who are developmentally on track, and they were ludicrous for this struggling second grader. Another second-grade spelling list included *routine*, *through*, *coupon*, *throughway* and *soup*, fourth- or fifth-grade spelling words that

Spelling List

1. routine routine routine routine routine routine

2. through through through through through

3. you you you you you you you you you you

4. soup soup soup soup soup soup soup soup

5. group group group group group group group

6. wound wound wound wound wound wound

7. coupon coupon coupon coupon coupon coupon

8. youth youth youth youth youth youth

9. throughway throughway throughway throughway

10. throughout throughout throughout throughout

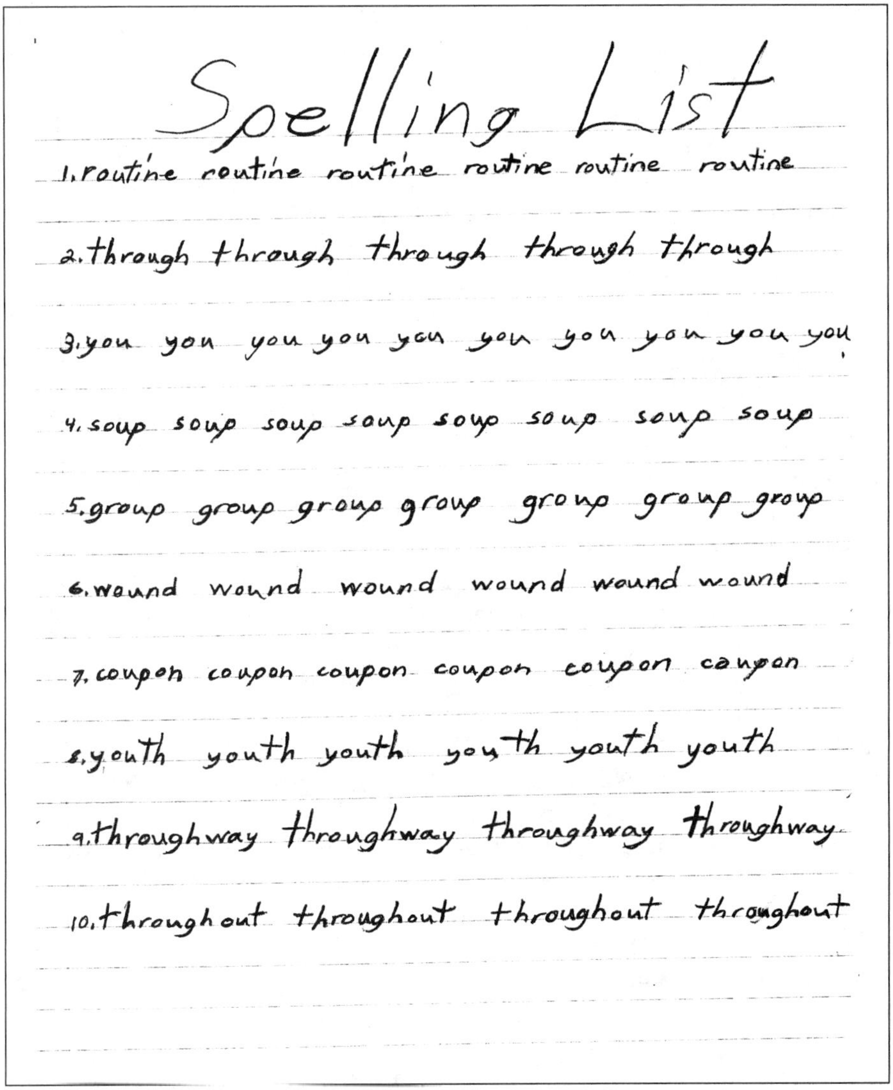

FIGURE 10.1 (continued)

she was required to copy. The floundering tadpole was being treated as if she were a frog.

It is very likely that many children in Daniella's second grade classroom were succeeding in school in spite of what was going on with Daniella. Her school was one of ninety-three elementary schools in a very large school district that "was making excellent progress" according to The No Child Left Behind Act guidelines. At the time of this writing, school-by-school grades based on the scores from the Florida Comprehensive Assessment Test (FCAT) were released on a yearly basis by then Florida governor Jeb Bush and the State

Department of Education. They always made the front page of the news. Daniella's school had received an "A" and the highly touted "yes" for annual yearly progress. But while the school was celebrating its "A" for the governor, the state department, the newspaper, and press conferences, Daniella was being hopelessly left behind. Regardless of grade level expectations or promotion mandates, I knew that my instruction had to start where Daniella was functioning.

Daniella's level of word knowledge was revealed in the independent writing sample that I found in the second-grade notebook collection—one of only three independent writing samples I found in her notebook. It is presented in Figure 10.2.

At the time that she was copying words such as *cough* and *petroglyphs,* Daniella could not spell *hat,* or *hot. Pepperoni* (pep-per-ro-ni) was spelled *papare.* I knew my instructional intervention would have to address Daniella's lack of knowledge about the English spelling code.

The Intervention Blueprint provides an easy plan for teachers or tutors who work with beginning readers and writers to follow, and the Blueprint's straightforward guidelines charted my course. After identifying her levels of development in reading, writing, and spelling, and checking against what was expected, I intervened and provided the right kind of instruction geared to Daniella's instructional levels. My work differed from her previous teachers' and tutors' work because for the first time, someone was teaching Daniella, not merely following a prescribed reading program or a set of prescribed tutorial materials. I set out to know Daniella as a reader, writer, and a speller and I allowed my observations of what she could and could not do guide my decisions for the type and timing of her instruction. I bonded with her and made it fun. I made sure I provided appropriate emphasis on all aspects of literacy—reading, writing, spelling, listening, and speaking. I tried to make our work interesting and to keep her motivated. I effected student-driven decision making based on the Instructional Blueprint—the kind of knowledgeable, conscientious, active decision making that should be the hallmark of all beginning reading and writing instruction.

There were two exceptions. I helped Daniella with a few homework assignments later in the year and noted that she was making great strides in becoming more prepared to handle the work independently. Secondly, in December and January, we did one practice exercise for the state test so that I might see if she was becoming better prepared to handle the test obstacle. She did amazingly well, with my mediation, and I was able to boost her confidence. I didn't know if Daniella would be able to pass the test in April, but the practice test experience along with my other observations gave me confidence that she would eventually meet the test requirement and be ready for fourth grade in August.

With appropriate ordinary reading, writing, and spelling instruction, Daniella's progress was miraculous.

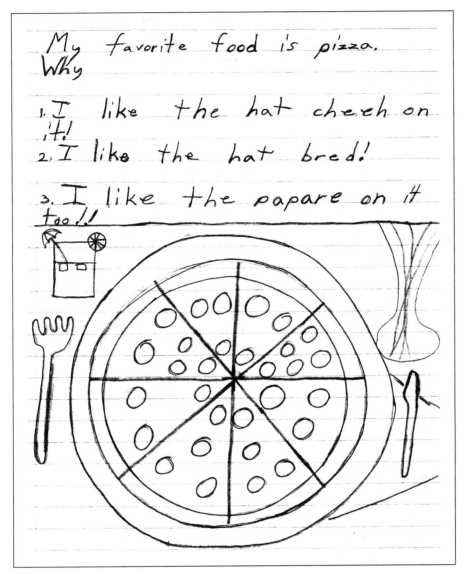

My favorite food is pizza.
Why

1. I like the hat cheeh on it!
2. I like the hat bred!

3. I like the papare on it too!!

FIGURE 10.2   Writing Sample from Daniella's Second-Grade Notebook

DANIELLA'S TUTORIAL PROGRAM—ORDINARY READING INSTRUCTION:

- I identifed Daniella's level of development.
- I provided appropriate intervention.
- I bonded with Daniella.
- I tried hard to make our tutoring sessions fun.

- We worked arduously. Each session was rigorous and nonstop. No breaks, because our time was too precious.
- I used teaching techniques that matched her level of development.
- I taught both the whole and the parts.
- I used good children's literature.
- We did authentic writing.
- I connected reading and writing instruction.
- We worked with high-frequency words and word chunks to facilitate accurate, automatic, word recognition.
- I taught spelling explicitly.
- I provided lots of repetition. Daniella read *The Foot Book* and *Green Eggs and Ham* literally scores of times over the next two or three months.
- We did repeated readings for fluency and worked on oral reading for confidence.
- We dramatically increased the volume and the amount of time Daniella spent reading. The neurons in her brain for words were firing, and firing, and firing.
- We enlisted the help of the teacher and the special reading teacher at school.
- Daniella's mother worked with her every night at home.
- I constantly kept a positive attitude and tried to build up Daniella's self-esteem.
- I nudged Daniella into more challenging material.
- I helped her with material that was too hard.
- We had celebrations.

Daniella was not an easy client. A climate of negativity had already been set. She hated reading and felt self-defeated. She had experienced tutoring sessions before and none of them had worked. Reading and writing were behaviors she was conditioned to try to avoid. She generally came to me after a long school day and sometimes she was tired. Initially we met weekly but we soon could meet for only one or two sessions per month. In spite of these obstacles, the Instructional Blueprint and a spirit of optimism and fun guided our work. I looked forward to my sessions with Daniella and found it personally gratifying. I knew my mission, I knew where I was going, and I felt a sense of accomplishment. Getting into the flow of our tutoring session was exhilarating.

Glimpses into Daniella's tutorial

The Parts and the Wholes Coexisted. Daniella needed both the wholes and the parts in order to succeed from the outset. She needed to know what it felt like to read whole text and at the same time she needed the chunking skills to allow for the express pathway for reading to be activated for accurate, automatic word recognition. When she first read for me, even in middle-first-grade-level material, the reading was slow and halting with lots of stumbles over words. She brought some materials left over from the expensive private tutoring clinic—an abysmal experience—she had attended during the spring and summer of her second-grade year and while those materials were indeed on her instructional level, the tutor had lashed out at Daniella for not doing her homework. The negative experience notwithstanding, Daniella liked the comic book stories about Cinderella that were on her instructional level:

> Yella, please sweep the front steps.
> Stella, please clean the garage.
> Ella, you do the dishes. And use soap this time!
>   (Kumon Institute of Education 3A 110b)

The problem was that the private tutor tried to herd Daniella through the little sets of comic books and didn't stick with any one of the stories long enough for Daniella to gain fluency and automatic word recognition, either through recognition of chunks, or by remembering the story through repetition. Daniella could not read these beginning first-grade-level stories fluently when she came to me in July.

At the outset of our sessions, Daniella needed a few high-interest, relatively short reading selections that she could read over and over and over to get into the flow. She had to *feel* like a reader. We started out with repeated readings of *The Foot Book*. We did lots of fluency work. We did echo reading, shared reading, repeated reading, and dramatic readings (readings with exaggerated expression and hand gestures while swaying with the rhythm and cadence of the text.) We read a few selections—the Dr. Seuss books, the stories that Daniella wrote, and the Cinderella comic books—over and over. Sometimes we worked through a small section to get it perfect—then we put it all together. We read lots and lots of ways—sometimes chanting line by line, page by page, echoing, sharing, laughing together when we got it right and joking at our inept stumbles. We did echo reading and individual reading mixing it up just to keep it interesting and just to keep it going. Daniella practiced these materials at home.

It worked. *The Foot Book* was the first book Daniella could read orally well enough to sound like a skilled reader. Of course she had memorized it, but *The Foot Book* gave her confidence and she loved reading it. She was able to recognize the words in text accurately and rapidly without conscious effort. Her phrasing and expression during reading aloud, for the first time, sounded like natural speech. The reading of it became easy for her and it thrilled her to read it and read it and read it. One day she told me, "I could read this for my class!" For the first time she knew she could read. *She could read! She could read! SHE COULD READ!*

More and More Books—Advancing Step by Step. Before *The Foot Book* (Level E) was completely mastered I made an announcement: "This one is too easy for you, Daniella. You need a challenge!" I gave her a choice of three higher-level books. She selected another Dr. Seuss book, *Green Eggs and Ham*, an end-of-first-grade Level J, five levels higher than *The Foot Book.* We both loved Dr. Seuss books for the clever content. Daniella loved the meter and rhyme, and the fun of it and I loved the repeated word families and chunks of spelling patterns that she so desperately needed to read automatically. In addition to a higher reading level, *Green Eggs and Ha*m had 688 more words than *The Foot Book.* (There are 810 words in *Green Eggs and Ham* versus 122 words in *The Foot Book.*) Few teachers would make a big deal of counting the words in a picture book, but it was a big deal for me. As I listened to Daniella read *The Foot Book* for what might have been her one-hundredth time, I imagined that the neurons in her brain had fired thousands and thousands of times for each reading of its 122 words. Marie Clay's wise counsel echoed in my brain: "Every time a child reads a sentence . . . every (single) word in the sentence profits by being used, . . . moving further towards fluency [to] automatic responding" (Clay 1982, 4). *The Foot Book* was charging up Daniella's brain to read automatically! She was discovering that accurate, automatic word recognition was in her grasp.

In my mind, *Green Eggs and Ham* wasn't just a delightful story, it was a speed drill for the 810 high-frequency words between its covers. Whenever Daniella read it I imagined electrical currents firing in the back of her left hemisphere. They were firing in all the right areas and the neural connections were growing. Every time she reread it, those "reading lights" in her mind were sparking. She was activating a shock wave of knowledge and understanding.

Celebrations. At the second tutoring session I invited Daniella's parents to come in at the end of the session when they came to pick up Daniella.

"Look at this," I said. "Come see a miracle!"

Daniella did a perfect rendition of *Green Eggs and Ham* as tears welled in her mother's eyes. It was the first of many celebrations.

Chunks and Chunks and Chunks. At the same time we were doing *The Foot Book* and *Green Eggs and Ham*, we were drilling with chunks of phonics patterns and sight words and we called it our spelling or word work.

"Let's work with some words!" I would say.

Daniella recognized a sizable number of words on sight when she came to me, but remarkably, it almost seemed as if she read them logographically. She didn't see a connection between *hat, bat,* and *cat*. Using the Zaner-Bloser first-grade spelling book as my resource (Gentry 2004c), I selected nine first-grade spelling pattern units, all with high-frequency words, and we did word sorts. We did teacher-led sorts and I showed her the pattern as we hand spelled the words: /h/ /-at/, *hat*; /c/ /-at/, *cat*; /h/ /-as/, *has*; /h/ /-is/, *his*; /d/ /-id/, *did*. We did buddy sorts, and speed sorts. Daniella picked up on this activity rapidly. She practiced the sorts at home. In two weeks she could spell fifty-four first-grade words perfectly and I hoped she was beginning to pay attention to their pattern relationships.

The Power List. We started work on what I called our power list—a list of forty word pairs that matched the important CVC and CVCe patterns that we had worked on since our first session. I used the list from the Sally Shaywitz book (2003, 214) because it made an easy speed drill and reality check to see if the patterns were being learned on a level of automaticity. (I used the term "reality check" because the word "test" traumatized too many third graders in Florida.) The list, presented in Figure 10.3, were forty pairs of short CVC words paired with the companion CVCe pattern such as *hop* and *hope,* and *bit* and *bite.*

Picking up on the empirical research from Brown and Morris that suggests that all second-grade-level learners need to recognize the short vowels, I had started work with short vowel patterns in our very first session. I added the

bit, bite	cub, cube	cut, cute
can, cane	cap, cape	cod, code
con, cone	Dan, Dane	dim, dime
fad, fade	fat, fate	fin, fine
fir, fire	hat, hate	hid, hide
hop, hope	kit, kite	Jan, Jane
man, mane	mad, made	mat, mate
not, note	pal, pale	pan, pane
pin, pine	rat, rate	rid, ride
rip, ripe	rob, robe	rod, rode
Sam, same	sid, side	sit, site
tam, tame	tap, tape	Tim, time
Tom, tome	tub, tube	van, vane
win, wine		

FIGURE 10.3   CVC and CVCe Matched Pairs

e-marker contrasting pattern to each short vowel combination and we worked with them until we learned them. Daniella could only get through the first eight pairs on August 19: *bit, bite; can, cane; con, cone; fad, fade*—and even through I was seeing them as chunks she was slow and analytical. By August 19 she was trying to read them letter-by-letter. We worked with these patterns at every session—though not just with the list, but whenever the patterns appeared in stories and she missed them, I would do short column drills:

hop   hope

at   ate

pet   Pete

bit   bite

Even though I described them as patterns and chunks from the beginning, I observed Daniella move from Phase 2 to Phase 3, before moving to Phase 4. It was interesting to watch Daniella go through the tadpole phases before discovering a chunking phase for decoding. She initially tried to read the patterns attending to beginning and ending letters. From this partial alphabetic strategy, she moved to sounding them letter-by-letter. From this full alphabetic strategy, she eventually moved to seeing them as chunks of phonics patterns. Even on August 31 she still might not recognize *bit, men, man,* or *bite* in isolation. But we continued to work and I tried to be patient to allow time for the last shift in her conceptualization of chunking these English spelling patterns. There seemed to be a glimmer of understanding as early as August 9—but the idea of how the alternating short and long chunks worked would take many months to become automatic. By September 31 Daniella could get through the first half of the list of forty CVC versus CVCe pairs getting most of them correct. For the first time, on Novermber 11, she got all forty pairs through analysis. (I imagined she was still using Area B, the parieto-temporal area for slow, letter-by-letter analysis.) On December 14 she improved and recognized more of the pairs automatically, but their recognition still was not automatic. In our first session in January Daniella aced the list. (Was Area C, the occipito-temporal area, now revving through the list automatically? It seemed plausible.) It had taken five months! It was disconcerting to note that slow recognition of these basic chunks seemed out of step with the rapid gains Daniella continued to make in reading level. I suspect that while the important redundancy and backup systems for reading were moving her forward, breaking the code was still holding her back. Getting the list was a breakthrough. She could use the chunks to break down words into syllables and pronounce them. These chunks gave Daniella access to literally thousands of single syllable and polysyllabic words: *smite, hope-ful, in-hos-pit-a-ble, e-man-ci-pate, re-fresh-ing!*

Reading and Writing Reciprocity. Reading cannot be separated from writing. It's neither research-based, practicable, nor sensible to read first without writing.

Students must connect reading and writing every day (Routman 2005). It has to be writing *and* reading first. That's how the brain works. Knowing this, I made writing a prominent aspect of our tutorial session. I combined shared writing and Language Experience Approach (Lee and Van Allen 1963) to allow Daniella to create meaningful personal written accounts on topics that were important to her and she learned to read these selections fluently. Daniella wrote her stories and I scaffolded and provided help with spelling as she wrote. On one day when she was too tired to write, I took dictation. It was clear to me that much of the same brain circuitry being activated for reading was activated for writing so every writing sample was construed as a reading opportunity. The chunking and spelling work in our writing made the decontextualized spelling, word sorting, and chunking work we did meaningful and concrete. Daniella understood the connection between reading, writing, and spelling. In spite of her low level of skills, she was able to think up meaningful and wonderful age-appropriate writing samples. I provided the help she needed to write them down.

The timeline—nine sessions

Here is a timeline showing part of our work together with commentary pointing out signals of Daniella's advancement including the peaks and plateaus:

July 26

We started work on *The Foot Book.*

Daniella couldn't read lots of first-grade-level words including words as simple as *try* and dozens of basic high-frequency short vowel (CVC) and e-marker patterns. We worked on *hop* versus *hope, at* versus *ate, pet* versus *Pete,* and *bit* versus *bite.* She didn't get it. I made up a game tailored somewhat after Making Words (Cunningham and Cunningham 1992; Rasinski and Oswald 2005), which we called Chunking Columns. In the game we practiced particular spelling patterns that Daniella missed in her reading and writing. Daniella wrote the words as I said, "If you can write *ho, ho, ho,* you can write *so!* If you can write *so,* you can write *no.* If you can write *so,* you can write *so long.* If you can write *no,* you can write *no-tice.* If you can write *so,* you can write *so-lu-tion.*" I helped her with the chunks such as *-tion* in *solution.* Then we practiced reading the list. It occurred to me that she liked being told "you can write . . . , you can write . . . , you can write!" Here's the first practice:

ho, ho, ho	feed	fed	day
so	feet	bed	bay
no	see	red	play
so long	seen	Ben	say
notice (no-tice)	bee	Ed	staying
solution (so-lu-tion)	green	Eddie	maybe

We enjoyed writing stories together. Each time she wrote a story we read it for several weeks until she could read it perfectly. I wanted her to feel like a writer and get into the flow so I spelled any words she couldn't get as she wrote. It was a tutorial form of shared writing and scaffolded writing. If she made a false start I would say "It's p-a-i-n-t-e-d" just to keep her going. We were using a variation of Language Experience Approach (Lee and Van Allen 1963) using the text of her stories as content for reading lessons. Daniella loved reading her stories over and over and I noticed that her stories grew in sophistication over the course of our tutorial and she grew in confidence. "My House" was from July 26.

MY HOUSE

My mom fixed it up.
First, she took down a wall.
Next, she took out the carpet.
Instead of the carpet she put down a tile. She painted the kitchen and the bathroom yellow and she painted the living room green. Finally, she painted her room blue. Now our house is beautiful!

August 3

Daniella still didn't understand the chunking principles underlying basic short and long vowels. She missed *met, smile, mile, Pete,* and *bit* from the previous week.

I did lots of talking about chunks. When we wrote together, I spelled out the patterns she needed and broke the words into syllable chunks like *shi-ny* and *spark-ling*.

She Wrote "My Beautiful Mom."

MY BEAUTIFUL MOM

My mom has a beautiful face and shiny beautiful blonde hair. Her eyes are like sparkling stars. Her personality is beautiful too. She's very nice, happy and has a sparkling smile. She's always laughing, singing, and smiling.
I love my mom!

Initially Daniella couldn't read *laughing* as a sight word but after rereading her story I challenged her to memorize the spelling. "*Laugh-ing.* L-a-u-g-h. L-a-u-g-h. L-a-u-g-h. Try to see this chunk in your mind," I said. "You don't see this spelling pattern very often in English." She closed her eyes, paused for a moment, and spelled it. We used the same process and she learned to spell *beau-ti-ful.* I told her these were big words and happy words and we would be using them a lot. I found it remarkable that she could spell *beautiful* before she could spell *hope.*

We read *Green Eggs and Ham* for the first time. She loved it so we practiced it over and over. She picked it up and started reading for her parents when they walked in to pick her up. Her Mother said, "Daniella, we have to go. Dr. Gentry's time is up." She read all sixty-two pages! She wouldn't stop!

August 9

Daniella remembered how to spell *beautiful* and she spelled *laughing* correctly with a little prompting.

She did her first "dramatic reading" of *Green Eggs and Ham*, standing across from me on the other side of the dining room table as if she were on a stage. She read it with such verve and expression, that it gave me goose bumps and made me laugh. I gave her a standing ovation!

Like most "only children" in a family, Daniella not only *liked* having choices, she *insisted* upon them. She was accustomed to getting her way. I suggested writing the story of Cinderella but she said, "Oh no, let's do *Green Eggs and Ham*." I thought condensing that sixty-two-page picture book into a one-page story would be difficult, so I suggest that we use a First-Then-Next-Last story map:

GREEN EGGS AND HAM!

The two characters meet and the
Boy says "I am Sam."
Sam tries to get the man to eat green eggs and ham. For example, in the dark. The Man yells "I do not like them Anywhere!" In the end he says, "I do like green eggs and ham."

Daniella misread *met* in isolation and still did not understand the concept of CVC versus CVCe, however, she caught on and read all the CVC an CVCe words correctly at the end of the session.

August 18

Daniella returned from a vacation to Disneyworld where she had been trapped in a hotel without electricity or water. I suggested her trip might be a great idea for a story but she chose to write about "The Jimmy Neutron Ride." Her topic was narrower and a better choice.

THE JIMMY NEUTRON RIDE

First you have to get in line. Then people who work there take you in. They show a movie and then they open up the doors and you have to sit in little jets. The automatic doors close. Then it gets dark. The chairs move up and move around, so it gets scary. You feel like you are inside the movie.

We started the Power List (refer back to Figure 10.3).

Daniella loved *Henry and Mudge,* a new book for her by Cynthia Rylant, and we celebrated her advancement to its second-grade reading level. I marveled at her latest renditions of *Green Eggs and Ham,* which she delivered like a Shakespearian thespian. Her reading of it was spiced with psychological asides to me, as she analyzed the characters. "Oh, he's very frustrated here," she commented. "I think he's angry. He's losing his patience." She brought a level of meaning and analysis to this very easy book that few first graders would have been capable of. It reminded me of Louise Rosenblatt's Transactional Theory (1938, 1978). Daniella was living through *Green Eggs and Ham* taking an aesthetic stance, not merely reading it for the basic story information. In reading the story for pleasure and bringing a high level of creative analysis and her own internal interpretation, Daniella was comprehending an easy book at a much higher than usual level. I was watching a transaction between the reader and the text in which the text conveyed meaning brought to it by the reader.

[Note: Everyone in Florida lost a month when four hurricanes pounded our state during August and September. We were under four evacuations and my work with Daniella was interrupted.]

September 31

Daniella started out with a perfect dramatic reading of *Green Eggs and Ham* but this time she informed me that she would be using a "narrator" and changing her voice to fit the character's changing moods. The repeated reading was never boring for Daniella because each session she cleverly invented creative and wonderful ways to make it stimulating and interesting. She got into the story. She did this of her own volition. It was a natural process for her.

Our making words and column formations with chunks was becoming pretty sophisticated, as illustrated in Figure 10.4.

Short *e* still gave Daniella a challenge. She could not spell *man* or *men* consistently, and she still might not recognize *bit* in isolation. She was attending to a letter-for-a-sound but not chunking when decoding words.

October 12

Daniella read *Nate the Great Goes Undercover* by Sharmat M. Weinman, which I had tried several weeks earlier and found too hard for her, but now she could read it. She missed the word *five,* and miscued on *saw,* which she called "was," but she self-corrected. We worked on her third-grade-level homework assignments and I noted that she was able to do them with my mediation. We did chunking graphosyllabic analysis with words like *im-me-di-ate-ly* and *tem-per-a-ture.* She could read words like *per-son-al-i-ty* if I pointed to the chunks. I gave

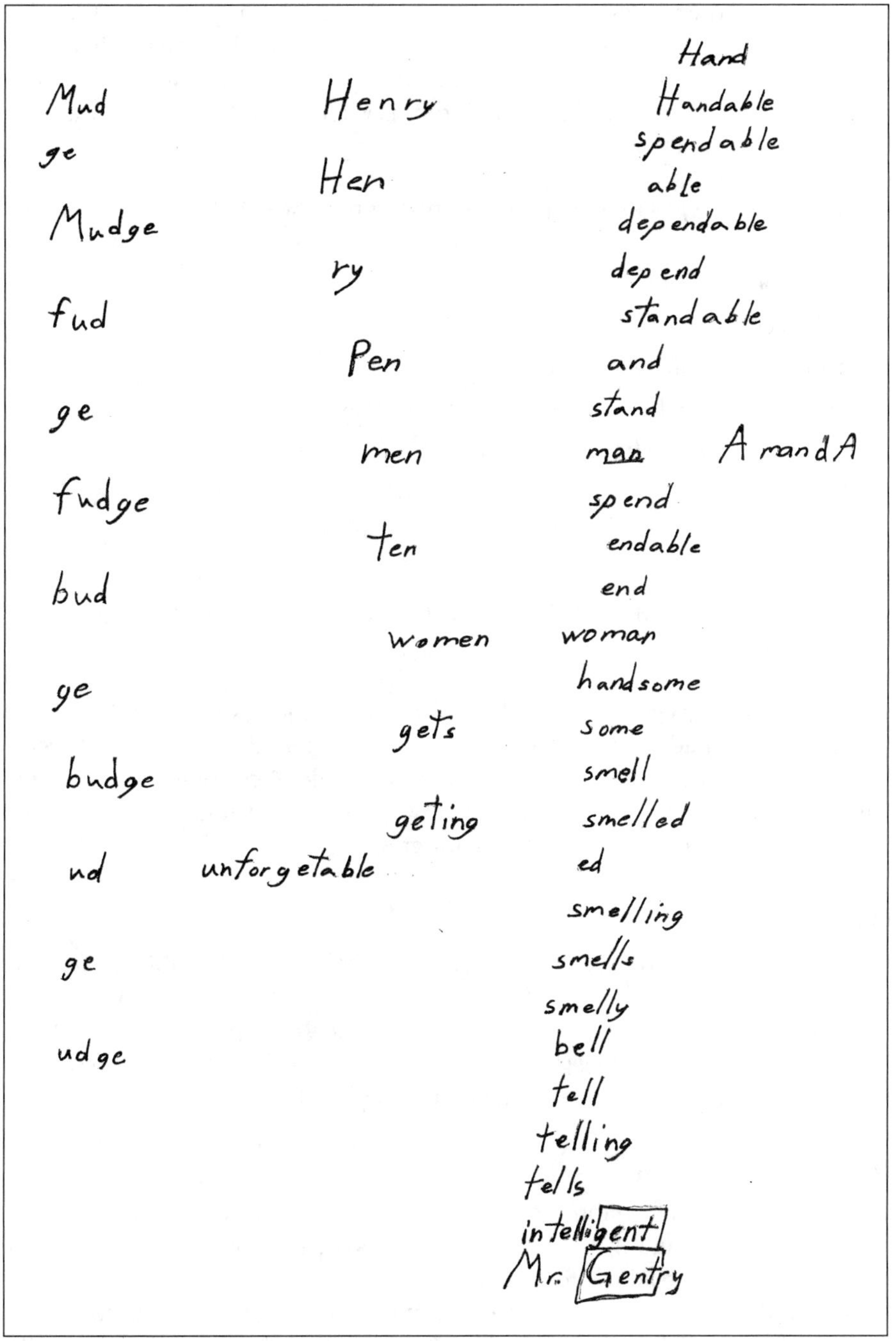

Mud
ge
Mudge

fud

ge

fudge

bud

ge

budge

nd

ge

udge

Henry

Hen

ry

Pen

men

ten

women

gets

geting

unforgetable

Hand
Handable
spendable
able
dependable
depend
standable
and
stand
man   A rand A
spend
endable
end
woman
handsome
some
smell
smelled
ed
smelling
smells
smelly
bell
tell
telling
tells
intelligent
Mr. Gentry

FIGURE 10.4   Column Formations with Chunks

Daniella the Monster Tests (see the Appendix) and it clearly revealed that she was moving from a letter-for-a-sound to spelling in chunks. For Daniella, the chunking strategy seemed to happen in her writing before it was happening consistently in her reading. She moved from Level 3 to Level 4 when I prompted her to spell *human* in chunks.

1. mostr (Level 3) to mos-ter (Level 3 due to preconsonaltal nasal ommision of n)
2. younithed (Level 4)
3. dres (Level 4)
4. bottom (Level 4)
5. hite for "hike" which she mispronounces (Level 4)
6. humn (Level 3) to hu-men with my chunking cue (Level 4)
7. egol (Level 4)
8. closd (Level 3)
9. bompt (Level 3)
10. tipe (Level 4) She did TIP first and self-corrected remarking, "No, that's *tip!*"

There were seven Level 4 chunked spellings on Daniella's Monster Test! As a speller Daniella had moved from Level 2 when we started on July 26 to Level 3 and now to Level 4 on October 12. We had a chunking celebration. I thought, "this is phenomenal!" as I watched what was happening on the test. The Monster Test made it easy to clearly see her progress.

October 25

On a homework exercise she miscued on *captain* and I said, "Read the first chunk."

"Cape," she said. "Wait let me think." The parieto-temporal area was firing!

When she read *Green Eggs and Ham* she said, "This is easy for me because I read it a hundred times!" She had great fun reading it.

December 14

We spent most of the session on what I believed to be a third-grade practice test exercise entitled "Dino Eggs by the Dozen," presented in Figure 10.5. Daniella told me she hadn't read it and that she needed to read it. She learned to read it fluently and amazed me by answering all of the comprehension questions after our first slow and labored mediated reading. I marveled that she could handle the piece this well, and for the first time I believed she might pass the state reading test in April.

Directions: Read the story.

Dino Eggs by the Dozen

It was more than 70 million years ago. A group of female dinosaurs roamed along a riverbank in South America. They were going to lay their eggs there. There were thousands of eggs! One by one, the baby dinosaurs started to hatch.

Then a giant flood washed over the land. They were lost forever.

Well, not quite forever. In November 1998, a group of scientists uncovered something. They found the eggs and babies.

Scientists were in a field. It was covered with rocks the size of grapefruits. They took a closer look. The "rocks" were really dinosaur eggs. "There were thousands of eggs all over the place," says Luis Chiappe, a team leader.

The eggs belonged to small dinosaurs. They had long necks and ate plants. They are called titanosaurs.

Of course, all of these dinosaurs were not really small. An adult titanosaur was more than 50 feet long. Babies were about 15 inches long. That's "the size of a small poodle," says Chiappe.

The flood buried the eggs in mud. The mud helped preserve the babies still inside the eggshells. One egg held 32 teeth. Each tooth is small enough to fit inside this capital "O." Others held patches of scaly skin.

Chiappe and his team returned to the area. They hoped to answer more questions. They wanted to know whether the mama dinosaurs made careful nests or laid their eggs just anywhere. With so many eggs yet to be studied, those answers may be just waiting to hatch.

Directions: Answer these questions. You may look at the story.

1. On what continent were the dinosaurs roaming the riverbank?

2. Why were the baby dinosaurs "lost forever"?

3. Why weren't the eggs and babies really lost forever?

4. Why do you think the scientists want to learn more about these dinosaurs?

5. How might this discovery helpful to scientists?

6. What would have happened to the babies if mud had not preserved them?

7. How were the eggs similar to grapefruits?

8. If the floods had not come, what would have happened to these dinosaurs?

9. Explain the importance of this discovery to scientists.

FIGURE 10.5   **"Dino Eggs by the Dozen" Test Practice Worksheet**

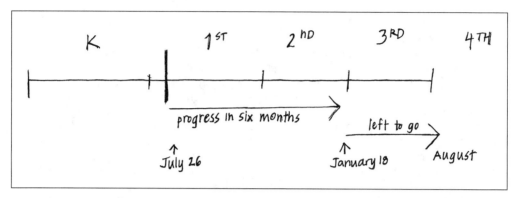

FIGURE 10.6   Daniella's Reading Improvement Chart

January 18

She read "Dino Eggs by the Dozen" in half the time it had taken the previous month. Her reading wasn't fluent but she read it independently. She now read

Daniella Working at the Author's Dining Table

words that she couldn't read a month ago such as *roam,* and *South America.* But she miscued on *giant, field,* and *enough.* She says pō-dle for poo-dle.

I made the chart in Figure 10.6 to show Daniella and her mother Daniella's reading progress over the last six months—from beginning first-grade level to roughly beginning of third-grade level.

I told Daniella's mother, "This child will be on fourth-grade level by August! We only have one more grade level to go!" We celebrated with presents.

My work with Daniella is continuing. Our infrequent work together the remainder of the spring of her third-grade year was preoccupied with testing to prove to the school team that Daniella could read. Our tutoring time was replaced by visits with the school staff. I saw my role changing from teacher/tutor to confidence builder and advocate. I plan to meet with her occasionally just to check in and give her a boost. Over the summer after third grade Daniella made a trip to Hungary. When I tested Daniella in April of her third-grade year she scored on fourth-grade level in both word recognition and comprehension.

Daniella's case study has helped me better understand how children learn to read and some of the complexities, nuances, and marvels of it. I think I learned more from Daniella than I taught her. I taught Daniella to read in eighteen hours. She had attended school for six hundred and thirty-one days.

Postscript

A Letter from My Mother

My mother taught me to read. She was my first grade teacher. Most of her thirty-four-year teaching career was spent teaching children to read in first grade. At that time, there were no kindergartens in the poor rural school district in North Carolina where she taught.

Mama always had a clear mission for first-grade teaching: "It's so important that I teach them to read." I heard these words over and over and she loved to talk about the particulars of it. Perhaps it's not coincidental that I developed the same passion for teaching reading and became a reading teacher myself. Eventually, I earned a Ph.D. in reading education, directed a university reading center, and placed reading instruction as the capstone of my career.

When Mama was eighty-four years old, she began to experience declining health that confined her to the exigencies of assisted living, a decline that would present unexpected challenges persisting into her nineties. One major disappointment was failing eyesight, which eventually left her unable to read. Soon after leaving her home and moving into assisted living, to my great amazement, my mother wrote me a wonderful letter written with clarity and grace. It was unexpected. I thought Mama had already lost the precision grip of the pen and the wherewithal to write letters. It had saddened me because over the years her letters to me had always been beautifully scripted, spelled perfectly, and poignant—a treasure trove of love, wise counsel, and joy that had begun in my college days and lasted into my fifties. The sparking jewel here was a letter to congratulate me for writing a book about teaching reading. It would be the last letter my mother would ever be able to write to me.

Dear Richard,

No words can express how proud I am of your new book — The Literacy Map. I am that you had the ability to write it. You have worked very, very hard to develop your talents and skills. That you chose your life's work "education" was certainly the right thing for you to do. (Like Mama: Like Son) You have contributed much to help children, teachers, your family, friends and ME. All has been recieved graciously and with deep appreciaton. We love you for it.

Reading your book is one of my chief joys now. How happy I would have been to have had a book like this when I began my first year teaching. Instead, they gave me about 40 kids, a book Dick and Jane, and said Teach them to Read — And I did! You were one of those little people. I loved everyone of them. I kept at it 34 years.

The joy of teaching is in later years — meeting former students and hearing about their present life now.

Always remember that you have made me very happy, with your writings, etc. I wanted to write a book — never had time. It's too late now. oh, oh, oh Yet maybe, there's a little bit of me on a page or two of yours.

I love you,
Mama

11-7-99

My Mom's Letter

There is more than a page or two from my mother in *Breaking the Code*. There is a passion for teaching literacy radiating from my Mom underlying every page in this book. There is recognition, for those of us who teach reading, of the importance of our work.

If you teach a child to read, or an adolescent or an adult, my mother would say you have given that person an extraordinary gift. Perhaps this gift will chart the person's brighter future. Perhaps it will lead him or her to discover their inner self. Reading may allow the person you teach to create a new vision, or in Albert Einstein's words, awaken joy in creative expression and knowledge. It may comfort him or her in loneliness. When you teach someone to read, your gift will sometimes make him or her cry, and sometimes laugh. Through reading some will unshackle brutal bonds of abuse, slavery, or oppression. Reading will help them find their way.

Reading may help your student dream better; it may help him or her pray. It may lead your student to deeper more profound thought making. Reading informs. When you give the gift of reading, you connect mankind to all humanity in the past and present. And for the reader who writes, that person's thought may transform future generations. Your student's written word may persist long after the writer is gone.

My mother would say to you who are reading teachers: "Your life has great purpose and meaning."

Honor the person who taught you to read. In teaching another or by moving them forward, you honor mankind. Reading teachers amplify our most profound human qualities. Reading teachers are in a class of their own.

Appendix

The Instructional Blueprint

This Appendix presents the Instructional Blueprint for writing, spelling, and reading that unfolds in nonalphabetic, pre-alphabetic, partial alphabetic, full alphabetic, and consolidated alphabetic phases. It shows in detail what should be expected at each level throughout the phase of development and shows expectations in writing, spelling, and reading separately, while highlighting their phase similarities. A "minimal competency benchmark" is assigned to each phase based on what one observes in the child's writing. A list of teaching techniques for each phase highlights the kind of instruction especially useful for helping the child move to the next highest level or phase of development. Specific information on the implementation and use of each of the teaching techniques is provided in more detail in Chapters 6 and 7. (Note: Phase descriptions are an adaptation of information reported in Gentry 2005; Expected behaviors are an adaptation of information reported in Gentry 1982, 2000a.)

Level 0—No Letter Use

Look at the four writing samples in Figure A.1. If the child's writing samples look most like these the child is likely to be Level 0. The child is at Level 0 if he or she is unable to write his or her own name and unable to write using letters.

Writing

Writing at Level 0 may be described as *nonalphabetic writing*. This is a symbol representation stage characterized by no use of letters. Writing is represented by marks, scribbles, and pictures and often may be referred to with children as "wavy writing" or "looping writing" (Feldgus and Cardonick 1999). No discernable letters are present. The Level 0 writer knows that writing has meaning and may be fascinated with the idea, but does not grasp how the system works.

FIGURE A.1   Level 0 Writing

Spelling

Spellings are not yet invented. The child may just now be learning to write his or her name. Learning to write one's name is a watershed event. Once children can write their name or other important words and form a few letters, they can easily move to Level 1.

Minimal competency benchmark

Minimal competency at Level 0 based on expected progress in writing is that the child would be functioning in this phase by the beginning of kindergarten. Children should learn to write their names in the beginning weeks of kindergarten if they cannot already do so.

Reading

No Level 0 Reading Phase has been reported.

Useful teaching strategies

Teaching strategies that support writing and reading reciprocity and are particularly useful for helping children understand the concepts needed in order to move from Level 0 to Level 1 include the following: Teach the child to write his or her name and important words. Teach the alphabet song. Begin teaching letter recognition and sounds. Once children can write their names encourage them to fill in the highlighted lines of writing scaffolds using letters to replace the formerly used squiggles, wavy writing or loopy writing (see Chapter 7). Use materialization techniques for phonological awareness, including clapping out syllables in names, and work with rhyming words. Introduce phonemic awareness with matching activities such as matching words that begin with the same sound in the child's name or a targeted letter-sound correspondence. Target rhyming words in nursery rhymes and poems. Use hand spelling activities with rhyming words targeting easy patterns such as *rat, cat, bat, sat, fat, mat* using hand spelling with the thumb going up to help the child recognize the beginning sound. (See Chapters 6 and 7 for a full description of teaching strategies appropriate for Level 0.) Make sure the child is exposed to lots of print via read-alouds and book handling experiences.

Key Techniques for Level 0: Writing workshop; writing one's name; letter formation and practice; use of invented spelling; scaffolded writing; adult underwriting; word play with rhyming words; clapping syllables; materialization techniques such as stretching out the sounds in the child's name while modeling with stretchable fabric; modeling beginning sounds by elongating and accentuating sounds; matching beginning sounds, particularly words that begin with the beginning sound of the child's name or a targeted letter-sound correspondence.

Level 1—Nonalphabetic Letter Use

Look at the four writing samples in Figure A.2. If the child's writing samples look most like these the child is likely to be Level 1.

Writing

Writing at Level 1 may be described as *pre-alphabetic writing*. The Level 1 writer begins to show some control of letters. Letters used by the Level 1 writer do not represent sounds and appear to be random letters. Level 1 writing cannot be read by others or by the writer out of context or after a lapse in time. The writer puts letters on the page to express meaning but he or she does not know how the system of print works and demonstrates no understanding of the regularity or alphabetic nature of print.

EXPECTED WRITING BEHAVIORS

1. Letters are used to represent a message.
2. No letter-sound correspondence is evident.
3. The writer may or may not know left-to-right directionality.
4. Letters may appear on the page in sporadic order—top to bottom, sideways, floating, etc.
5. Alphabetic knowledge may be minimal or substantial ranging from a few known letters to substantial production of many letters.
6. Letters may often be repeated in letter strings.
7. There may be a preference for uppercase letters.
8. Uppercase and lowercase letters may be interspersed indiscriminately.

(Adapted from Gentry, 1982)

FIGURE A.2   Level 1 Writing

Spelling

Level 1 is precommunicative spelling.

At least half of the invented spellings are precommunicative: Spellings appear to be random letters. Messages and words may be spelled in strings of letters but there are no letter-sound matches. Spacing may not occur between words. Phonemic awareness is not evident.

Monster Test

Spellings in the Monster Test look like this:

1. monster: socvnefh (any combination of random letters with no letter-sound correspondence)

2. united: kducn (any combination of seemingly random letters with no letter-sound correspondence)

3. dress: pncrnstw (any combination of seemingly random letters with no letter-sound correspondence)

4. bottom: lpvduz (any combination of random letters with no letter-sound correspondence)

5. hiked: xpvrn (any combination of random letters with no letter-sound correspondence)

6. human: dlmxxt (any combination of random letters with no letter-sound correspondence)

7. eagle: ctwk (any combination of random letters with no letter-sound correspondence)

8. closed: eihhc (any combination of random letters with no letter-sound correspondence)

9. bumped: kjfn (any combination of random letters with no letter-sound correspondence)

10. type: lcne (any combination of random letters with no letter-sound correspondence)

EXPECTED SPELLING BEHAVIORS

1. *At least half* of the invented spellings in a volume of writing (several writing samples) or half of the invented spellings on an instrument such as the Monster Test are *precommunicative.*

2. No letter-sound correspondence is evident.

3. Child uses individual letters or strings of letters for words or phases.

4. Letters may appear to be floating on the page.

5. Numerals may be used as letters.

6. Letters may be interspersed with scribbles or indecipherable letter forms.

7. The invented spelling may represent entire messages or it may represent specific words.

Minimal competency benchmark

Minimal competency at Level 1 based on expected progress in writing is that the child would be functioning in this phase or exhibiting the expected behaviors by the middle of kindergarten. Intervention may be needed if the child cannot write some letters, cannot write his or her name and has not progressed to Level 1 writing/spelling by the middle of kindergarten. (Under optimal conditions, many children should go beyond this benchmark by the middle of kindergarten.)

Reading

Reading at Level 1 may be described as *pre-alphabetic*. Level 1 readers are far from having mastered a system of chunking spelling into patterns, a core mechanism of reading. When they encounter a new or unknown word, they rely upon nonalphabetic information to decode the word. This strategy is unsystematic and often leads to guessing, reliance on pictures, or sometimes use of context cues remembered from having heard the story over and over. These readers may not be able to do the voice-to-print match. Words tend to be remembered as visual logos, which is very inefficient since each word must be remembered as a separate entity and no alphabetic cues are used to help the Level 1 reader remember words. Level 1 readers may memorize rhymes, poems, easy books, and short selections, but their paucity of understanding of the alphabet system puts great limitations on them. They must begin to unlock the mysteries of the English alphabetic system including learning about the function of sounds and letters for reading before they may be expected to advance much farther as readers.

A number of factors may influence reading level so the following description and levels represent what is probable though individual variation may exist and should be expected. The basic strategy at this level is to echo-read or memorize text that has been read over and over to the child. (Other beginning reading techniques include whole word approaches that start out by having children memorize individual words such as the famous Scott, Foresman and Company "Dick and Jane" series, and synthetic phonics approaches that start out by having children memorize letter-sound correspondences and move through graduated, often, unnatural highly decodable text.) Starting out by having children echo-read meaningful text along with appropriate phonics instruction or balanced literacy instruction that includes contextual reading, phonics, spelling, and writing is currently the preferred method supported by research (International Reading Association and National Association for the Education of Young Children 1998; Morris 2003; Snow, Burns and Griffin 1998). In the balanced reading context as children start out by echo-reading meaningful text, it should be noted that even as the child is relying a great deal on memory of story or support from the illustration, the Level 1 reader is not cueing from the letter symbols. Level 1 readers may be successful with memorizing environmental print, names, signs, labels, short easily memorized nursery rhymes, verses, short poems, or song lyrics, and they are often very successful memorizing adult underwriting of labels, phrases, sentences, lists, short directions, very short stories, or summary charts that use their oral language patterns to describe their own writings and drawings (a version of Language Experience Approach [Van Allen 1976]). They may memorize keep books, caption books, pattern books, and enjoy alphabet books, pop-up books, board books, and concept books about animals, colors, numbers, plants, and shapes, and other topics. A great deal of repetition of reading and rereading the same material from memory is highly beneficial at this level. Probable reading level begins with environmental print, names, words, labels, and phrases and moves to a few Level A–B easy books, which have three to five words on a page, focus on a concept the child is familiar with, often have a repeated sentence stem, have a clear picture-to-text match, and are meaningful, easy and fun for the child to read over and over. Examples of material that may be read after repeated rereadings at Level 1 include selections such as "Jack Be Nimble," "Roses Are Red," *I Paint,* by Jon Madian, and *The Pancake,* by Roderick Hunt.

EXPECTED READING BEHAVIORS

1. There is no systematic letter-sound processing.
2. Logo matches for word reading is evident.
3. No attention is paid to letter-sounds.
4. Attention is paid to nonalphabetic information.
5. There is possible phonological awareness (e.g., clapping syllables; recognizing rhyming words).
6. There is no phonemic awareness.

Useful teaching strategies

Teaching strategies that support writing and reading reciprocity and are particularly useful for helping children understand the concepts needed in order to move from Level 1 to Level 2 are summarized here and fully explicated in Chapters 6 and 7. Once children can write their names, increase the volume of writing with frequent opportunities to write using invented spelling. Use adult underwriting and scaffolded writing, encouraging a couple of written productions each week. Adult underwriting in writing journals should be read over and over until memorized. Continue focus on teaching letter recognition and matching sounds. Once children can fill in the highlighted lines of writing scaffolds using random letters, nudge them to replace random spellings with Level 2 spelling by matching beginning or ending sounds in words with appropriate letter-sound matches (see Chapter 6). Continue materialization techniques for phonological awareness including clapping out syllables in names and work with rhyming words. Remember that it is easier for children to work with rhyming words and syllables than with individual sounds (phonemes) that make up a word. Move from rhyming words and syllable work to onsets and rimes. Continue phonemic awareness with matching activities such as matching words that begin with the same sound as the child's name or a targeted letter-sound correspondence. Hand spelling activities with rhyming words and onset and rime patterns are ideal for Level 1, especially with the introduction and targeted focus on new letter-sound correspondences. For example, in focusing on the letter *H* and the /h/ sound one might introduce "A House Is a House for Me" and hand spell words such as *h-ouse, h-ive, h-ill, h-ole*. (See Chapters 6 and 7 for a full description of hand spelling and other teaching strategies appropriate for Level 1.) Model initial sounds by elongating and accentuating the sound. Use strategies to help the child develop the concept of word. Once a child understands that the printed word represents a spoken word, it's easier to teach the concept that the word is an entity with a beginning, middle, and ending. Do beginning and ending letter sound-matching activities first and move to the more difficult tasks such as isolating medial sounds and segmenting sounds in the word as the child moves to Level 2. In general, the progression from easiest to hardest phonemic awareness tasks is as follows: from matching, to sound isolation, to sound substitution, to blending, to sound segmentation, and finally to sound deletion (Yopp and Yopp 2000). The following directives illustrate the progression from easier to harder tasks:

1. *Matching.* "Which words begin with the same sound?"
2. *Sound Isolation.* "What sound do you hear at the beginning of *Jack?*"
3. *Sound Substitution.* "What word would you have if you changed the /J/ in Jack to /b/?"
4. *Blending.* "What word would you have if you put these sounds together: /J/ plus /-ack/? Once students are successful with onsets and rimes, challenge them with phonemes: "What word would you have if you put these sounds together: /j/-/a/-/k/?
5. *Sound Segmentation.* "Tell the sounds you hear in *Jack.*"
6. *Sound Deletion.* "Say *Jack* without the /j/" (-ack). "Say *Jack* without the /k/ at the end" (/ja/).

Key Techniques for Level 1: Writing workshop; scaffolded writing; use of invented spelling; adult underwriting; hand spelling for new sounds and letters; materialization techniques such as stretching out the sounds in words while modeling with stretchable fabric; modeling by elongating and accentuating sounds; teaching concept of word; modeling the space between words; finger spelling may be introduced as children move into Level 2 signaled by their ability to stretch out the sounds in a word; letter boxes/sound boxes may be introduced as children move into Level 2.

Level 2—Using Beginning and Ending Letters

Look at the four writing samples in Figure A.3. If the child's writing samples look most like these the child is likely to be Level 2 (a phase when the child gets most beginning and some ending sounds).

Writing

Level 2 writing may be described as *partial alphabetic writing*. When inventing a spelling, the writer does not provide full phonemic representation of words but often writes words in abbreviated spellings using one to three letters. Another variation of Level 2 is the use of a few letter-sound matches mixed with random letters. Prominent sounds in words such as the beginning and ending sounds are more often represented than medial sounds. Directionality is present. A few correct spellings may appear in the message. The Level 2 writer begins to make the connection that letters may represent some of the sounds within a word or message.

FIGURE A.3   Level 2 Writing

EXPECTED WRITING BEHAVIORS

1. The writer knows that letters represent sounds.

2. The writer has rudimentary knowledge and is able to provide partial but not complete representations of the sounds in words such as KT for *cat,* and MTBT for *motorboat.*

3. Some sounds are left out, particularly letters for representing the sounds in the middle of words.

4. A letter may be chosen to represent a word, sound, or syllable that matches the name of the letter such as R for *are,* U for *you,* and L-E for the first two syllables of *elephant.* These are called letter-name spellings.

5. Word segmentation may or may not be in evidence; however, the writer begins to move toward stabilization of the concept that a printed word is representation for a spoken word. Thus the concept of word begins to materialize. There may be little evidence of concept of word as a child first moves into Phase 2 but use of spaces between words and evidence of concept of word generally become more apparent towards the end of Phase 2.

6. The child begins to grasp the left-to-right sequential arrangement of letters for spelling. Left-to-right directionally for spelling is in evidence.

7. Alphabetic knowledge and letter formation become more complete. The child learns many letters and can better discriminate upper and lower case.

Spelling

Level 2 invented spelling is called *semiphonetic spelling.* Prominent sounds are now spelled with letter-sound matches. Some of the sounds in the invented word are not represented. This is the first level at which the child's spelling and writing show evidence of some (but not full) phonemic awareness.

Monster Test

Spellings in the Monster Test look like this:

1. monster: MTR (any combination of partial letter-sound correspondence)

2. united: U (any combination of partial letter-sound correspondence)

3. dress: JRS (any combination of partial letter-sound correspondence)

4. bottom: BT (any combination of partial letter-sound correspondence)

5. hiked: HT (any combination of partial letter-sound correspondence)

6. human: UM (any combination of partial letter-sound correspondence)

7. eagle: EL (any combination of partial letter-sound correspondence)

8. closed: KD (any combination of partial letter-sound correspondence)

9. bumped: B (any combination of partial letter-sound correspondence)

10. type: TP (any combination of partial letter-sound correspondence)

EXPECTED SPELLING BEHAVIORS

1. *At least half* of the invented spellings in a volume of writing (several writing samples) or half of the invented spellings on an instrument such as the Monster Test are *semiphonetic.*

2. Expect partial but not full representations: RUDF (Are you deaf?), HAB (happy).

3. Beginning and ending sounds are more likely to be represented than medial sounds: DP (dump), DF (deaf), OD (old); polysyllabic example: GABJ (garbage).

4. Expect letter-name spellings: R (are), U (you), L-EFT (elephant), B (bee), C (see).

Minimal competency benchmark

Minimal competency at Level 2 based on expected progress in writing is that the child would be functioning in this phase or exhibiting the expected behaviors by the end of kindergarten. Intervention may be needed if the child cannot make some letter-sound matches and fails to exhibit substantial alphabet knowledge by the end of kindergarten (Gentry 2000a, 2000b, 2004, 2005; International Reading Association 1998; Snow, Burns, and Griffin 1998). (Under optimal conditions, many children go beyond this phase by the end of kindergarten.)

Reading

Reading at Level 2 is called *partial alphabetic.* Level 2 readers make giant steps as readers by using the alphabet to cue word reading and this increases their word-reading skills. For the first time they begin to pay attention to some of the letter constituents of words to help them cue a word in memory. They are not yet transforming spelling chunks (graphosyllabic analysis) into pronunciations but they may be using beginning and ending letters to cue the words. The representations of words stored in memory at Level 2 are likely to be rudimentary and incomplete. Level 2 readers read new words by forming partial letter-sound representations, often linking initial and final letters to the sounds to form recognizable words but not paying attention to the medial letters. The brain may be forming an association matrix connecting beginning and ending letters with sounds allowing for effective cueing of *hot* versus *sun* but not so effective for *hot* versus *hat* or *hut.* The new understanding that letters represent sounds has transformative power, however, and moves the child to a new level of conceptualization of how the system works and makes it easier to read more books from memory. The child begins to see the rudiments of regularity and the rudiments of a pattern system as he or she matches some letters to sounds.

The approach that dominates when a Level 2 reader reads a novel word or unfamiliar word is that he or she often relies upon rudimentary alphabet knowledge and sometimes only a few known letter-sound matches but does begin to see some regularity in the system. The grapheme sound cue is information that previously was not being used. For the first time the reader comes to rely upon alphabetic information to help him or her read. While attention is on beginning and ending letters with little focus of attention on middle letters, it not surprising that attention to the middle of the word is limited because the middle is often constituted of vowels or vowel patterns that are more complex than most consonant letter-sound correspondences and tend to require more knowledge about how words work and are harder to read. Letters are decoded individually rather than in chunks at Level 2. The reader may not know all the letters of the alphabet and may know some letters but not their sounds, thus letter-sound correspondence is incomplete so new words are processed by partial-letter cues, sometimes in a kind of default strategy when the word being read contains letters that the child does not know.

When Level 2 readers encounter a new or unknown word, they may now rely upon some alphabetic information to decode the word, thus they are beginning to bring some sense of a system to the process as they search for regularity. These readers become more successful with the voice-to-print match. Like Level 1 readers, Level 2 readers rely heavily on memorization, but with the new strategy of cueing from partial alphabetic information it is easier to memorize rhymes, poems, easy books, and short selections. The basic strategy at Level 2 continues to be echo-reading and memorizing text that has been read over and over to making use of the same printed materials as are effective for Level 1, including environmental print, names, signs, labels, short easily memorized nursery rhymes, verses, short poems, and song lyrics. The idea is to increase the repertoire of materials that can be read from memory and allow the child to practice, further develop, and stabilize the newfound strategy of cueing from letters as well as develop a concept of word. The volume increases for memorizing adult underwriting of labels, phrases, sentences, lists, short directions, and a few lines of stories or messages that use the child's oral language patterns to describe their own writings and drawings. Memorization and practice of easy books, caption books, pattern books, alphabet books, pop-up books, board books, and concept books continue as the volume of books that are memorized increases. A great deal of repetition reading and rereading the same material from memory continues to be highly beneficial.

Probable reading level moves from labels and captions to more substantive material, usually with an increase in ability to read Level A–C easy books. By Level C the books tend to increase to more than five words on a page, but still focus on a concept the child is familiar with, often have a repeated sentence stem, have a clear picture-to-text match, and are meaningful, easy and fun for the child to read over and over and memorize. Students at Level 2 may start out at book Level A but may be expected to move to book levels B and C. Examples of material that Level 2 readers can read successfully include more sophisticated selections such as *Cat on the Mat,* by Brian Wildsmith, and the poem, "A House Is a House for Me," by Mary Ann Hoberman, eventually moving to books at the level of *Brown Bear, Brown Bear* (1970), by Bill Martin.

EXPECTED READING BEHAVIORS

1. Except cueing from beginning and ending letter matches.

2. Some phonemic awareness is evident.

3. Initial knowledge is of only a few letters and sounds.

4. Growth is seen in letter and sound knowledge.

5. There is limited memory for letters within a word.

6. A lack of attention is paid to medial letters in words.

7. The student has difficulty distinguishing between similarly spelled words.

8. There is development of the voice-to-print match.

9. The student doesn't use analogues unless the analogue (word family) is in view.

Key Techniques for Level 2: Writing workshop; scaffolded writing; use of invented spelling; adult underwriting; hand spelling for new sounds and letters; materialization techniques such as stretching out the sounds in words while modeling with stretchable fabric; modeling by elongating and accentuating sounds; finger spelling and letter boxes/sound boxes. As children move toward the end of Level 2, increase finger spelling and the use of letter boxes/sound boxes. Use three materialization techniques in this order: (1) stretch out the sounds, (2) finger spell the word, (3) use letter/sound boxes. First stretch out the sounds in a new word to be spelled by modeling with stretchable fabric. Next finger spell the word beginning with the thumb and providing a finger and a letter for each sound in the word. Then use letter/sound boxes allowing the child to write a letter in the box for each sound in a word.

Level 3—Full Letter–Sound Processing in Words— A Letter for a Sound

Look at the four writing samples in Figure A.4. If the child's writing samples look most like these the child is likely to be at Level 3 (a phase when the child uses a letter for each sound he or she hears in a word).

Writing

Writing at Level 3 may be described as *full alphabetic writing.* Level 3 writing is easy to read phonetically. The Level 3 writer's main strategy to invent a spelling is to use one letter for each sound in a word representing all the phonemes or surface sound features of the word being spelled. (A few exceptions are noted in

The three Pig's Lillte
one bay a Mut
hr. Pig Sent.
her three Lillte
Pig's Ot inot
The WoD's.
The Frst Litl Pig
Met a MaN With
a BuNDL uV.
tAte Ctor to Bild my
MaN GiV mE huse

OL vb At BLAce
BLAce iSA BLAC AND yiT
DOG. He CHASES me.
He GoT LosT. YE FAND Hm.

All About Blackie
Blackie is a black and white
dog. He chases me.
He got lost. We found him.

Halluween
I like halluween
bceus it is fun!
I Wet crecrcetin
  trick|or|treat   ing
I di z|up|in sd men
  dressed   as
  six   houses
I Wet to Sex haSe?

Fed x

FIT X
TRIC

Truck

FIGURE A.4   Level 3 Writing

the spelling section that follows.) Level 3 writers have full phonemic awareness.
Level 3 pieces may be quite lengthy. Sometimes Level 3 spellings such as ATE for
eighty do not look like English spelling but the spelling does represent each of
the sounds in the word that the Level 3 writer is attempting to spell, in this case
a blending of the three letter names /a/ + /t/ + /e/. Generally, many more words

are spelled correctly at Level 3 because the Level 3 writer has more word-specific knowledge and has usually begun to amass a repertoire of quite a few known spellings.

EXPECTED WRITING BEHAVIORS

1. The writer moves beyond rudimentary letter-sound knowledge and is able to provide full representations of the sounds in words such as MOTR BOT for *motorboat,* BOTM for *bottom* and UNITD STATZ for *United States.*

2. With only a few exceptions, all sounds are represented in every word.

3. Letter-name spellings may be present.

4. Word segmentation is generally in evidence.

5. The child has a more stabilized concept of word.

6. Alphabetic knowledge may be complete.

7. The child has phonemic awareness.

Spelling

Level 3 invented spelling is *phonetic spelling.* The Level 3 speller provides a letter for each sound in a novel word. Virtually all of the sounds in the word are represented, including vowels. Full phonemic awareness is evident. Medial short vowels are often misspelled at Level 3 with *a* for short *e, e* for short *i, i* for short *o,* and *o* for short *u* as in PAT for *pet,* PET for *pit,* PIT for *pot* and POT for *put.* Correct spelling of CVC short vowels signals recognition of the regularity of CVC as a pattern and usually comes as writers move into Level 4. The Phase 3 spellings such as PAT for *pet* are generated one letter for each sound such as /p/+/e/+/t/, which may result in PAT for *pet* because short *e* sounds more like the letter name "A" than the letter name "E." Level 3 is the perfect time to devote much attention to teaching medial short vowels.

Monster Test

Spellings in the Monster Test look like this:

1. monster: MOSTR (a letter for each sound except the preconsonantal nasal)

2. united: UNITD

3. dress: JRAS; JRES; DRAS

4. bottom: BODM; BOTM; BIDM, BITM

5. hiked: HIKT; HICT; HIKD; HICT

6. human: HUMN

7. eagle: EGL

8. closed: KLOSD; CLOSD; KLOST; CLOST

9. bumped: BOPT; BUPT; BOMPT; BUMPT

10. type: TIP

EXPECTED SPELLING BEHAVIORS

1. *At least half* of the invented spellings in a volume of writing (several writing samples) or half of the invented spellings on an instrument such as The Monster Test are *phonetic.*

2. The speller invents by using a letter of the alphabet to represent each sound in a word. Certain sound features may allow one letter to represent two sounds at Level 3. This creates a few exceptions to the letter for a sound rule including *r*-controlled vowels such as BRD for *bird* in which the *r* carries the vowel sound; syllabic sonorants such as TABL for *table* and PISM for *possum* in which the *l* and *m*, respectively, carry the vowel sounds; and preconsonantal nasals where the *m* or *n* is systematically left out when it represents a nasal sound that comes before a consonant in words such as STAP for *stamp*, and BOP for *bump.*

3. Letter-name spellings may be common as children transition into Level 3 but this practice tends to diminish as children transition out of Level 3 into Level 4.

4. Spellings such as EGL for *eagle* are common.

5. Nasals are not represented before consonants (STAP for *stamp*).

6. The vowel is omitted before syllabic *R* (MOSTR for monster)

7. Vowel digraphs (i.e., *ai, ea, ay, ee, ow*) are generally spelled with one letter (PLA for *play* and KEP for *keep*).

8. The *e*-marker CVCe silent *e* pattern is often spelled using a letter-name strategy (TIP for *type*; BIK for *bike*).

9. Sound spellings may not look like the correct spelling (ATE for *eighty*).

10. Inflectional endings *s, 's, -est, -ing,* and *-ed* are often spelled like they sound (RATZ for *rats*).

11. Inflectional ending *-ed* is spelled like it sounds with *-T, -D,* and *-AD* or *ID* as in PEKT (*peeked*), CLOSD (*closed*), and CHRADAD (*traded*).

12. *Tr* may be spelled *ch* (CHUK for *truck*).

Minimal competency benchmark

Minimal competency at Level 3 based on expected progress in writing is that the child would be functioning in this phase or exhibiting the expected behaviors by the middle of first grade. Intervention may be needed if the child does not have full phonemic awareness and generally does not provide a letter for each sound when inventing a spelling by the middle of first grade. (Gentry 2000a, 2000b, 2004, 2005; International Reading Association, 1998; Snow, Burns, and

Griffin 1998). (Under optical conditions many children will exceed the minimal competency benchmark by the middle of first grade.)

Reading

Reading at Level 3 is called *full alphabetic*. At Level 3 readers really take off using the alphabet to cue full word reading by paying attention to all the letters in words. The representations of words stored in memory at Level 3 are more complete. The primary strategy to figure out a new word is to read new words by forming full letter-sound representations; however, when the child encounters a new word he or she is likely to sound the word out letter-by-letter rather than recognize chunks of spelling patterns. The brain may be forming more complex association matrices using all the letters in words. It is in this phase that readers generally discover the process of analogizing. Readers at this level begin to take a great leap in building the number of words they recognize automatically on sight, which increases exponentially once they begin analogizing or using word families. They may not use chunks for graphosyllabic analysis of novel words or polysyllabic words; rather, they are more likely to try to decode these words letter-by-letter. Level 3 readers often respond particularly well to Word Wall activities for building new sight vocabulary.

Level 3 readers generally have full control of the alphabet and they move into full phonemic awareness. The approach that dominates when a Level 3 reader reads a new word or unfamiliar word is that he or she relies upon much more complete alphabet knowledge, and attempts complete letter-sound matches making use of a great deal of regularity in the system. The grapheme-to-sound cue is information that is being used extensively. As at Level 2, letters tend to be decoded individually rather than in chunks but the full spelling is processed. With attention on all the letters, the Level 3 reader is much more successful reading similarly spelled words than at previous levels.

With much more letter-sound regularity recognized in the spelling system and an increasing number of words being recognized automatically (often a result of word study with Word Walls), the Level 3 reader may be expected to increase both the volume and level of reading noticeably. While echo-reading and memorizing text that has been read over and over is still a primary strategy for learning to read new material, the reader is expected to make much more use of decoding and generally has enough alphabet and word-specific knowledge to do so. At the same time, the child is using syntactic and semantic systems reciprocally to cue reading. Keeping in mind the increasing variation in individuals with each increase in complexity of reading levels, a rough guage is that Level 3 readers may be expected to move through book Level C through about book Level H with concomitant changes in text complexity ranging from "Jack ran away from the giant. Run, Jack, Run. The giant wants to eat you" (from *Run! Run!* (1995) by JoAnn Vandine—Level C, *Guided Reading,* Fountas and Pinnell

1996) to text such as "In the great green room there was a telephone and a red balloon and a picture of—the cow jumping over the moon" (from *Goodnight Moon* by Margaret Wise Brown—Level H, Guided Reading, Fountas and Pinnell 1996). The Level H text tends to have a higher vocabulary load, more variation in vocabulary, and more sentence complexity, having moved from repetition of one or two sentences (Level C) to varied sentence patterns with some repeated phrases or refrains and a move from direct support to moderate support provided by illustrations (Peterson 1998). Level 3 readers flourish in materials that help them learn medial vowels, word families, and chunks of spelling patterns. Examples include *"Pop" Pops the Popcorn* (1996) by Bob Egan, which is a partially decodable text matching Fountas' and Pinnell's criteria for book Level D. Notice how the text gives the Level 3 reader lots of practice with the short *o* sound and the matching CVC spelling pattern: "Get a box. Get a mop. The popcorn is popping over the top. 'Pop' pops the popcorn. When will it stop?" Eight CVC short *o* words are included in the story: *Bob, box, lot, mop, pop, pot, stop,* and *top,* with additional variations such as *pops, popping,* and *popcorn.* Much repetition in text is particularly beneficial to Level 3 readers. Likewise, very popular books such as Mem Fox's *Zoo-Looking* (1996) and the Dr. Seuss books are wonderful for Level 3 readers because these texts make use of lots of word families, onsets and rimes, and chunks of spelling patterns such as *back, black, crack, smack, whack,* and *snack*—the repeated words and patterns in *Zoo-Looking* (book Level G). These books should be read over and over to support fluency, pattern recognition, and word recognition.

EXPECTED READING BEHAVIORS

1. The student pays attention to all letters in the word.
2. The reader pays attention to complete letter-sound correspondences.
3. The reader achieves full phonemic awareness.
4. The child stabilizes concept of word.
5. He distinguishes among similarly spelled words.
6. He learns to read similarly spelled words easily.
7. The student begins to read new words by analogy.
8. The reader uses fingerpoint reading successfully.
9. He begins to recognize spelling patterns in words.

Useful teaching strategies

The following teaching strategies are particularly useful for helping children understand the concepts needed in order to move from Level 3 to Level 4. You will find a full description of how to implement these techniques in Chapters 6 and 7.

Key Techniques for Level 3: Writing workshop; scaffolded writing moving to more complex forms; use of invented spelling with encouragement to invent in chunks; moving to phase out adult underwriting because the Level 3 writing is easily read; hand spelling for new onset and rime patterns; continue a three-step use of materialization techniques in this order: (1) stretching out the sounds in new words while modeling with stretchable fabric followed by (2) finger spelling the word, followed by (3) letter/sound boxes for the same word. Extensive use of word families; making and writing words; extensive pattern recognition work in many formats with many basic patterns. Extensive medial vowel work especially with short vowel patterns. Extensive onset and rime work; extensive word sorting of basic vowel patterns such as the CVC pattern with the same vowel in words such as *pop, mop, stop, top;* the CV pattern as in *by, my, sky,* and *fly;* the CVCe pattern as in *bake, make, lake, rake, fake;* and contrasting short vowels with CVC patterns such as *nat, tap, rat, stamp* versus *not, top, rot, stop.*

Level 4—The Move to Pattern Recognition

Look at the two writing samples in Figure A.5. If the child's writing samples look most like these the child is likely to be at Level 4 (a phase when the child spells sounds in chunks of letters based on phonics patterns).

Writing

Writing at Level 4 may be described as *consolidated alphabetic writing.* The Level 4 writer writes in chunks of spelling patterns and moves away from providing one letter for each sound as the primary strategy, moving toward consolidating groups of letter combinations into chunks. The general shift is to think of the components of sound in a word such as *interesting* as *in-ter-est-ing* and inventing each syllable in chunks such as IN-TUR-REST-ING as opposed to the Level 3 strategy of inventing each sound separately which might result in an invented spelling such as E-N-T-R-A-C-T-NG. We see the same move from Level 3 to Level 4 that was noted in the reading phases: from processing the word *interesting* virtually as individual letters (*i-n-t-e-r-e-s-t-i-ng*), to processing it in chunks (*in-ter-est-ing*). The only difference is that the writer is encoding while the reader is decoding and since it is easier to read a word than to spell a word, one generally observes the child decoding patterns in reading before encoding the patterns in writing. This isn't always the case, however, because some of the patterns are discovered through writing, which further underscores the importance of reading and writing reciprocity.

The Level 4 writer has consolidated his or her knowledge into a more sophisticated understanding of how the alphabetic system works to include the concept that reading and writing works in chunks of regular spelling patterns. What typifies Level 4 spelling is that the writer doesn't have enough word-specific knowledge to use the correct chunks because English is so complex that

Good THING to Eat

I like STRALBARES and i like ORRANGE.
I like tomato SUPE and I like PECHIS.
I like apples and I like BROCLE.
I like COLEFLAWORE TO, you know.
I like corn and I like green BENES.
I like FRIDE CEKEN and I like BARBO Q CEKEN TO.
But most of all I like HO MAED SPOGATE.
THOSS things are good for you.
That's why I put them down.

THE RUN AWAY CAR

My mom was taking TO long so I WANT to the FRUNT SEET. I didn't MENA to
but I TURND on the car. My mom ran and ran. She KOT up to the car. I OPINDE
the DOUR. She got in. I was in TRUBUL. She was mad!

FIGURE A.5   Level 4 Writing

it takes most children a number of years of spelling and word study to learn
all the correct forms. Nevertheless, children move into Level 4 with a lot of
word knowledge. Generally about two-thirds of the words in a writing piece
are spelled correctly as children move into Level 4, which for many children
happens near the beginning of second grade. By end of third grade and the
middle of fourth grade many writers who have had appropriate instruction are
able to spell more than 90 percent of the words they use in writing correctly and
they can generally find and correct almost all of their spelling mistakes in edit-
ing (Gentry 2000b). The Level 4 writer applies more sophisticated phonics
patterns in writing. Due to reading/writing reciprocity, observation of the patterns used in Level 4 writing is often a good measure of a child's understanding
of phonics. It's very easy to look at Level 4 writing and determine whether a
child is using basic patterns such as CVC short vowel patterns and VCVe long
vowel patterns correctly or incorrectly (Gentry 2000a). At the beginning of Level
4 the writer has not yet fully developed a sense of whether or not a spelling
"looks right" probably because the word form area of the brain is not yet processing large numbers of words that it will eventually recognize and produce
automatically.

EXPECTED WRITING BEHAVIORS

1. Writers consolidate individual phonemes into chunks of regular phonics
   patterns when inventing spellings.
2. Writers spell many more words and word parts by analogy.

3. The students spell more words conventionally than invented in more lengthy pieces of writing.

4. There is potential for more elaborate extended pieces of writing; however, quantitative aspects of writing are highly dependent on exposure, experience, and instruction and may not be in line with qualitative developmental levels.

Spelling

Level 4 invented spelling is called *transitional spelling*. The Level 4 speller knows many spelling patterns and invents spelling in chunks of spelling patterns. Short vowels are spelled conventionally. One-syllable long vowel patterns such as CVCe and CVVC are recognized and used but the Level 4 speller may not have developed the word-specific knowledge to choose the correct pattern for phonetically viable options, so there are likely to be many spellings such as *mene* or *meen* for *mean*.

Monster Test

Spellings in the Monster Test look like this:

1. monster: MONSTUR; MONSTAR; MUNSTUR; MUNSTAR
2. united: YOUNIGHTED; UNIGHTED; YOUNITED;
3. dress: DRES; DREAS
4. bottom: BOTTUM; BODDUM
5. hiked: HICKED; HITKED; HIKDE
6. human: HUMUN; HUMON; HUMEN
7. eagle: EGUL; EGOL
8. closed: CLOSSED; CLOESD
9. bumped: BUMPPED; BUMTED
10. type: TIPE; TIEP

EXPECTED SPELLING BEHAVIORS

1. *At least half* of the invented spelling in a volume of writing (several writing samples) or half of the invented spelling on an instrument such as the Monster Test are *transitional.*

2. Vowels appear in every syllable (EGUL replaces Level 3 EGL for *eagle*).

3. Nasals are represented before consonants (STAMPP or STAMPE replaces Level 3 STAP for *stamp*).

4. The letter-name strategy drops out (ELLEFONT replaces Level 3 LEFUT for *elephant*).

5. A vowel is represented before syllabic *R* (MONSTUR replaces Level 3 MOSTR for monster).

6. Chunks of letter combinations are used (YOUNIGHTED for *united*, STINGKS for *stinks*).

7. Vowel digraphs (i.e., ai, ea, ay, ee, ow) are used liberally but often incorrectly such as PLAID for *played* and KEAP for *keep*.

8. The *e*-marker CVCe silent *e* pattern begins to stabilize (TIPE replaces Level 3 TIP for *type*).

9. Visually recalled spellings replace sound spellings (EIGHTEE replaces Level 3 ATE for *eighty*).

10. Inflectional endings *s, 's, -est, -ing,* and *-ed* are more likely to be spelled like they look, not as they sound.

11. Visually recalled spellings may appear in mixed-up letter order (e.g., TAOD for *toad*, HUOSE for *house*, OPNE for *open*).

12. Many alternatives may be used for the same sound such as five alternatives for long *a* (EIGHTE for *eighty*, ABUL for *able*, LASEE for *lazy*, RANE for *rain*, SAIL for *sale*).

13. Correctly spelled words are used in greater abundance.

14. Numerous spelling principles remain to be learned including influences of graphemic environment of the unit, influences of the position of the letter chunk in a word, stress influences to spelling, morpheme boundaries, likely positions for double consonants, and meaning constancy in words such as *too, two,* and *to* or *by, buy,* and *bye* as well as information about homophones and compound words. Some stress pattern relationships, principles of syllable juncture, obscure patterns within polysyllabic words, contributions to English from other languages such as Greek and Latin forms, and certain complex concepts such as consonant assimilation may not be learned until upper elementary and middle grades. (An example of consonant assimilation is when the prefix *in-* meaning *not* becomes *im-* when added to base words such as *-mobile* and *-modest* to form *immobile, immodest,* as opposed to being spelled INMOBILE and INMODEST. Due to consonant assimilation, *ad-* assimilates to *ac-* in *account* rather than ADCOUNT).

Minimal competency benchmark

Minimal competency at Level 4 based on expected progress in writing is that the child would be functioning in this phase or exhibiting these expected behaviors by the end of first grade. Intervention may be needed if the child cannot demonstrate chunking knowledge in spelling and automatic recognition of over one hundred sight words by the end of first grade (Gentry 2000a, 2000b, 2004; International Reading Association 1998; Snow, Burns, and Griffin 1998).

Reading

Word reading at Level 4 is called *consolidated alphabetic,* reflecting the reader's move to consolidating or chunking groups of letters into phonics patterns or graphosyllabic constituents. These spelling chunks are transformed into pronunciations and blended to match words. This is the level at which the child has mastered the core mechanism of the English spelling system and likely the level that has sufficient regularity that the word form area of the brain may become fully activated and begin to process many more words and word parts automatically. The quality of representations stored in memory is likely the same as in the adult reader but with the adult reader having stored many more words. Understanding the chunking system and bonding the spelling chunks to pronunciations in memory enhances word reading so much so that word-reading skills may become automatic and many more words can be retrieved on sight. The child has in a sense become a grown-up reader, having moved from novice to experienced and practiced reader, and is much more independent, no longer relying upon echo-reading and memorizing text to learn new material. The reader's potential increases for volume and complexity of material and many Level 4 readers move into reading chapter books. Over one hundred words are likely to be recognized automatically on sight at this level. The reader accurately decodes nonsense words representative of various syllable patterns such as *dit, nuv, buf, yode, shi, fler,* and *cleef* (Bryant 1975) and makes use of this ability in breaking polysyllabic words into pronounceable units. He or she also makes use of hundreds of one-syllable words that are recognized as syllable units in polysyllabic words such as *man* in *man*ual, com*man*d, un*man*ageable, *man*ipulate, *man*date, hu*man*, *man*agement, dor*man*t and the like. The brain activates the word form area forming complex association matrices using automatic recognition of chunks of spelling patterns to activate words automatically. These complete connections between known words or syllable letter-chunks and appropriate sounds enable the child's brain to do the work of the mature reader so that when he or she sees a word a unique constellation of neurons fire triggering the word's meaning, sound, and spelling for upwards of one hundred or more words. The Level 4 reader routinely uses chunks for graphosyllabic analysis of polysyllabic words. The child now has enough word-specific knowledge to allow self-teaching to kick in when he or she reads new material. This enables the child to learn many more vocabulary words by reading and to be less dependent on activities such as using word walls for learning new vocabulary.

Although reading levels may vary greatly, Level 4 readers become fluent, proficient readers of more complex text often moving from mid-first-grade levels to end-of-first-grade levels and beyond. Level 4 readers often are observed reading text such as "Long, long ago, before there were people, dinosaurs lived on Earth. The word dinosaur means 'terrible lizard.' Some dinosaurs were very small, but other dinosaurs were huge," which includes the words *compsognathus* and *brachiosaurus* in the illustration (from *Dinosaurs* [1995] by Michael

Collins—Level K, *Guided reading,* Fountas and Pinnell 1996). Words such as *compsognathus* are read because the reader can now read them in chunks—*comp-sog-na-thus.* Once the brain recognizes the cluster of chunks in *compsognathus* a number of times and has attached it to the word's pronunciation and meaning, the recognition of *compsognathus* may become automatic. Reading should become more proficient and fluent at Level 4 with a great increase in the number of words that the child reads, and with each reading of a word a staggering increase in the number of times reading related neurons are firing in the brain, as the brain actively reinforces the neural pathways for each specific word module, makes new connections, and builds automaticity.

Level 4 readers are likely to move into chapter books such as *Little Bear* (1957) by Elsa Minarik (Level J), *Frog and Toad Are Friends* (1970) by Arnold Lobel (Level K), and *Amelia Bedelia* (1963) by Peggy Parish (Level K, *Guided Reading,* Fountas and Pinnell 1996) and even more challenging material with literary language, elaborated episodes and events, unusual and challenging vocabulary, extended descriptions, and with much less support needed from illustrations (Peterson 1998).

EXPECTED READING BEHAVIOR

1. The reader consolidates letters into chunks of spelling patterns such as *tel-e-phone* and *el-e-phant.*
2. The reader is processing in chunks.
3. The child has increased sight-word recognition of 100 or more words.
4. The student uses analogizing by using many common words and patterns.
5. She is reading mutisyllabic words in chunks.
6. The reader is much less dependant on echo-reading for word learning (though echo-reading is useful at Level 4 for fluency development).
7. She increases the volume of reading including a move to easy chapter books.
8. The reader is more independent for reading new material.

Useful teaching strategies

The following teaching strategies are particularly useful for helping children understand the concepts needed for Level 4 and beyond. You will find a full description of how to implement these techniques in Chapters 6 and 7.

Key Techniques for Level 4: Comprehensive reading instruction with emphasis on comprehension and fluency; writing workshop; scaffolded writing moving to more complex forms; story frames for more elaborate productions; use of invented spelling with encouragement to invent in chunks; extensive pattern recognition work in many formats with new patterns. Extensive word sorting of basic vowel patterns such as CVC with the same vowel such as *pop, mop, stop top;* CV in *by, my, sky,* and *fly;* CVCe as in *bake, make, lake, rake, fake;* and contrasting short vowels with CVC patterns such as *nat, tap, rat, stamp* versus *not, top, rot, stop.* Extensive vowel pattern study moving to the myriad of vowel digraphs once short vowel patterns and basic *e*-marker long vowel patterns are mastered. Making and Writing Words; explicit spelling instruction.

References

Adams, M. J. 1990. *Beginning to Read: Thinking and Learning About Print.* Cambridge, MA: MIT Press.

Allington, R. L. 2001. *What Really Matters for Struggling Readers.* New York: Addison Wesley Longman.

Atwell, N. 1987. *In the Middle: Writing, Reading and Learning with Adolescents.* Upper Montclair, NJ: Boyton/Cook.

Bear, D., M. Invernizzi, S. Templeton, and F. Johnston. 2000. *Words Their Way.* Columbus, OH: Merrill/Prentice Hall.

Beers, J. 1974. *First and Second Grade Children's Developing Orthographic Concepts of Tense and Lax Vowels.* Unpublished doctoral dissertation, University of Virginia, Charlottesville.

Beers, J. W., and E. H. Henderson. 1977. "A Study of Developing Orthographic Concepts Among First Graders." *Research in the Teaching of English* 11: 133–48.

Bhattacharya, A., and L. Ehri. 2004. "Graphosyllabic Analysis Helps Adolescent Struggling Readers Read and Spell Words." *Journal of Learning Disabilities* 37 4: 331–48.

Bissex, G. 1980. *GNYS at WRK: A Child Learns to Write and Read.* Cambridge, MA: Harvard University Press.

Blachman, B. 2000. Phonological Awareness. In *Handbook of Reading Research,* edited by M. Kamil, P. Mosenthal, P. D. Pearson, and R. Barr (vol. 3), 483–502. Mahwah, NJ: Lawrence Erlbaum Associates.

Bodrova, E., and D. J. Leong. 1998. "Scaffolding Emergent Writing in the Zone of Proximal Development." *Literacy Teaching and Learning* 3(2): 1–18.

Bosman, A. M. T., and G. C. Van Orden. 1997. "Why Spelling Is More Difficult Than Reading." In *Learning to Spell,* edited by C. A. Perfetti, L. Rieben, and M. Fayol, 173–94. London: Lawrence Erlbaum Associates.

Brown, J., and D. Morris. 2005. "Meeting the Needs of Low Spellers in a Second-Grade Classroom." *Reading and Writing Quarterly* 21: 165–84.

Bruner, J. 1981. *Vygotsky and Language Acquisition.* Cambridge, MA: Harvard Graduate School of Education.

Bryant, N. D. 1975. *Diagnostic Test of Basic Decoding Skills.* New York: Columbia University, Teachers College.

Byrnes, J. P. 2001. *Minds, Brains, and Learning: Understanding the Psychological and Educational Relevance of Neuroscientific Research.* New York: The Guilford Press.

Calkins, L. 2005. *The Nuts and Bolts of Teaching Writing.* Portsmouth, NH: Heinemann.

Clay, M. 1982. *Observing Young Readers.* Exeter, NH: Heinemann Educational.

Collins, M. 1995. *Dinosaurs.* New York: MONDO Publishers.

Cunningham, A. E., and K. E. Stanovich. 1998. "What Reading Does for the Mind." *American Educator* 22: 8–15.

Cunningham, P. M., and J. W. Cunningham. 1992. "Making Words: Enhancing the Invented Spelling—Decoding Connection." *The Reading Teacher* 46: 106–15.

Dyson, A. H. 1989. *Multiple Worlds of Child Writers: Friends Learning to Write.* New York: Teachers College Press.

Egan, B. 1996. *"Pop" Pops the Popcorn.* Parsippany, NJ: Modern Curriculum Press.

Eggers, D., N. Calegari, and D. Moulthrop. 2005. *"Teachers Have It Easy": The Big Sacrifices and Small Salaries of America's Teachers.* New York: The New Press.

Ehri, L. C. 1998. "Grapheme-phoneme Knowledge Is Essential for Learning to Read Words in English." In *Word Recognition in Beginning Literacy,* edited by J. Metsala and L. Ehri, 3–40. Mahwah, NJ: Lawrence Erlbaum Associates.

———. 1997. "Learning to Read and Learning to Spell Are One and the Same, Almost." In *Learning to Spell,* edited by C. A. Perfetti, L. Rieben, and M. Fayol, 237–69. London: Lawrence Erlbaum Associates.

———. 1992. "Reconceptualizing the Development of Sight Word Reading and Its Relationship to Recoding." In *Reading Acquisition,* edited by P. Gough, E. C. Ehri and R. Treiman, 107–43. Hillsdale, NJ: Lawrence Erlbaum Associates.

Ehri, L., and C. Robbins. 1992. "Beginners Need Some Decoding Skill to Read Words by Analogy." *Reading Research Quarterly* 27: 12–26.

Ehri, L. C., and I. Wilce. 1985. "Movement into Reading: Is the First Stage of Printed Word Learning Visual or Phonetic?" *Reading Research Quarterly* 20: 163–79.

Feldgus, E. G., and I. Cardonick. 1999. *Kid Writing: A Systematic Approach to Phonics, Journals, and Writing Workshop.* Bothell, WA: The Wright Group.

Fletcher, R. 1993. *What a Writer Needs.* Portsmouth, NH: Heinemann.

Fountas, I. C., and G. S. Pinnell. 2001. *Guiding Readers and Writers Grades 3–6.* Portsmouth, NH: Heinemann.

———. 1996. *Guided Reading: Good First Teaching for All Children.* Portsmouth, NH: Heinemann.

Fox, M. 1996. *Zoo Looking.* New York: MONDO Publishing.

Galperin, P. Y. 1969. "The Role of Orientation in Thought." *Soviet Psychology* 18(2): 84–89.

Gambrell. L. 1996. "Creating Classroom Cultures That Foster Reading Motivation." *The Reading Teacher* 50: 14–25.

Gentry, J. R. 2005. "Instructional Techniques for Emerging Writer's and Special Needs Students at Kindergarten and Grade 1 Levels." *Reading and Writing Quarterly* 21: 113–34.

———. 2004a. *The Science of Spelling: The Explicit Specifics That Make Great Readers and Writers (and Spellers!).* Portsmouth, NH: Heinemann.

———. 2004b. *Spelling Connections: Kindergarten.* Columbus, OH: Zaner-Bloser.

———. 2004c. *Spelling Connections: First Grade.* Columbus, OH: Zaner-Bloser.

———. 2000a. "A Retrospective on Invented Spelling and a Look Forward." *The Reading Teacher* 54 (3): 318–32.

———. 2000b. *The Literacy Map: Guiding Children to Where They Need to Be (K–3).* New York: MONDO Publishing.

———. 1987. *Spel. . . . Is a Four-Letter Word.* Portsmouth, NH: Heinemann.

———. 1985. "You Can Analyze Developmental Spelling." *Teaching K–8* 15: 44–45.

———. 1982. "An Analysis of Developmental Spelling in *GNYS at WRK.*" *The Reading Teacher* 36: 192–200.

———. 1981. "Learning to Spell Developmentally." *The Reading Teacher* 34: 378–81.

———. 1978. "Early Spelling Strategies." *The Elementary School Journal* 79: 88–92.

————. 1977. *A Study of the Orthographic Strategies of Beginning Readers.* Unpublished doctoral dissertation, University of Virginia, Charlottesville.

Gentry, J. R., and E. H. Henderson. 1978. "Three Steps to Teaching Beginning Readers to Spell." *The Reading Teacher* 31: 632–37.

Gentry, J. R., L. Nanez, and D. Benavides. 2005. *Rescuing "Starving Writers":* Addressing the Spelling Issue with English Language Learners and Struggling Writers. Manuscript submitted for publication.

Goodman, K. 1993. *Phonics Phacts.* Portsmouth, NH: Heinemann.

————. 1965. "A Linguistic Study of Cues and Miscues in Reading." *Elementary English* 42: 639–43.

Gorman, C. 2003. "The New Science of Dyslexia." *Time,* July 28, pp. 52–59.

Goswami, U. 1996. *Rhyme and Analogy Teacher's Guide.* New York: Oxford University Press.

Graves, D. H. 1978. *Balance the Basics.* New York: Ford Foundation.

Harste, J. C., C. L. Burke, and V. A. Woodward. 1982. "Children's Language and World: Initial Encounters with Print." In *Reader Meets Author/ Bridging the Gap,* edited by J. A. Langer and M. T. Smith-Burke, 105–31. Newark, DE: International Reading Association.

Harste, J. C., V. A. Woodward, and C. L. Burke. 1981. *Language Stories and Literacy Lessons.* Portsmouth, NH: Heinemann.

Henderson, E. H. [1985] 1990. *Teaching Spelling* (2d ed.). Boston: Houghton Mifflin, International Reading Association.

Henderson, E. H., and J. W. Beers, eds. 1980. *Developmental and Cognitive Aspects of Learning to Spell: A Reflection of Word Knowledge.* Newark, DE: International Reading Association.

Hendrex, S. 2005. "Why Stevie Can't Spell," *The Washington Post Magazine,* February 20, pp. 26–45.

Holdaway, D. 1979. *The Foundations of Literacy.* Portsmouth, NH: Heinemann.

International Reading Association. 1998. "Learning to Read and Write: Developmentally Appropriate Practices for Young Children." *The Reading Teacher* 52: 193–214.

Johns, J. 1997. *Basic Reading Inventory: Pre-Primer through Grade Twelve & Early Literacy Assessments.* Dubuque, IA: Kendall/Hunt.

Kher, U. 2001. "Blame It on the Written Word." *Time,* March 26, p. 56.

Kozol, J. 1991. *Savage Inequalities.* New York: Crown.

Lee, D., and R. Van Allen. 1963. *Learning to Read Through Experience.* New York: Appleton-Century-Crofts.

Lewkowicz. N. 1980. "Phoneme Awareness Training: What to Teach and How to Teach It." *Journal of Educational Psychology* 72: 686–700.

Liberman, I. Y. E. Shankweiler, F. Fischer, and B. Carter. 1974. "Explicit Phoneme and Syllable Segmentation in the Young Child." *Journal of Experimental Child Psychology* 18: 201–12.

Lobel, A. 1970. *Frog and Toad Are Friends.* New York: HarperCollins.

Martin, B. Jr. 1970. *Brown Bear, Brown Bear, What Do You See?* New York: Holt.

Mattingly, I. 1972. "Reading: The Linguistic Process and Linguistic Awareness." In *Language by Ear and by Eye,* edited by J. Kavanaugh and I. Mattingly, 133–47. Cambridge, MA: MIT Press.

McGuffey, W. H. 1957. *McGuffey's New Fourth Eclectic Reader: Instructive Lessons for the Young.* New York: Wilson, Hinkle & Company.

McKenzie, M. G. 1986. *Journeys into Literacy.* Heddersfield, England: Schofield & Sims.

Minarik, E. 1957. *The Little Bear Treasury.* New York: HarperCollins.

Morris, D. 1981. "Concept of Word: A Developmental Phenomenon in the Beginning Reading and Writing Process." *Language Arts* 58: 659–68.

Morris, D., J. W. Bloodgood, R. G. Lomax, and J. Perney. 2003. "Developmental Steps in Learning to Read: A Longitudinal Study in Kindergarten and First Grade." *Reading Research Quarterly* 38: 302–28.

Moustafa, M. 1997. *Beyond Traditional Phonics.* Portsmouth, NH: Heinemann.

National Institute of Child Health and Human Development. 2000. *Report of the National Reading Panel. Teaching Children to Read: An Evidence-Based Assessment of the Scientific Research Literature on Reading and Its Implications for Reading Instruction* (NIH Publication No. 00–4769). Washington, DC: U.S. Government Printing Office.

Orton, J. L. 1964. *A Guide to Teaching Phonics.* Cambridge, MA: Educators Publishing Service.

Paulesu, E., J.–F. Demonet, F. Fazio, E. McCrory, V. Chanoine, N. Brunswick, S. F. Cappa, G. Cossu, M. Habib, C. D. Frith, and U. Frith. 2001. "Dyslexia: Cultural Diversity and Biological Unity." *Science* 291(5511, 16 March): 2165.

Parish, P. 1963. *Amelia Bedelia.* New York: HarperCollins.

Peterson, B. 1998. *Characteristics of Texts That Support Beginning Readers.* Columbus, OH: The Ohio State University.

Rasinski, T., and R. Oswald. 2005. "Making and Writing Words: Constructivist Word Learning in a Second-Grade Classroom." *Reading & Writing Quarterly* 21: 151–63.

Read, C. 1986. *Children's Creative Spelling.* London: Routledge and Kegan.

———. 1975. *Children's Categorizations of Speech Sounds in English.* Urbana, IL: National Council of Teachers in English.

———. 1971. "Pre-school Children's Knowledge of English Phonology." *Harvard Educational Review* 42: 1–34.

Rosenblatt, L. M. 1978. *The Reader the Text the Poem.* Edwardsville, IL: Southern Illinois University Press.

———. 1938. *Literature as Exploration.* New York: Noble and Noble Publishers.

Routman, R. 2005. *Writing Essentials.* Portsmouth, NH. Heinemann.

———. 2000. *Conversations.* Portsmouth, NH. Heinemann.

———. 1991. *Invitations.* Portsmouth, NH: Heinemann.

Shaywitz, S. 2003. *Overcoming Dyslexia.* New York: Alfred A. Knopf.

Shaywitz, S., and B. Shaywitz. 2001. "The Neurobiology of Reading and Dyslexia." In *Focus on Basics* 5(A): 1–11.

Smith, C., R. Constantino, and S. Krashen, 1997. "Differences in Print Environment for Children in Beverly Hills, Compton, and Watts." *The Emergency Librarian* 24 (4): 8–9.

Snow, C. 2005. Special Feature Address: "English Language Learners: What Do Teachers Need to Know?" 2005 Association for Supervision and Curriculum Development 60th Annual Conference. April 4, 2005. Orlando, Florida.

Snow, C., M. W. Burns, and P. Griffin. 1998. *Preventing Reading Difficulties in Young Children.* Washington, DC: National Academy Press.

Sousa, D. A. 2000. *How the Brain Learns.* Thousand Oaks, CA: Corwin Press.

Stauffer, R. 1980. *The Language Experience Approach to Teaching Reading.* New York: Harper & Row.

———. 1969. *Directing Reading Maturity as a Cognitive Process.* New York: Harper & Row.

Strickland, D. 1998. *Teaching Phonics Today: A Primer for Educators.* Newark, DE: International Reading Association.

Teal, W. H. 1986. "Home Background and Young Children's Literacy Development." In *Emergent Literacy: Writing and Reading,* edited by W. Teale and E. Sulzby. Norwood, NJ: Ablex.

Templeton, S., and D. Bear, eds. 1992. *Development of Orthographic Knowledge and the Foundations of Literacy: A Memorial Festschrift for Edmund H. Henderson.* Hillsdale, NJ: Lawrence Erlbaum Associates.

Van Allen, R. 1976. *Language Experiences in Communication.* Boston: Houghton Mifflin.

Van Allen, R. V., and C. Van Allen. 1966. *Language Experiences in Reading: Teachers' Resource Book.* Chicago: Encyclopedia.

Vandine, J. 1995. *Run! Run!* New York: MONDO Publishing.

Venezky, R. 1970. *The Structure of English Orthography.* The Hague, Netherlands: Mouton.

Vygotsky, L. S. 1987. *The Collected Works of L. S. Vygotsky.* Translated by R. W. Rieber and A. S. Carton. New York: Plenum Press. (Original work published in 1930, 1933, 1935.)

———. 1978. *Mind in Society.* Cambridge, MA: Harvard University Press.

Welch J., and S. Welch. 2005. *Winning.* New York: HarperCollins.

Wells, G. 1986. *The Meaning Makers.* Portsmouth, NH: Heinemann.

———. 1985. "Preschool Literacy-Related Activities and Success in School." In *Literacy, Language, and Learning,* edited by D. Olson, A. Hildyard, and N. Torrance. New York: Cambridge University Press.

Wilde, S. 1992. *You Kan Red This! Spelling and Punctuation for Whole Language Classrooms, K–6.* Portsmouth, NH: Heinemann.

Wood, D., J. C. Bruner, and G. Ross. 1976. "The Role of Tutoring in Problem Solving." *Journal of Child Psychology and Psychiatry* 17: 89–100.

Yopp, H. K., and R. H. Yopp. 2000. "Supporting Phonemic Awareness Development in the Classroom." *The Reading Teacher* 54 (2): 130–43.

Zutell, J. 1992a. "An Integrated View of Word Knowledge: Correctional Studies of the Relationships Among Spelling, Reading, and Conceptual Development. In *Development of Orthographic Knowledge and the Foundations of Literacy: A Memorial Festschrift for Edmund Henderson,* edited by S. Templeton and D. R. Bear, 213–30. Hillsdale, NJ: Lawrence Erlbaum Associates.

———. 1992b. "Sorting It Out Through Word Sorts." In *Voices on Word Matters,* edited by I. Fountas and G. S. Pinnell, 103–13. Portsmouth, NH: Heinemann.

———. 1978. "Some Psychololinguistic Perspectives on Children's Spelling." *Language Arts* 55: 844–50.

———. 1975. *Spelling Strategies of Primary School Children and Their Relationship to the Piagetian Concept of Decentration.* Dissertation Abstracts International, 36908A, 5030. (University Microfilms No. AAG7600018).

Index